Dwis Taylor

Capacity-Building

An Approach to People-Centred Development

Deborah Eade

Oxfam
(UK and Ireland)

First published by Oxfam UK and Ireland 1997

Reprinted by Oxfam GB 1998, 2000, 2003

© Oxfam UK and Ireland 1997

ISBN 0 85598 366 3

A catalogue record for this publication is available from the British Library.

Available from:

Bournemouth English Book Centre, PO Box 1496, Parkstone, Dorset, BH12 3YD, UK
tel: +44 (0)1202 712933; fax: +44 (0)1202 712930; email: oxfam@bebc.co.uk

USA: Stylus Publishing LLC, PO Box 605, Herndon, VA 20172-0605, USA
tel: +1 (0)703 661 1581; fax: +1 (0)703 661 1547; email: styluspub@aol.com

For details of local agents and representatives in other countries, consult our website:
www.oxfam.org.uk/publications
or contact Oxfam Publishing, 274 Banbury Road, Oxford OX2 7DZ, UK
tel: +44 (0)1865 311 311; fax: +44 (0)1865 312 600; email: publish@oxfam.org.uk

Our website contains a fully searchable database of all our titles, and facilities for secure on-line ordering.

Published by Oxfam GB, 274 Banbury Road, Oxford OX2 7DZ, UK.

Printed by Information Press, Eynsham.

Oxfam GB is a registered charity, no. 202 918, and is a member of Oxfam International.

Contents

Acknowledgements

Many people have helped this book to reach the light of day, including those who contributed to *The Oxfam Handbook of Development and Relief* on which much of it is based. Robert Cornford, Briony Harrison, Chris Jackson, Ben Rogaly, Ines Smyth, and Sarah Totterdell all gave valuable support, while Caroline Knowles did much to make it possible. Very special thanks are due to Lilly Nicholls and Chris Roche whose detailed comments and ideas were immensely useful. My deepest acknowledgement is, as ever, to my *comadre* and most exacting critic, Suzanne Williams.

Deborah Eade
October 1997

Preface

Oxfam is embarking on a process of more systematic analysis of what it does well and what it does poorly. In short, we are learning how to learn more effectively. This book is an attempt to take stock in one broad area of our work that has always been important to Oxfam, namely, supporting individuals, groups, and organisations to promote social justice. It therefore should be seen as a contribution to an ongoing debate from a particular perspective, not a 'state of the art' review or the definitive answer on what capacity-building means and how it is achieved. As Deborah Eade states in the first chapter, it is more a 'why to' than a 'how to' book.

Much of the literature on 'learning organisations' and change processes in organisations tends to dismiss learning from the past as at best irrelevant and at worst a handicap for thinking imaginatively about the future. Many people in Oxfam would take issue with this view and argue that the process of critically analysing new ideas and concepts and examining them in relation to existing knowledge is an essential step in the generation of genuinely useful frameworks of analysis.

As such, the recent interest, or in some cases, renewal of interest, in the concepts of capacity-building, civil society, social capital, and exclusion need to be rigorously tested against the notions of entitlements, equity, human rights, and empowerment. If not, there is a grave danger of NGO faddism taking on a new repertoire of jargon that contributes to an already alarming degree of amnesia.

The ever-shifting balance of relationships between state, market, civil society, and household is not a new phenomenon. Issues of power, interests, marginalisation, and conflict remain central. The concept and practice of capacity-building has to be tested against whether it can contribute to creating the synergy between different actors which can confront and challenge existing imbalances of power We hope this book will contribute something to that debate.

Chris Roche
Gender and Learning Team, Oxfam

1

Introduction

> *Our lack of an adequate theory of capacity building reduces our own capacity to engage in the practice. We lack the theory because we are not thinking through what we see before us. And we are avoiding thinking things through because to face the obvious will be to radically transform our practice. We are avoiding genuine accountability* (CDRA, 1995).

> *What is 'capacity building? That is the problem. It includes everything that was covered by the different definitions of 'institution building', and much more besides ... Aid agencies would be wise to have no truck with the new jargon of 'capacity building' and to insist on using language and terms that have identifiable and precise meanings* (Moore, 1995).

Capacity-building: saying what we mean, or meaning what we say?

If 'scaling-up' was all the rage in the late 1980s, the latest fashion for maximising NGO impact is 'capacity-building'. Along with 'empowerment', 'participation', and 'gender-equity', capacity-building is seen as an essential element if development is to be sustainable and centred in people.[1]

Capacity-building is increasingly seen as important by official donors and multilateral agencies. No UN Summit goes by without ritual calls for *capacity-building programmes* for NGOs and other social organisations:

> *in critical areas, such as participatory planning, programme design, implementation and evaluation, economic and financial analysis, credit management, research, information and advocacy ... [and strengthening] networking and exchange of expertise and experience among such organisations.*[2]

1

The World Bank follows suit:

... Bank-NGO collaboration also presents an opportunity to build the capacity of the NGO sector. The building of social capital and the emergence of a strong civil society are essential ingredients in achieving long-term, sustainable development at the national level. Enhancing the capacity of indigenous NGOs through operational collaboration may well generate a development impact which surpasses immediate project goals. [3]

This view is mirrored in the NGO world, at least in the North. A survey among European and North American development NGOs reported — not entirely surprisingly, given the growing dependence of many Northern NGOs on channelling government funding — that nine out of ten respondents identified 'capacity-building' in the South as a core activity (James, 1994). Fewer of these were able to define what it means in practice. But most would place capacity-building somewhere on a spectrum ranging from 'helping people to help themselves', at a personal, local or national level, to strengthening civil society organisations in order to foster democratisation, and building strong, effective and accountable institutions of government.

What does such across-the-board consensus imply? Does the World Bank really envisage the same process as does the South African NGO which also regards 'the building of capacity [as] an essential development intervention towards the strengthening of civil society'? [4] If it means so much to so many, does 'capacity-building' really mean anything to anyone? Do people build their own capacities, or do they need to contract the job out to professional builders — in which case, how professional are NGOs? Is capacity-building a precondition for, or a by-product of, international cooperation? Is it synonymous with development? A means or an end, or both? Or is capacity-building just another piece of unwieldy jargon whose very imprecision disguises its emptiness?

Oxfam is a relatively late arrival in this discussion, its first serious use of the term 'capacity-building' not appearing until 1995, in *The Oxfam Handbook of Development and Relief*.[5] Oxfam's thinking is shaped not so much by academic debate — valuable though this is in offering analytical tools and access to a wider body of thought — as by its own experience as a poverty-focused British NGO that works in over 70 countries around the world.[6] Oxfam's analysis thus derives principally from efforts to reflect on and deepen its understanding of that changing body of experience.

Oxfam's definition of capacity-building is marked by its own fundamental beliefs: that all people have the right to an equitable share in the world's resources, and to be the authors of their own development; and that the denial of such rights is at the heart of poverty and suffering. Strengthening people's capacity to determine their own values and priorities, and to act on these, is the basis of development. It follows, then, that for Oxfam, *capacity-building is an approach to development* rather than a set of discrete or pre-packaged interventions. So while there are certain basic capacities (social, economic, political, and practical) on which development depends, Oxfam seeks to support organisations working for sustainable social justice. In supporting its counterparts within their diverse contexts, Oxfam aims to combine a detailed focus on each specific situation with a broader and longer-term strategic vision.

This dual approach has several implications. The first is that capacity-building cannot be seen or undertaken in isolation. It is (for reasons that we will explore later in this book) deeply embedded in the social, economic, and political environment. Understanding this environment is critical in order to understand who lacks what capacities, in any given context; why; and why this matters. Which leads us to the second point. Women and men, however poor or marginalised, always have many capacities, which may not be obvious to outsiders, and which even they themselves may not recognise. It may take time to discover these capacities and potential. But to intervene without doing so is not only disrespectful; it also wastes an opportunity to build on these existing capacities, and — even more importantly — risks undermining them, and so leaving people even more vulnerable than they were before. This danger is heightened in fast-moving emergency relief programmes, as we shall discuss in Chapter 8.

The third implication is that an individual's capacities and needs — and the opportunity to act on them — depend on the myriad factors that differentiate human beings from each other and shape social identities, relationships, and life experiences: most obviously gender, age, and disability, but also cultural identity and socio-economic status. For capacity-building to generate a genuinely inclusive form of development, interventions must therefore take into account the different (and potentially negative) ways in which their impact will be felt by individuals and social groups.

Fourth, while capacity-building is designed to promote change, project-based interventions themselves take place within far wider processes of social and economic transformation. Hence the importance of being flexible enough to respond to a changing situation, while maintaining a sense of direction.

And finally, capacity-building is not 'doing development' on the cheap, or against the clock. Nor is it risk-free. Quite the reverse. It implies a long-term investment in people and their organisations, and a commitment to the various processes through which they can better shape the forces that affect their lives. For instance, both the former British Overseas Development Administration (now the Department for International Development, DfID) and USAID 'estimate that a realistic time frame for organisational strengthening [is] over ten years'.[7]

The principles underlying Oxfam's approach are summarised below:[8]

Oxfam's basic principles for development and relief work

People-centredness: Development and relief work is about improving the lives of women, men and children. Interventions must *always* be measured in terms of how they affect people's lives, in ways which are meaningful to the people concerned.

Human rights: The active promotion of human rights is central to development and relief work. These rights include the civil, political, economic, social, and cultural rights — individual and collective, personal and public — of all women, men and children.

Empowerment: Gaining the strength, confidence and vision to work for positive changes in their lives, individually and together with others, is the process of empowerment. Women and men become empowered by their own efforts, not by what others do for them. When development and relief programmes are not firmly based on people's own efforts to work for change, their impact may be disempowering.

Participation: Effective participation means people's right to shape decisions which affect their lives. Women and men are disempowered when they cannot exercise this right. Development and relief work should strengthen people's capacity to participate positively in social change, in terms both of personal growth and public action.

Interdependence: Societies depend on the inter-relations between women, men, and children, whose needs are distinct, and vary according to cultural, political, and economic factors. Development and relief interventions cannot isolate or 'target' one set of people without also having an impact on the lives and well-being of everyone who relates to them.

Change: Development and relief work takes place within a context of wider processes of social change, which are drawn on a far broader canvas than that of NGO interventions. Such processes are messy: social change does not have a clear beginning, middle or end, nor is it predictable or evenly-paced. Social change is always differentiated by gender. To be a positive force, NGOs must understand, and be committed to, the processes of change in which they choose to intervene.

Sustainability: To be sustainable, the processes of change must promote equity between, and for, all women and men; and enhance their ability to gain a decent living, both now and in the future. Sustainability is more than a matter of financial self-reliance: it depends on people's social and economic capacity to withstand and surmount pressures on their lives, and ways of life.

Risk: Development and relief are not risk-free. Women and men take risks when they try to change their lives, and to shape the decisions and processes affecting them. They cannot be certain about the outcomes of their efforts. Likewise, NGOs cannot demand certain returns from the support that they give.

(Eade and Williams,1994, pp 17–19.)

___

Some working definitions

Every organisation needs a clear conceptual framework for its activities — 'a set of concepts which allows the organisation to make sense of the world around it, to locate itself within that world, and to make decisions in relation to it' (CDRA,1995:6). Formulating such a framework requires an organisation to identify and define ideas and values that it finds most meaningful. Below, we offer some definitions of terms used in this book. Some are widely accepted, but others are either inherently difficult to define, or are currently used in widely divergent ways by different agencies. For this reason, where a broadly acceptable definition exists, this is what we have adopted here.

Civil society: '[T]ogether with state and market, one of the three 'spheres' that interface in the making of democratic societies. Civil society is the sphere in which social movements become organised. The organisations of civil society, which represent many diverse and sometimes contradictory social interests, are shaped to fit their social base, constituency, thematic orientations (eg environment, gender, human rights) and types of activity. They include church-related groups, trade unions, co-operatives, service organisations, community groups and youth organisations, as well as academic institutions and others' (UNDP, 1993, *UNDP and Organizations of Civil Society: Building Sustainable Partnerships*, New York:UNDP, *quoted in* Bebbington and Riddell, 1995).

NGOs: '[P]rofessional (though not always salaried), intermediary non-governmental groups channelling financial, technical, intellectual and further support to other groups within civil society' (Bebbington and Mitlin, 1996:8). NGOs often also provide similar forms of support to government entities, such as ministries of health or education. International NGOs are also widely involved in operational programmes, where their assistance may be direct or coordinated by another agency, such as the UN High Commissioner for Refugees (UNHCR). In addition, NGOs may undertake advocacy work or public education activities without having any immediate link with other groups within civil society.

In this Guideline, we use 'NGO' to refer only to those civil society organisations that are involved in development and humanitarian work (sometimes called NGDOs — non-governmental development organisations). We make no intrinsic distinction between Northern and Southern NGOs, but because the former tend to dispense financial and other resources to the latter, the relationship between them is essentially that of donor and recipient.

Community-based organisations (CBOs) and membership organisations: These are organisations whose membership is voluntary and who claim some representational function on behalf of their members (or, in the case of membership organisations who exist to support others — such as Amnesty International — their beneficiaries). They may also be known as 'people's', 'popular', or 'social organisations', or 'civics'. Common examples include unions, cooperatives, village-based or neighbourhood associations, and church- or mosque-based social committees.

Many CBOs run development programmes, with or without going through intermediary NGOs. Many international NGOs and a rising number of official donors directly fund such CBOs or membership organisations.

Donors: This refers to official (ie bilateral or multilateral) donor agencies, such as the Department for International Development (DfID) of the British government, formerly the Overseas Development Administration (ODA), or the European Union (EU). While the international financial institutions, such as the International Monetary Fund or the World Bank, are not donors, they are classified for the purposes of this book as official agencies. International NGOs are also funding agencies, and often channel official aid to Southern organisations.

Institutions: Applying this term to formal organisations or 'deliberately constructed human groupings' (Goldsmith, quoted in Moore:1995), we use 'institutional development' to refer to efforts that are intended to improve the functioning of a given institution (or set of institutions) so that they can perform more effectively, eg by improving their financial management systems, or training their staff. This is sometimes called 'institution-building'.

Organisational development: While organisational and institutional development overlap, we use the former to refer to processes and systems for achieving greater effectiveness within a given structure or group of people, such as decision-making and policy-formulation, appraisal, planning, evaluation and 'institutional learning', and training. While institutional development refers to activities aimed at formal structures, organisational development is equally relevant to informal or nascent associational forms.[9]

Partners and counterparts, recipients, clients, and beneficiaries:
Most Northern NGOs refer to those whose work they fund in the South as their 'partners'. This is, however, usually an inaccurate way to describe the relationship between Northern NGOs and the Southern organisations to whom they make grants. Here, we use instead the term 'counterparts' or 'recipients'. Although it is increasingly used in the literature, we avoid the term 'client' because of its ambiguity: it both implies patronage, and yet suggests that Southern organisations can freely 'shop around' to find the best supplier — something they are seldom able to do. By 'beneficiaries', we mean the people ultimately intended to benefit from a given intervention.

The purpose of this book

This Development Guideline is derived from *The Oxfam Handbook of Development and Relief* (Eade and Williams, 1995). It necessarily adopts a narrower focus in addressing a single topic, though one with far-reaching ramifications. However, it differs from the *Handbook* in two respects. The first is in introducing various concerns and dilemmas arising from NGO involvement in capacity-building. As Chris Roche mentions in his Preface, Oxfam is continually grappling with ways to learn more systematically from its own experience. In the area of capacity-building, this also demands a critical awareness of various conceptual frameworks — from a range of cultural backgrounds. The second major difference is that, in keeping with the aim of this series to offer accessible best-practice guidance for development professionals, the book makes liberal use of illustrative material, most of which is drawn from Oxfam's own publications. This material is set apart from the body of the text in the form of textboxes.

The opening three Chapters introduce the topic, and identify issues that should be borne in mind throughout the more practice-oriented section of the book. Chapter 2, 'Capacity-building: where does it come from?' suggests some of the factors that have contributed to the current interest in capacity-building, and identifies some of the conceptual and practical dilemmas that may in turn generate new thinking. Chapter 3, 'What is capacity-building?' introduces various definitions used by organisations and commentators and explains Oxfam's own approach to capacity-building — including what Oxfam aims *not* to do! Chapter 4, 'Whose capacities?' looks at how social diversity affects the capacities of people and their organisations, focusing on the impact of discrimination and exclusion on the basis of gender, ethnic and cultural identity, age, and disability.

The following four Chapters cover the kinds of capacities that are critical for development, irrespective of the group or organisation in question. Such capacities can be divided broadly into social, organisational, and material, though of course these categories are far from watertight. Chapter 5, 'Investing in people', deals with human development within an organised social setting. It focuses specifically on education and skills training, training for employment, and personal development. Chapter 6, 'Investing in organis-ations', examines various ways of supporting organisational capacity, looking at issues such as appraisal, planning, institutional learning, and financial manage-ment. The following Chapter, 'Investing in networks', looks at networking and alliance-building in the context of capacity-building, and the rapid develop-ments in information technology. Chapter 8, 'Building capacity in crisis', discusses the importance of focusing on existing social and organisational capacities during a major crisis, so that these are not undermined by any relief intervention.

A final Chapter, 'Building the capacities of others: questions for donors' draws out the major themes from the book, and poses a number of questions for donor agencies and development NGOs who provide funding and other resources for capacity-building. The book concludes with a Bibliography of works referred to in the text, and recommended further reading.

Who is this Guideline for?

Essentially, this book is for anyone with an interest in capacity-building and people-centred development. It is written from Oxfam's own perspective, and does not in that sense aim to be 'neutral' or non-committal: Oxfam is inspired by a vision of a world without poverty, where all human beings have an equitable share in the world's resources. However, Oxfam's vision is limited by the fact that it is a British NGO that works internationally. A Southern NGO or grassroots organisation would have a very different perspective. Equally, the approaches to capacity-building taken by a government agricultural exten-sion department, a Northern academic researcher, or an organisational management consultant from the business sector, would all be very different.

However, we hope that this Guideline will be relevant to anyone who is involved in the policy and practice of development and relief work, particularly within the NGO sector, but also within other organisations and institutions that are in some way engaged in the capacity-building process. As a 'why to' rather than a 'how to' book, if it enables readers to reflect more critically about their role(s) in this process, it will have succeeded.

2

Capacity-building: where has it come from?

No matter how understanding the donor may be, the fact that the Northern NGO is the one with the money means that the Southern NGO must be the one with the begging bowl. No matter how good the personal relationship between the Northern and the Southern NGO, the latter must accept the humiliation of being the receiver of charity. Perforce, there is a relationship of unequals. And inequality never built capacity (Manji, 1997).

Capacity-building: just another fad...?

Like most development jargon, capacity-building is now used so indiscriminately that any meaning it once had may soon evaporate. Indeed, some commentators argue that the term was never really intended to mean anything anyway and should be jettisoned, since 'it is likely to spawn confusing controversy and undermine the morale of aid agency staff concerned with institution building by weakening their sense of working to a clear mission' (Moore, 1995:92).

As we shall see in Chapter 3, definitions of capacity-building are sometimes vague and inconsistent, though not necessarily incompatible in practice. It is easy to be irritated by the speed with which development jargon catches on and is bandied about so uncritically — until it goes out of vogue. But why is it that 'capacity-building' has risen to such prominence in the mid-1990s? Surely not only because of institutional self-interest or linguistic fashion.

In this Chapter, we identify and discuss various significant trends in thinking, policy, and practice that have contributed to this interest in capacity-building for development, particularly in relation to NGOs (whether these are donors, channels, or ultimate recipients of assistance). Drawing on material that is essential and accessible reading for practitioners, we will attempt to indicate the breadth of writing on the topic.

...Or a response to a changing context?

Today's thinking about 'capacity-building' is influenced by earlier ideas concerning participation, empowerment, civil society, and social movements (see, for example, Escobar and Alvarez, 1992; Williams et al, 1994; Eade and Williams, 1995; Rowlands 1995; Carmen, 1996; White, 1996; Rowlands, 1997; UNDP); and these in turn have been significantly shaped by the work of Paulo Freire, and the impact of Liberation Theology (Freire; Gutiérrez). There is also a substantial literature on the role(s) of NGOs, both from within the NGO sector and from outside observers (see, for example, Korten, 1990; Clark, 1991; Pearce, 1993; Edwards and Hulme, 1992; Edwards and Hulme, 1995a; Edwards and Hulme, 1995b; Sogge, 1996; Smillie, 1995; Fowler, 1997).

Development for liberation: critical capacities for change

Two inter-weaving strands of thought emerged from Latin America during the 1970s and 1980s, influencing more than a generation of popular organisations, revolutionary movements, political actors, and development NGOs, and they continue to shape the intellectual and moral framework for defining human development and empowerment. They are the *conscientisation* or awareness-creation approach to adult literacy of the Brazilian educationalist Paulo Freire; and Liberation Theology. These concepts flourished during a period when political and military repression were at their height throughout Latin America: Freire was himself forced into political exile, while many hundreds of priests, *catequistas* (lay-preachers), and members of religious communities were persecuted by right-wing forces throughout the sub-continent, particularly in Central America. The involvement of the proponents of these ideas with poor people's daily struggles to resist oppression, and to achieve social justice, helped to make these ideas profoundly influential.

Today, the Freirean focus on popular mobilisation is sometimes considered outdated, especially among NGOs that have become sceptical of social movements and would now see income-generation and economic production projects as the first priority. And the Vatican has clamped down firmly on Liberation Theology since its heyday in the 1980s. However, these linked ideas inspired and mobilised poor and excluded people on a scale far greater than any other development 'ideology' has succeeded in doing either before or since. What follows below is a summary of some of the central ideas as these relate to capacity-building.

Freire's seminal works *Pedagogy of the Oppressed* (1972) and *Education for Critical Consciousness* (1973), argue that the process of learning to read and the act of reading are deeply political: our reading of the word is shaped by our reading of the world. Rather than seeing education as a means by which knowledge is handed down from an omniscient teacher to the ignorant student, Freire maintained that 'education for liberation' must be a process of problem-solving and dialogue among equals.

There have been many critiques and refinements of Freirean methods of literacy teaching; and some recent attempts to revive these in combination with other more modern participatory research techniques (these are discussed in Chapter 5). But we can identify three lasting contributions to development thinking, and specifically to thinking about capacity-building and empowerment. First, that the learners and their own experience and knowledge are of crucial importance; second, that awareness, learning, self-esteem, and the capacity for political action are mutually reinforcing. And third, that poor and marginalised people have the right, and the capacity, to organise and challenge authority in order to create a society that is not based on exploitation and oppression.

Within the Catholic Church, Liberation Theology represented an attempt to reclaim the *humanity* of Jesus Christ and the *divinity* of every human being; and to situate Christianity within the everyday reality of poverty and suffering. Whereas the traditional reading of the Bible had for centuries served to justify the oppressive actions of the rich and the powerful, Liberation Theology sought to re-discover Christ's authentic 'gospel of the poor'. Many biblical texts assumed a powerful political significance, once poverty, oppression, and suffering were related to material conditions in the here and now. Christ thus became a symbol of personal, collective, and even national liberation: someone who would challenge injustice and poverty in the real world, even at the expense of his own life.

The Second Vatican Council had encouraged the Church to consolidate its mission by incorporating local values and recognising the importance of the lay-preachers, often known as Catechists or Delegates of the Word. Liberation Theology was endorsed by the Latin American Council of Bishops at their 1968 meeting in Medellín. The Medellín Documents laid out the belief in 'a third way' between capitalism and communism — an argument that strongly favoured the growth of Christian Democracy throughout the region. But the Documents also stressed that Christ had come 'to set at liberty them that are bruised' (Luke 4:18); and to cleanse the world of sin — defined also as poverty, injustice, ignorance, institutionalised violence, and economic neo-colonialism. In their Letter from Puebla, the Bishops reinforced this position, stating that the church in Latin America would henceforth exercise a 'preferential option for the poor'.

In the political and economic context of Latin America, where 90 per cent of the people are Catholic, and where wealth and power are in most countries concentrated in the hands of a tiny few while the vast majority live in poverty, such a message was dynamite. It inspired many of those who took up arms in the various revolutionary movements throughout the region. It also encouraged an unprecedented level of social organisation. In rural areas and city slums alike, Christian Base Communities brought people together to reflect on the teachings of Christ, and relate these to their own lives. There was a huge upsurge in the membership of popular organisations, such as peasant associations and unions; and a corresponding investment in popular education, training centres, radio schools, and so on.

Feminist theologians and Christian activists expanded the meaning and scope of Liberation Theology, making it a powerful tool for working with poor women (see, for example, Pixley, 1986; Tábora, 1992). In a social context which is suspicious and fearful of 'feminism', it was important to be able to 'ground' this work in women's own Christian faith — often with the support of the official church structures.

My reference points were in the Bible: the roles played by Esther and Judith in the Old Testament, and by Mary in the New Testament. This, and my own practical experience as the only woman cooperative leader, were what gave me an awareness of gender. As I participated in the otherwise all-male cooperative, I felt uneasy: why was I the only woman there? Why weren't there more women? I was for ever asking myself: where are the other women?
(leader of education programme for rural Christian women, quoted in Tábora, 1992:43, my translation).

The current emphasis on empowerment and participation in development thinking has been deeply influenced by these experiences.

Development in crisis: new thinking, new approaches

The concept of development began to come under serious fire from the late 1980s, the so-called 'lost decade' in which many of the earlier gains and achievements of development either stagnated or went into reverse. Even to summarise the debates is well beyond the scope of this Guideline, but influential critiques include those of outstanding scholars and activists such as Samir Amin, Peggy Antrobus, Robert Chambers, Gustavo Esteva, Paulo Freire, Susan George, Ivan Illich, Devaki Jain, Martin Khor, David Korten, Rajni Kothari, Mahmood Mamdani, Manfred Max-Neef, Wolfgang Sachs, Amartya Sen, and Vandana Shiva.

In various ways, such scholars maintain that the Western model of development is intrinsically unsustainable and undesirable. Arturo Escobar sums up this position, describing 'development' as a post-1945 construct within which to shape and manage relationships between nations and peoples, 'an apparatus that links forms of knowledge about the Third World with the deployment of forms of power and intervention, resulting in the mapping and production of Third World societies', (Escobar in Crush, 1995:213). Global institutions such as the World Bank and IMF, the UN, the regional development banks, as well as the bi-lateral agencies — and indeed most NGOs — operate within and reinforce a world-view that regards development as 'paving the way for the achievement of those conditions that characterise rich societies: industrialisation, agricultural modernisation, and urbanisation' (ibid. 214). In Escobar's analysis, this discourse has been so powerful and seductive that it succeeded (and still succeeds) in colonising all space for thought and action. However, 'fashionable notions such as "sustainable development", "grassroots development", "women and development", "market-friendly development" and the like' are no more than 'attempts to salvage development' by updating the terminology, while leaving the concept intact. As Northern thinkers grapple with 'the impasse in development' (Schuurman, 1992), Escobar argues that Southern scholars are abandoning the search for 'development alternatives' and instead 'speak about "alternatives to development", that is, a rejection of the entire paradigm' (Escobar, op cit, p 215).

Also emerging in the late 1980s, Capacities and Vulnerabilities Analysis (CVA) signalled a shift in the perceived relationship between development and crisis (Anderson and Woodrow, 1989). CVA drew on a number of case-studies, some relating to 'natural' disasters, and others to wars and political violence, and helped to show how the former (and responses to them) are necessarily social and political in their impact: a disaster may be natural, but never neutral. It also offered a conceptual alternative to the 'relief-rehabilitation-development continuum' just as the nature of 'complex political emergencies' was rendering such linear notions redundant.[1]

CVA is an analytical framework based on three main assumptions:

• *Development is the process by which vulnerabilities are reduced and capacities are increased.* If equality and equity are the goals of development, then interventions must address the causes of people's weakness and recognise their sources of strength; and understand the dynamic relationships between these.

• *No one 'develops' anyone else.* People and societies develop themselves, with or without the help of external agencies.

• *Relief programmes are never neutral in their developmental impact.* Relief efforts which do not strengthen people's existing capacities necessarily intensify their vulnerabilities, ie those long-term factors which affect their ability to respond to adverse events, or which make them susceptible to calamities.

The CVA matrix divides capacities and vulnerabilities into three categories: material, social, and attitudinal. These are differentiated by variables such as gender, age, ethnicity, and socio-economic status. A change within any category inevitably alters the situation overall: if an aid programme enlists men to undertake tasks, such as food distribution, from which women drew status and identity, the overall impact may be to damage women's self-esteem and organisational capacity. CVA thus brings a sharper awareness that aid can have unintended negative effects. Identifying and strengthening the capacities that people and organisations already have, and tackling the causes of their weakness — causes which may well lie outside the immediate community, or national borders (Anderson, 1994:330-331) — provides a framework for making decisions about short- and long-term responses.

CVA demonstrated that development (that is, positive changes in people's well-being and ability to control their lives) does not wait for an emergency to end, but goes on *in the midst of crisis, and may help to shape the outcomes.* Conversely, interventions that reinforce inequality and exclusion may themselves generate various forms of crisis. NGO thinking and practice has since built on these perceptions (see Eade and Williams, 1995; Eade, 1996b). Aid agencies have come to see that turbulence and uncertainty define the context for their work. To confine 'development' to those activities that require stability is not only misguided, but may lead to action (or inaction) that is harmful for those who are least able to mobilise resources.These points are taken up in Chapter 8.

In the wake of structural adjustment policies throughout many regions of the South, the late 1980s and early 1990s saw a growing awareness that the goal of economic growth and industrialisation at the expense of massive indebtedness, rising unemployment, and widening gaps between rich and poor, was itself responsible for some of the problems that were erupting in conflict and crisis. Ideas on sustainable livelihoods (Chambers and Conway, 1992), and Participatory Rural Appraisal (PRA) and its derivatives offered a way to understand development (and aid interventions) in a more dynamic, disaggregated, and systemic way: who loses and who benefits, how, and with what long-term implications for society as a whole. Answering these questions helps in deciding whose capacities need to be strengthened, and in what ways.

A focus on people, diversity, and rights

The impact of neo-liberal economic policies caused increasing disquiet within some of the UN specialised agencies, notably UNDP, UNICEF, and UNRISD. A broad-based and vocal consensus around the idea of human or people-centred development (Nicholls, 1996:4–5) began to emerge, which also included citizens' groups (such as the Freedom from Debt Coalition in the Philippines, the Self-Employed Women's Association, and the Latin American Forum on Debt and Development) and various influential NGOs. Development could not be delivered by markets or by economic growth alone, which might, indeed, undermine it; and it required something quite distinct from the re-distribution of financial and material resources. The constraints on development were in large measure social, political, and cultural. The assumption that 'development would trickle down to all income classes — and that it was gender-neutral in its impact' was thus widely discredited (UNDP,1995:1).

The 1985 Nairobi Conference to review progress made during the UN Decade for Women marked a turning-point in 'putting gender on the agenda'. Gender-based oppression was seen to be universal. Several UN agencies began to pay more systematic attention to what UNICEF in its 1992 *The State of the World's Children* called 'the apartheid of gender', by disaggregating data to reveal the huge gulf in the life-experiences and opportunities of women and girls, compared with men and boys. The international women's movement had also gained prominence, especially in the South, since the 1975 conference in Mexico which launched the International Decade for Women. The growth of feminist analysis in many relevant fields, including economics, anthropology, social and political science, and cultural studies, also influenced the policy environment within official agencies and NGOs.[2]

A book co-written by Richard Jolly, then Deputy Executive Director of UNICEF (and now Special Adviser to the Administrator of UNDP) was influential in putting the case for 'adjustment with a human face' (Cornia et al 1989). The UNDP took the intellectual lead in developing some of the analytical tools and statistical data by which to assess the quality of development from a human perspective. Since 1990, its *Human Development Report* series has argued that 'people are the real wealth of a nation', and contrasted conventional economic indicators (such as Gross National Product or per capita income) with others (such as food security, employment, military expenditure, and educational performance), to produce a composite Human Development Index (HDI). This drew on earlier efforts to measure and promote development, bringing together social and economic analysis; what UNRISD in 1974 had termed 'capacitation':

... a 'capacitating' operation [which] does not try so much to define or control the future as to establish present conditions or capacities which will permit a given society to meet its problems in the future. The emphasis in such an approach is not on setting future appropriate output targets but on

15

diagnosing current weaknesses and potentials, finding appropriate policies, and constantly monitoring the course of development (Wolfe, 1996:40).

A 'capabilities approach' to defining development was also propounded by the economist and philosopher Amartya Sen, whose work on 'entitlements' has been influential in shaping the analysis of famines and their prevention. Sen argues that the true purpose of development is to enhance people's quality of life, which is best achieved by giving them access to a wider spectrum of capabilities: 'the capabilities approach is related to, but fundamentally different from, characterising development as either (i) the expansion of goods and services, (ii) an increase in utilities, or (iii) meeting basic needs'.[3]

The 1990 UNDP *Report* stated that 'civil and political rights tend broadly to correlate with equitable economic arrangements ... [and] therefore ... that civil and political freedom are an essential element of human development, not an optional extra' (quoted in Eade and Williams, 1995:35). UNDP's 1995 *Report*, published to coincide with the Fourth World Conference on Women in Beijing, introduced the Gender-related Development Index (GDI). This was based on factors such as the female share of earned income, as well as educational performance and participation in public and political life. The GDI graphically demonstrated what feminists had been saying for decades: that 'gender-neutral' analyses and policies mask — and reinforce — systematic biases in access to power and resources, favouring men. For instance Canada dropped from first position in world HDI ranking to ninth, once gender differentials were taken into account. Conversely, several poorer countries did better: for instance, Thailand outranked Spain in the GDI, although its per capita income is less than half that of Spain.

UNDP has, therefore, helped to show that economic growth is a necessary but insufficient condition for human development. If the aim is to enlarge the capacity for choice, so that all women and men can become agents of change, equality of opportunity becomes a litmus test for human development:

[which is] unjust and discriminatory if most women are excluded from its benefits. And the continuing exclusion of women from many economic and political opportunities is a continuing indictment of modern progress
(UNDP, 1995:1).

In a post-modern intellectual climate that stresses diversity, difference, and 'freedom of choice', and rejects notions of universality, it is vital also to examine the many ways in which choices are denied. Too easily, 'an appreciation of differences' is translated into 'total cultural relativism'; while, conversely, 'a programmatic emphasis on difference and diversity has, in some cases, supported tendencies towards social disintegration and divisiveness'.[4]

The major UN Conferences during the 1990s,[5] although marked by dissent and disillusion, also gave unprecedented opportunities for official development agencies, NGOs, citizens' groups and others to learn more about their differences and similarities, to organise together on the basis of shared needs and experiences, to strategise and make common cause for changes in national and international institutions and policies so that all human beings can enjoy their full political, economic, social, and cultural rights.

NGOs and the 'new policy agenda'

Hastened by the end of the Cold War, the now dominant neo-liberal framework for global economic policy has been associated not only with a 'rolling back of the state' (or even with the virtual collapse of government in some countries), but also with a spectacular growth in the development NGO sector. This phenomenon has, in part, been a spontaneous response to the damaging side-effects of economic structural adjustment programmes: increasing poverty and social exclusion, and the growing numbers of 'new poor'.

But in a climate of privatisation and 'out-contracting', NGOs have also become the channel of choice for many official donors. This may be because donors believe that NGOs perform better than governments in delivering aid: in terms of reaching 'the poor', or in their accountability, cost-effectiveness, efficiency, or ability to innovate. Many donors have also assumed that if NGOs are accountable to their 'beneficiaries', then they can also represent the interests of these people, and so hold governments more democratically accountable to the poor. Thus, donors may want to strengthen NGOs so that they in turn can mobilise their respective constituencies within 'civil society', in order to promote 'democratisation' and 'good governance' at the local or national level.[6]

Thus, against a background of steady decline in government-to-government aid (German and Randel, 1996) NGOs are competing for contracts to provide health-care programmes, education projects, agricultural extension services, training courses, evaluations, organisational management consultancies, and so on. Further, in 'scaling-up' the scope and diversity of their work, many NGOs have increased their own dependence on channelling official aid money, both in long-term development programmes and in emergency relief work. So much so, that it is now almost a cliché to ask at what point an NGO stops being *non*-governmental.[7]

These trends have far-reaching implications both for the non-governmental sector as a whole, and in terms of the survival strategies that individual NGOs adopt — itself a subject of lively debate (see for example Zetter, 1996; Edwards and Hulme, 1995a, 1995b; Stewart, 1995; Bebbington and Riddell,

1995; Bebbington and Mitlin, 1996). As NGO-state relations are re-aligned, it is not only an NGO's programmes that are affected, but also its functioning, organisational ethos, and relationship with its own constituency — donors as well as 'clients' or contractors. For example, it is one thing for an NGO to support health projects that complement an existing public health service which defines policies and regulates standards. It is quite another to assume formal responsibility for providing health care in lieu of the state — and to depend on an uncertain mixture of user-fees, grants, and charitable donations in order to do so. To whom does accountability lie? To the donors? The state? The other contracted service-providers? The health professionals? The tax-payers? Or to the patients?

In a context of rapid change, an NGO must be all the more clear about its own purpose and values and the role(s) it wishes to play. This is a complex issue (for two excellent overviews, see Bebbington and Riddell, 1995; Bebbington and Mitlin, 1996); but even if NGOs cannot do everything that has been claimed of them, there are five critical issues they must address if they are to retain their credibility as 'capacity-builders'.

First, if as Caroline Moser maintains, NGOs are 'identified as the institutional solution for "alternative" development models' because of 'their capacity to reach the "grass-roots" where the "real people" are',[8] this capacity may be undermined by the demands associated with channelling aid from official donors. As Firoze Manji suggests in the opening quotation to this Chapter, 'partnerships' that are mediated by money are characterised by tension and inequality. When international or national NGOs become channels for official assistance, tensions often arise about a range of issues: rapid or poorly managed expansion, in response to the priorities of donors; the need to become more 'professional', even at the expense of a voluntarist ethos; the adoption of systems for planning, appraisal, and reporting that may conflict with more flexible, informal, or participatory approaches; and an emphasis on cost-effectiveness, efficiency, and measurable impact, which reduces local consultation and involvement in shaping the programme. Such tensions may occur at each link in the chain of dependency joining the donor, the Northern NGO, and the Southern NGO or counterpart organisation. So-called 'capacity-building' begins to look like an elaborate charade:

Some Northern agencies clearly include within capacity building the skills that they require within Southern agencies, so that the agency staff can meet the Northern agencies' requirements for reporting and accounting. More fundamentally, there are also concerns that the types of issues and questions raised with capacity building ... are all Northern perceptions of Southern needs' (Bebbington and Mitlin, 1996:16).

In fact, these researchers found that although Northern NGOs have taken on the language of capacity-building, 'in many cases the focus of their work appears to be more on *capacity building as a means to securing on-going activities*, rather than to secure more 'ends' oriented objectives' (ibid:18 my italics).

Second, it may actually be self-defeating to see capacity-building as a way of equipping Southern NGOs to be 'better vehicles for the simple delivery of programmes defined by donors', since doing so may erode their central identity and sense of purpose:

By imposing an agenda and objectives, the donors can distort the links between an NGO's value base, organisation and activities, and thus ultimately weaken the NGO even at the same time as increasing its financial, technical and human resources in the short term (Bebbington and Mitlin, 1996:16).

This problem was identified by NGOs in Bolivia and Peru who became involved in handling the Emergency Social Funds, the so-called 'safety-nets' designed to accompany World Bank and IMF economic structural adjustment programmes. In addition to the bureaucratic impositions already mentioned, some of them found that the 'contract culture', whereby they were contracted to undertake specific time-bound projects for 'client' groups, often fitted uneasily with their existing relationship with their constituencies in poor communities (Whitehead, 1995).

Third, it is unwise to take it on trust that NGOs are accountable to or can represent the social sectors or organisations whose interests they serve. Indeed, there is evidence that some NGOs (Northern and Southern) have improved their own capacity to survive in a changing environment, while the organisations that originally gave them legitimacy are either marginalised, or just as dependent and insecure as before. Whatever the donors' intentions, the overall effect of building the capacity of certain NGOs has sometimes been the further disempowerment and exclusion of the poorer and weaker members of civil society with whom they work:

Chile is the classic case, but not the only one. Here, the return to civilian rule ... has been accompanied by the disempowerment of the social movements of the 1980s. The Chilean NGO world is split between those who opted to engage with the centre-left government programme — and so have succeeded in institutionalising themselves in the new circumstances — and those who remain critical of the failure of the government to meet the needs of the poorest sectors. The latter remain small, under-resourced, fragmented, and politically marginalised. And, as the larger NGOs have come closer to the national and formal 'political' world, their links with the social world have become very weak (Pearce, 1993:223–4).

Jenny Pearce recommends that donors analyse the mechanisms of 'downward accountability' before concentrating resources within a particular NGO or CBO. They should also be aware of the cumulative impact of their support. There are many examples of local organisations being flooded with grants from various international donors, none of whom takes responsibility when their counterpart collapses under the weight of over-funding.

Fourth, it is dangerous to base capacity-building strategies on the assumption that the state and 'civil society' are monolithic, and dichotomously opposed, with the former seen as intrinsically 'bad' or oppressive, and the latter as inherently 'good' or consensual. 'Civil society' may be an arena for conflict and the abuse of power, while the state may provide a regulatory framework for mediating conflict and penalising abuse. The existence of, a Commission for Racial Equality, an Equal Opportunities Commission, or a European Court of Human Rights, demonstrates this. More bluntly, in the words of Susan George, 'Who will make sure the good guys win, in so far as business interests, gun-lovers and the Ku Klux Klan also figure in civil society?'[9]

Further, an active and 'enabling' state is seen by many as a precondition for a vibrant civil society. Jenny Pearce argues that the emergence of 'social movements' in Chile under the Pinochet régime 'emphasised the *weakness* of "civil society", not its arrival on the scene. People had taken to the streets, precisely because the appropriate channels for political participation did not exist for them' (Pearce, ibid:225). Researchers in Brazil found that the high performance of government health workers was partially due to the trust and respect in which they were held by local people, as well as to the relative autonomy with which they could respond to local needs. These experiences challenge the prevalent assumption that the state is an obstacle to participatory development, or that the public sector is necessarily opaque and unaccountable (Tendler and Freedheim, 1994).

In terms of how NGOs engage with the state, thinking and practice have moved beyond the alternatives of confrontation or constructive engagement, towards a range of inter-weaving opportunities. A single NGO may simultaneously have a variety of relationships with the state, each of which may be re-negotiated or evolve over time (Farrington and Bebbington, 1993). But for international NGOs the fundamental question remains whether the promotion of non-governmental institutions that replace public provision of basic services (or draw public employees into a better-paid NGO sector) will ultimately weaken or strengthen civil society.

Given that Northern NGOs, Southern NGOs, and governments in the South are today competing for the same aid resources, an approach that encourages co-operation between them may be the sounder and more sustainable option. If NGOs are in competition with a diminished state — and at the same time depend on funding from the North — this will not only fuel resentment, but may ultimately create major difficulties for the NGOs and their sponsors. The real losers will be those who most need support, and whose voice is least likely to be heard:

It is not only projects which enhance local NGOs which can claim to be strengthening civil society. Those which also strengthen the provision of welfare services by the state also enable a degree of contact between state and citizen which may enhance the prospects for civil society (Whaites, 1996:243).

Fifth, if capacity-building aims to create sustainable Southern institutions, then the withdrawal of the state from areas such as education, training, research, health, housing, transport, or existing subsidy or benefit systems, compromises any related services that are provided through NGOs — especially if these are for low-income populations. Like the commercial private sector, NGOs themselves depend on the public sector in a host of ways. It is therefore illogical for donors to focus on building the capacity of the non-governmental sector, as though it could function autonomously, while promoting macro-economic policies that undermine the government's existing capacity to provide effective social welfare services. Doing so may not only create hardship, but also focus public discontent on the government:

Zimbabwe is widely cited by the World Bank as an example of its new, poverty-focused approach to structural adjustment. Under its 1990 structural adjustment programme, the Government of Zimbabwe committed itself to reducing the national budget deficit from 10 per cent to 5 per cent of national income by 1995. There was an agreement with the World Bank that it would do so in a way which would not only protect public expenditure in health and education, but restore cuts made since 1988, when per capita spending in both areas began to decline... In practice, however, budgets for health and education declined dramatically in real terms during the first three years of the structural adjustment programme ... These expenditure patterns have threatened the impressive social welfare improvements made in Zimbabwe since Independence. Their effects have been deeply felt by many of Oxfam's project partners, who have seen their opportunities for education and health care diminish. There is widespread and justifiable anger at the failure of the World Bank and the Zimbabwean government to consider more equitable ways of reducing the budget deficit (Watkins,1995:80–81).

In conclusion, what each of these paradoxes demonstrates is the danger of looking at capacity-building in isolation from the wider social, economic, cultural, and political fabric of which it must form a part. Capacity-building does not begin and end with NGOs, or with donors. Nor is 'civil society' independent of, much less an alternative to, the state. Rather, capacity-building involves the whole network of relationships in society: within, between, and among households, neighbourhoods, grassroots or community-based organisations, unions, religious confessions, training institutions, research bodies, government ministries, the private sector, NGOs, and donor agencies — whether official or non-governmental, Northern or Southern. Capacity-building is also concerned with creating new relationships of mutuality and reciprocity within a given society and beyond, at a time when the advances in communication technology are increasing the potential for global alliances (a subject we explore more fully in Chapter 7).

In terms of outside agencies, it is important to remember that capacity-building is a multi-directional, multi-dimensional process and not, as one Oxfam colleague puts it, 'a one-way street'. This means that external agents need to focus on enhancing the quality of existing and potential relationships within civil society, not just increasing the number of local organisations or implementing 'partners'. Essentially, agencies must recognise their own capacities and limitations before deciding how best to build the capacities of others, a point to which we shall return at the end of this book.

3

What is capacity-building?

Strengthening people's capacity to determine their own values and priorities, and to organise themselves to act on these, is the basis of development (Eade and Williams, 1995:9).

Introduction

Given the all-embracing scope often attached to the ubiquitous references to 'capacity-building' in many development agency documents, it is common to open a discussion on what it means by reeling off a set of competing definitions. In this way, readers can pick and choose, or even assemble their own. Alternatively, they simply become so bewildered that they are happy to let the author do this for them.

Here, we shall take a different approach, not providing a rigid definition of capacity-building, but rather certain principles and beliefs about the world, and about the role of NGOs. Oxfam's 'vision', 'mission', or 'organisational mandate' has evolved over its 55-year history, but its day-to-day interpretation of how best to work for 'the relief of poverty, distress and suffering' will vary from one setting to another. Oxfam's thinking on capacity-building as on any other topic, is shaped by the dynamic relationship between its formal purpose and its efforts to reflect on its own experience as a poverty-focused NGO. Like development itself, capacity-building is concerned with social and political relationships. It cannot, therefore, be viewed in isolation from the wider social, economic, and political environment — governments, markets, and the private sector as well as CBOs, NGOs and other institutions, right down to the community, household, and personal level.

It is critical to understand the context in order to know how change can best be stimulated. This will depend on a whole range of circumstances. For instance, a review of Oxfam's work over 20 years or more years in South India found that in some cases support for women's existing economic activities had given them the confidence to become involved in the social and political arena. In others, efforts by Dalits to pursue leadership training and organisational work had actually resulted in violent reprisals against them. (Parasuraman and Vimalanathan, 1997). Having the skills and sensitivity to assess such risks, and the flexibility to change direction if things are going wrong, is vital, and will be a recurrent theme of this Guideline.

This Chapter will firstly describe what Oxfam believes to be the essential principles that underpin capacity-building for development: what Allan Kaplan calls its 'working understanding of the world'. Given the many meanings in common usage, it will also clarify what Oxfam does *not* mean by capacity-building.

The Chapter then summarises some of the dilemmas arising from differing approaches to capacity-building. Much of the confusion about what capacity-building means is the result of donors and NGOs being woolly-minded about their own agendas or unrealistic about their own capacities. A schematic characterisation of contrasting approaches in Oxfam's own current programmes and interventions is given, to show that while there are no context-free recipes for capacity-building, a conscious framework for intervention can help in understanding diverse needs and opportunities, and in forming longer-term strategies.

Capacity-building: an approach to development

A capacity-building approach to development involves identifying the constraints that women and men experience in realising their basic rights, and finding appropriate vehicles through which to strengthen their ability to overcome the causes of their exclusion and suffering.

Development is about women and men becoming empowered to bring about positive changes in their lives; about personal growth together with public action; about both the process and the outcome of challenging poverty, oppression, and discrimination; and about the realisation of human potential through social and economic justice. Above all, it is about the process of transforming lives, and transforming societies (Eade and Williams, 1995:9).

Thus *capacity-building is an approach to development* not something separate from it. It is a response to the multi-dimensional processes of change, not a set of discrete or pre-packaged technical interventions intended to bring about a pre-defined outcome. In supporting organisations working for social justice, it is also necessary to support the various capacities they require to do this: intellectual, organisational, social, political, cultural, material, practical, or financial.

The most appropriate intervention will reflect the *diversity* of the groups and organisations within a given setting. For Oxfam, a single country pro-gramme may include contacts with government agencies as well as with organisations that are independent or even critical of government; with religious or cultural societies, farmers' cooperatives, labour unions, committees of refugees or displaced persons, human rights organisations, feminist research groups, training institutions, publishers, radio stations, neighbourhood or village committees, local or national NGOs. It may also include support for nationwide or international alliances among all or some of these.

The tasks of an intermediary NGO or donor agency are first, to assess what kind and level of support is most likely to promote a more inclusive and equitable society; and second, to monitor and modify any negative outcomes of that support. An agency's responsibility for its interventions does not stop with its final grant cheque, although the project-based mentality encourages this way of thinking.[1] For example, Oxfam funded dozens of Guatemalan producer and consumer cooperatives throughout the 1970s. These people and their communities were among the earliest targets of growing political violence. Survivors fled either to become fugitives in the forests and mountains of Guatemala, to its towns as internally displaced, or as refugees to Mexico or the USA. These people were persecuted largely because of their newly-acquired capacities: to organise, to communicate, to strategise, and to question. How can any agency that has been directly or indirectly involved in such a capacity-building process then ignore a moral claim on its continued solidarity? And can it justify withholding such support because its 'partners' now need material assistance in order to survive, rather than funding for training as cooperativists? These are rhetorical questions, but they illustrate that if projects have any meaning, it is as part of a wider and deeper process of change. Success in the short-term may not always be maintained in the longer term. Hard-won gains can be lost, or can give rise to many unforeseen problems as a situation evolves.

Capacities will not just 'trickle down'
No group is entirely homogeneous: within a household or family group, the situation of men may differ sharply from that of women; within a community, lone mothers are likely to have different concerns (and constraints) than do people with no dependents. These 'personal' dynamics need to be contin-ually assessed to see how they fit into a wider pattern. For instance, if women are reluctant or unable to participate openly in public or 'community' decision-making processes, then it may be harmful to strengthen the organisational structure in question without first exploring these inequalities. Capacities will not 'trickle down' through a power structure unless active steps are taken to ensure that they do.

As with any other resources, if activities intended to build capacities are introduced into a skewed environment of access to skills or opportunities, they may *de facto* reinforce existing forms of power and exclusion (Stewart and Taylor, 1995). To bring about sustainable change may mean having to take several steps back before moving ahead — spending time to work through the problem areas rather than throwing money at them in the hope that this will somehow resolve them. This kind of 'critical accompaniment' can be hard for agencies to provide when they are required to spend their budgets and show results. But the failure to do so can be damaging.

The growing literature on gender in institutions — much of it focused on development agencies — shows how these 'do not just passively mirror gender differences in social organisation, but ... also *produce* gender differences through their structures and everyday practices' (Goetz, 1996:3). The latter include everything from 'the gendering of authority symbols' to the lack of 'a *strategic presence* for women representing women's interests in policy-making processes' (ibid., p8). (See also Chapters 4 and 6).

It is doubtful whether an organisation that itself maintains oppressive social structures can be a reliable vehicle for transforming these in a liberating way, whatever its rhetoric. And this is equally true for donors and NGOs:

> *We all know the classic development cliché ... 'Give a man a fish, feed him for a day; teach him how to fish, feed him for a lifetime'. This is a laudable senti-ment, but it becomes more complex on two counts. The first we have known for some time— it does not help to teach people to fish when they are denied equal access to the resource base... But the second complexity is more intractable. What if those of us who claim to do the teaching do not know how to fish? This is not at all far-fetched. Can we — as NGOs, as donors, as governmental extension services— honestly claim to have achieved that much capacity in our own organisations, we who strive to teach others? Have we really mastered what we teach, have we been able to organise ourselves sufficiently to achieve meaningful impact? Clearly we have not* (CDRA, 1995: 2).

Finally, there is no guarantee that individuals or groups will use their strengthened or new capacities for the benefit of the whole; and experience shows that it is unwise to assume that they necessarily will.

Peeling off the labels

Because of the uniqueness of an organisation and its history, and its part in a wider context, decisions about what and when to support must be made on the basis of analysis rather than assumptions or labels. In deciding on the allocation of resources, it would be just as wrong to assume, for instance, that CBOs or intermediary NGOs are uniquely equipped to 'deliver development' or to guarantee 'civil society', as to assume that co-operatives are inherently superior to small businesses, that governments are always 'inefficient', while landlords and money-lenders are 'wicked', families are 'good', men are 'wife-beaters', and women-maintained households are invariably 'poor'. Categories and labels may be useful as descriptive shorthand, but they do not accurately define the people or organisations to which they are attached. The key questions are: *Who are poor and oppressed in this society, why, and in what ways? How will supporting structure X or activity Y help to change the overall balance in favour of those who lack access to power and resources?*

A cautionary tale from Tanzania

Bwana Ngo'a discovered very soon after his arrival at Kilimani that one of the most pitiable things which demonstrated women's oppression by men was the fact that they were still grinding millet and sorghum on stones and pounding millet in mortars. He felt that if women were to even begin talking about their rights, this Stone Age situation had to be remedied at once. That is what he set himself to do.

To effect the necessary change, he talked with the chairman and asked him to convene a women's *baraza* council, so that he could discuss their plight with them. The chairman dutifully complied, but secretly told the women that they should impress upon Bwana Ngo'a that their priority need was a diesel-powered grinding mill. This, he argued with the women, would not only help them with grinding, but also provide them with an income.

Ngo'a, as a sensible development agent, thought otherwise. He was convinced that what the women needed most was something which would bring them together and build their solidarity, so that they could challenge the men's oppression, which forced them to do the hard labour of grinding. Hence his suggestion to the women was to form themselves into cell groups of up to ten. Each cell would be given a manually powered grinding mill to ease their work-load, and so provide them with a meeting point to begin discussing development issues ...

Bwana Ngo'a had his meeting and sold his idea, which seemed to be universally accepted. He therefore went ahead and proposed that the women collect token funds at least to pay for the transportation of the hand mills to the village. The women accepted this readily, and the mills were duly imported and distributed to the cells. But to date none has been paid for, let alone fixed. In fact, they have had to be removed from the village, because nobody now seems to want to use them. Ngo'a cannot understand why the women deceived him...

Had Ngo'a taken time to understand the cultural dynamics of the Kilimani community, the grinding-mill project may have gained the consent of both men and women. As it was, by being gender-exclusive, the project alienated the men and provided no support to the women whom it had been intended to help (Anacleti, 1995:236–238).

Making the links

The same questions apply when looking at which capacities are needed, by whom, to do what. There are no standard ingredients or recipes (find some landless farmers or women refugees, start with income-generation, then stir in some literacy classes followed by a drop of social organisation, a pinch of conscientisation, and finally a sprinkling of management training). Human rights education, for example, may be something that urban NGO profession-als need so that they can lobby for the rights of landless farmers, but does this mean that the farmers themselves do not need it? Clearly not. For, if people are subjected to human rights abuses, the question is how best to enable *them* to deal with it.

Sometimes a composite response may be required: training for the NGO staff, a legal aid office attached to a rural labour union, and human rights education work at the grassroots. In Honduras, for example, Oxfam supported education in human rights at several levels during the 1980s, both with training for the leadership of rural and industrial workers' unions as well as local NGO staff, and by funding a series of workshops for parish committee members who were involved in social promotion work. These church activists had been impeded from holding meetings, or even walking the long distances from one hamlet to another, by the heavy military presence in the area. Some had been detained and tortured in the course of doing things such as encouraging villagers to attend a class on dental hygiene, or new tech-niques in tile-making. Oxfam's multi-track approach sought to provide those who needed it most urgently with access to basic information about their rights. However, it also helped the middle-class professionals who were providing the training to broaden *their* awareness of the problems facing people in the remote rural areas, to develop better communication skills, and in so doing to consolidate support for human rights work across a wider social spectrum. Over the years, Hondurans were also able to share their experience in popular education with other human rights workers in Central America. Thus, capacity-building focused not on a particular organisation, but rather on the capacities needed by a range of different people working in the same environment, and addressing a common concern.

A range of inputs

Over time, a single organisation may require a range of interventions from several sources, as needs and contexts change. A local NGO may be working with small farmers in a marginalised region that suddenly becomes home to thousands of refugees. UN agencies, foreign experts, TV crews, and international NGOs then rush into a context of which they may have only a superficial knowledge. The local NGO naturally wishes to become involved in shaping their various interventions. The refugees are from the same ethnic groups and social background as the population with whom the NGO works, and may even have attended some of the NGO's training courses over the years. The NGO staff also know the area well and have a good level of trust with the local population. The NGO will rapidly need to assess how it can best help. If it is to channel goods and services, it may need training in warehouse administration and food distribution, money to pay salaries for extra staff, or political back-up to protect it against security problems. On the other hand, its input may best be at a policy level — such as convening inter-agency discussions on the problems faced by humanitarian aid workers, or producing a newsletter or a radio slot to disseminate reliable information to the refugees and local community. What commonly happens, however, is either that the NGO is assigned a role as a local implementing agency (for which large amounts of money will be forthcoming, which will distract it from its normal activities for months to come, only to dry up once the 'emergency' is over); or it is assumed to be irrelevant. After all, its expertise is in managing a revolving loan fund for peasant farmers, not with refugees in transit camps.

This is an extreme (though real-life) example to illustrate that a capacity-building approach does not automatically privilege one kind of activity over another. 'There are no watertight formulae, and no straight line between cause and effect. Capacity building is an art, not a science' (CDRA, 1995). The stress may at times be more on delivery than on transformation, or more on funding for core items (such as administration and capital expenses) than on training. There are many ways to enable women and men to improve their quality of life, and exercise their 'right to effective participation in all aspects of development and at all stages of the decision-making process' (United Nations, *The Realisation of the Right to Development*, 1991). Of course, a sustained shift in the overall balance of its work will affect the organisation's basic direction. Thinking moves on, and old methods of working may become inappropriate. What is important is that the organisation (all those concerned with its work, not only its staff and funders) should be conscious of such shifts — being flexible does not mean drifting or improvising.

To be sustainable, capacity-building needs to be patient and flexible. It is not a short-cut to development, or a quick-fix way to make an organisation 'sustainable'. Behind every apparent problem lies a deeper one. Taking a capacity-building approach may mean starting several steps behind the 'obvious' point of entry in order to avoid generating resistance. For instance, starting up a female literacy class without first understanding *why* so many more women than men are illiterate, may even be counter-productive. Taking time to find this out, and to talk with the men of the community so that they will respect and support this work with women, is more likely to pay off in the long term.

Hence, this Guideline resists offering hard-and-fast rules about what to do and when to do it. While there may be major opportunity costs and trade-offs between one course of action versus another, these can only be assessed on a case-by-case basis according to the agency's own reading of the context, and its organisational strengths and priorities. However, experience suggests both that some organisational purpose and capacity need to exist before investing in training, or the establishment of particular structural forms (eg co-operatives); and that these need to be reinforced alongside such specific inputs.

For instance, a comparative analysis of efforts to encourage women's 'empowerment' in Honduras found that a programme that hoped that women who received training in community health would thereby be equipped to take on wider public roles, failed even after several years to move beyond a fairly rudimentary level of technical input. By contrast, an education programme that invested in developing rural women's intangible capacities in social organisation and analysis before moving any further had thus laid down the foundations on which to manage highly ambitious economic projects (Rowlands, 1997). Community leaders in post-war Central America are also clear about which comes first, as they complain that aid agency priorities have switched abruptly from organisational work to economic production:

If we don't have any organisational structure, then we might just as well go it alone. We don't need to work on projects with each other— what we need is to unite together in order to seek alternatives. (Nicaraguan community leader).

Now [the funding agencies] say they can no longer support much in the way of organisation. So what do we want the money for? If the idea is that we go it alone, we might be better off to do just that and see how we get on. (Leader of a Guatemalan popular organisation) (both quoted in Ardón, 1997; my translation).

As two NGO researchers from Bangladesh put it:

individual economic gains are fewer on the whole for groups linked with social mobilisation NGOs. But the focus of social mobilisation efforts is to change the rules of the game and to make existing systems accountable to the poor (Rao and Hashemi, 1995).

Further, capacity-building is *continual*. There are no magic wands: a one-off workshop session for staff on race-awareness, for example, will not on its own eliminate racist attitudes or behaviour within an organisation:

It does not help to train individuals when organisational vision is unclear, organisational culture is unhelpful and structure is confusing or obtuse. It does not help to secure resources when the organisation is not equipped to carry out its tasks. It does not help to develop information management systems when the basic organisational attitude is one which rejects learning through monitoring and evaluation in favour of frantic activity (CDRA, 1995:9).

Organisational (and individual) self-appraisal and self-monitoring are critical. Within a systematic commitment to address racism, for example, an awareness-training programme may indeed contribute to an organisational environment in which racism becomes unacceptable. And these new insights may, in turn, lead the organisation to confront other issues (such as sexuality or disability), or to re-focus its work altogether.

This represents a challenge for donors and development agencies, particularly those seeking concrete outcomes within pre-determined timespans. It may take years to reach a point where poor women and men can successfully make use of capacities they have been acquiring over this time, even assuming that the external environment is favourable. How long should it take for action to follow on awareness? How long does an organisation take to internalise its stated commitment to gender equity? One answer is 'for ever': growth and learning are intrinsic to healthy development. There is no inherent or ideal limit to our capacity for empowerment or participation — for these are processes as well as goals. How, then, can we measure them? How much participation is 'enough', and who has the right to say?

We can make comparisons over time, or in relation to other indicators, but not in absolute terms. For instance, villagers may now feel more confident than before in challenging the municipal authorities; war-widows may have started out as a mutual support group, but may go on to campaign for the perpetrators of human rights abuses to be brought to justice. These people have become sufficiently confident and equipped to do things that they could not have done before; but that does not mean that they could not become even more 'empowered' or 'capacitated' (Rowlands, 1997). Nor does it mean that people's sense of empowerment is diminished if they are unable to achieve their goals. The Mothers of May Square in Argentina may not have succeeded in forcing the military to return the bodies of their sons and daughters, but they continue to draw strength and confidence from each other — and to inspire others in their refusal to abandon their struggle for justice.

However, powers and capacities that are not used are likely to atrophy. Many children leave school knowing how to read and write, but become functionally illiterate as adults. Similarly, people who are told that their opinions are of no value (because they are women, or dark-skinned, or immigrants, or old, or illiterate, or simply because they are poor) internalise this, and may 'have no opinions'. Capacity-building for development, therefore, not only meets concrete needs for skills or resources, but responds to the *feelings* that come from people's experience of poverty or oppression. It is necessarily concerned with a long-term investment in people.

What capacity-building is not: four caveats

It may be helpful at this point to illustrate the nature of capacity-building, by means of four negative examples:

Capacity-building should not create dependency: Increasing dependency and vulnerability are the very opposite of capacity-building. Yet much development aid has resulted in institutions and activities which are dependent on continued grant-funding, partly because development co-operation is perceived largely as the one-way transfer of resources, rather than a process of 'critical accompaniment'.

Capacity-building cannot mean the creation of institutional structures that are grafted onto the local context, with no shared commitment to their survival. Such structures may serve a short-term interest, such as channelling relief resources. And some individuals may learn new skills or increase their earning capacity as a result. But where the central purpose of the exercise is determined by the donor's need to find the most expedient and efficient way to achieve a particular goal, these are essentially by-products (see Zetter, 1996).

Capacity-building does not mean weakening the state: Nor is capacity-building supporting CBOs or intermediary NGOs in ways that weaken the capacity of the state, or citizens' claims on it. 'Good governance' and 'democratisation' are not well served when governments abdicate their responsibilities to their citizens, or transfer these duties piece-meal to institutions that are not themselves accountable to those who use their services.

Capacity-building is not a separate activity: Capacity-building is not something to be done *instead of* supporting or undertaking health or education programmes. It is as wrong to see capacity-building as an independent or self-contained activity as to assume that it must always take certain forms. There are times when ensuring physical survival must take precedence over more consultative processes, just as there are times when people may be more motivated to analyse their situation than simply to achieve material gains. Development depends as much on *how* we do things as *what* we do.

Capacity-building is not solely concerned with financial sustainability: Although capacity-building should enhance sustainability, this is not synonymous with financial self-reliance. Reducing dependence on grant-funding is critical for any organisation that is working towards future independence, but not all activities can become entirely self-funding — health and education provision being the most obvious.

More important for capacity-building are the less tangible areas of social, political, organisational, and managerial sustainability. An organisation is just as likely to collapse for lack of a shared and coherent vision among its members, or a loss of confidence and commitment among its 'stakeholders', as because next year's grant is cut. Growing too fast, or over-diversifying in an attempt to 'scale-up' can be equally damaging. Getting the right fit between the organisation's size, scope, and structure are critical to managing changes in scale. This investment cannot be achieved with money alone: for 'experience has shown that it is easier to build capacity than to maintain and use it' (Maselli and Sottas, 1996).

Capacity-building: differences and dilemmas

Capacity-building is an approach that necessarily reflects an agency's philosophy of development, as well as how it interprets its own role(s). It requires an agency to work with its existing and potential counterparts in a way that responds coherently to a shared reading of the context, compatible criteria for evaluating results, and a mutual understanding of their respective mission and goals. There are many ways of developing this basic 'match'. However, a relationship of trust, or 'critical accompaniment' (what the US NGO World Neighbors calls 'a co-learning relationship'), is the only basis upon which to develop relationships and strategies that can both respond to and manage change. The various formal mechanisms for financial accountability make sense within the context of such mutual trust: without it, they may be little more than an unwelcome intrusion.

...development practitioners and funders need to pay close attention to the process and understand what they are seeing. If capacity building occurs through the development of long-term relationships which are marked by shifts in strategy and attitudes, those wishing to build capacity need to continually be observing, reflecting on, changing and improving those relationships (CDRA, 1995:15).

Unfortunately, agencies often miss out some of these critical steps, going straight into activities falling under their own general rubric of capacity-building.

This is as true of Southern NGOs as of Northern funding agencies, whether these are operational, or providing funds of their own or on behalf of other donors. At best, this is likely to lead to a confused or uneven programme whose potential is thus dissipated. At worst, it may fuel conflict, or undermine those it was intended to help.

On behalf of the former British Overseas Development Administration (ODA), Anthony Bebbington and Diana Mitlin reviewed nine NGO-related research studies into NGO capacity and effectiveness that had received funding from its Economic and Social Council for Overseas Research (ESCOR) (Bebbington and Mitlin, 1995). The survey aimed to draw out common themes and dilemmas rather than to reach firm conclusions. In doing so, it identified various issues that are often ignored, some of which are:

• Capacity-building is often used simply to mean enabling institutions be more effective in implementing development projects. Institutions are thus the instrument by which certain goals can be reached, and may be governmental or non-governmental.

• Capacity-building may also refer to support for organisations whose activities are geared towards catalysing political dialogue and/or contributing to development alternatives. This view stresses the democratising role in 'civil society' of NGOs and CBOs.

• If capacity-building is a means to an end, then the intended end of the intervening agencies, ie the chosen development path or model, must be explicit in order to compare options or evaluate progress. The focus is likely to be on improving the links between the structure, processes, and activities of the organisation that is receiving support, and the quality and quantity of its outputs and outcomes. Criteria for effectiveness will therefore concentrate on impact(s) at the local level.

• If capacity-building is an end in itself (eg strengthening the quality of representation and decision-making within civil society organisations, and their involvement in socio-political processes), such political choices demand a clear purpose and contextual analysis on the part of the intervening agency. The focus is likely to be on the counterpart's organisational mission, and the mesh between this, its analysis of the external world, and its structure and activities. Criteria for effectiveness will therefore relate to the extent to which the mission is perceived to be appropriate, coherent, and fulfilled.

• If capacity-building is a process of adaptation to change 'and of internal reaffirmation, that gives an organisation both the resources to deal with challenges as they arise, and the will to continue acting', it is questionable whether this is truly compatible with a conventional project-funding approach. The focus is likely to be on assisting the counterpart to become a more self-reliant and autonomous actor within a long-term alliance or 'critical accompaniment' with the donor and other relevant agencies. Criteria for effectiveness will therefore be developed jointly and will evolve over time. They will concentrate on the quality of the alliance, and on mutual learning as well as on the appropriateness of specific inputs.

These issues are summarised in matrix form below (op cit, p11).

	Capacity building as means	Capacity building as process	Capacity building as ends
Capacity building in the NGO	Strengthen organisation to perform specified **activities** (one of which may be to build capacity among primary stakeholders	Process of reflection, leadership, inspiration, adaptation and search for greater **coherence** between NGO mission, structure and activities	Strengthen NGO to survive and fulfil its **mission**, as defined by the organisation
Capacity building in civil society	Strengthen capacity of primary stakeholders to implement defined **activities**	Fostering **communication:** processes of debate, relationship building, conflict resolution and improved ability of society to deal with its differences	Strengthen capacity of primary stakeholders to participate in political and socio-economic arena according to **objectives** defined by them

In reality, the differences between these points on the matrix are often a question of emphasis or degree rather than of kind. Funding agencies and their local counterparts will pursue more than one purpose simultaneously, seeing these as inter-related rather than distinct. For example, in any one country, Oxfam is likely to support organisations and activities across this matrix, some focused on improving people's material security, others geared more to long-term social change. Indeed, a given organisations may work on several planes or levels, the balance between these shifting over time.

The matrix is not a way to pigeon-hole organisations or activities; But it is a useful tool for disentangling the central objectives from the secondary aims within a capacity-building programme; if these are muddled, it is impossible to form a coherent strategy or to agree criteria for effectiveness.

Models of capacity-building [2]

An NGO's programmes in any given country or region depends, among other things, on its analysis of how the following factors are affecting people who are poor or marginalised:

- macro-policy environment (structural adjustment programmes, debt-servicing and balance of payments, main export sector)
- nature of the state (powerful/effective, weak/ineffectual; all-encompassing, patchy, non-existent)
- economic and production systems (industrial, service; rural [nomadic or settled]; public, private, informal)
- role and nature of domestic market relations (monetary and informal or reciprocal); participation in regional markets such as MERCOSUR, NAFTA, EU, EFTA
- strength and cohesiveness of civil society (range of organisations, freedom of expression and association, extent of popular participation through organised forms)
- social relations (class, gender, culture/religion, ethnic, age differences), including intra-household relations.

The following seven archetypes or idealised models, within which Oxfam's programmes generally fit, each provide a framework for seeing a programme as a system (and not merely a cluster of self-contained projects), and being aware of the connections within it. The models were set out in an internal discussion paper by Chris Roche, of Oxfam's Gender and Learning Team. Seeing things in this way takes us away from thinking about capacity-building in terms of categories, compartments, and mechanistic progression.

To bring about change in favour of the poorest sectors of society requires a combination of interventions at several complementary levels (nationally and internationally). A shift in one part of the system will have an impact (not always positive or uncontested) on other parts of it.

Model 1: Working through intermediaries

Working through intermediary organisations, often in the form of local NGOs or CBOs, and sometimes international NGOs such as ACORD in Africa or ICD (the operational wing of CIIR) in Latin America and the Caribbean, is a standard way of working for international agencies such as Oxfam. There is little or no direct linkage between NGO and state. The relationship between an NGO and its counterparts here is often mediated via the provision of grant-funding for specified purposes, but may also involve other forms of support (such as advice, information, or contacts).

The lines between the organisational types in the following six
diagrams reflect different types of relationships:

Key to types of relationship

campaigning

networking

material aid / support

lobbying

representation
and lobbying

funding and
non-funding support

funding

advice

Working through intermediaries

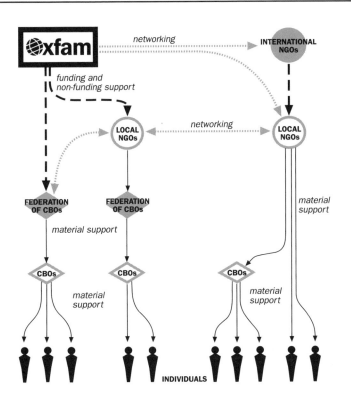

Oxfam has actively encouraged linking and networking between and among its counterpart organisations in-country and beyond. A good example of this way of working is the Campesino a Campesino initiative in Central America. This began life in the 1970s as a project by the Mexican NGO SEDEPAC to foster 'horizontal learning' among peasant farmers from the State of Tlaxcala and from Guatemala. In the mid-1980s, with support from Oxfam, SEDEPAC established links with the Nicaraguan farmers' union, UNAG. In addition to knowledge-sharing across national boundaries, this gave rise to UNAG's extensive soil-conservation programme in Nicaragua.

When Oxfam launched its South-South Environmental Linking Programme in 1991, UNAG became its Central American regional counterpart. The South-South programme drew on the existing capacity of UNAG, SEDEPAC, and other organisations throughout the region, and supported various Campesino a Campesino regional exchanges and training programmes. The South-South structure served 'as an umbrella organisation to scale up and regionalise Campesino a Campesino activities' (Nelson, 1995:13). In this case, even after the South-South Environmental Linking Programme had been wound up, there was still 'an active, dynamic network' in the region that was

having an impact in terms of improving livelihoods and encouraging farmer experimentation, building the capacity of NGOs and CBOs, and raising the profile of environmental issues on their agendas, and [whose] lobbying and advocacy activities are influencing governmental policies (Nelson, 1995:1).

Model 2: Generating synergies

A more focused variation is the synergy model, in which an NGO works with a specific combination of counterparts in order to generate changes at several levels. In its work with the artisanal fishing sector in the Philippines, for example, Oxfam supports grassroots CBOs in coastal resource management (CRM) activities, such as replanting mangroves and developing artificial reefs. At the same time, Oxfam assists national fishery organisations which provide support to CBOs and represent their interests. Oxfam encourages links between them and more specialist lobbying organisations in order to change national legislation. Enlarging the zone of municipal waters from which commercial trawlers are excluded is an example of change at a national level having a significant impact on local livelihoods.

The external evaluation of this aspect of Oxfam's work in the Philippines identified some of the ingredients that have helped to make this approach relatively successful:

[T]he collective impact ... was found to be positive not only because it was used to support several projects but, more importantly, because these projects fell into

Generating synergies

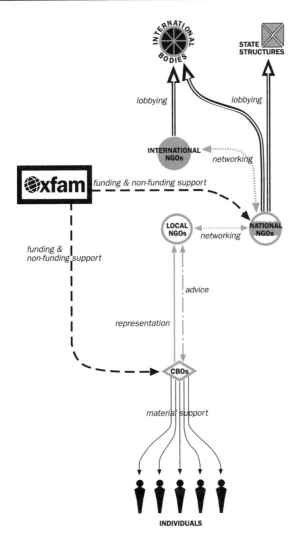

areas of work that had been identified as strategic aspects in the Community-based CRM movement. The existence of a comprehensive and coherent programme framework on the part of Oxfam enabled the ... integration of these areas of work and specific projects. Critical interventions in project design, objectives, and implementation were made ... with a clear purpose in mind.

This ... made it possible for Oxfam to be responsive to emergent or innovative project concepts ... as well as to the complexities in the institutional environment. All of these assured a higher degree of overall impact within the realm of NGO-People's Organisation relations and their continuing role in the advancement of the Community-based CRM movement in the country (Francisco, 1996:59 *et seq*).

Significantly, the evaluator also commented that since its funding capacity is relatively limited, this is 'one major incentive' for Oxfam to 'know exactly what it wants' so as to utilise its modest resources in an optimal and strategic way:

Creating an impact and becoming a strategic player is dependent more on informed planning and flexibility, than on having an enormous amount of resources. The strategic relationship with a selected group of partners must, however, be managed within a defined operational framework that clearly states when a partnership would be terminated or sustained in a different way (ibid. piii).

Model 3: Promoting representative organisations

A common model for both operational and non-operational programmes is one based on facilitating the emergence of federated CBOs into, for instance, farmers' unions, or NGO alliances, or trades union federations. It is hoped that as these structures gain in strength they will be better able to demand adequate public services as well as develop their own funding and non-funding relationships with other bodies. Support for capacity-building processes and organisational development are often the foundations of such programmes, alongside technical assistance in appropriate areas (credit, paravets, legal training).

An example of this kind of approach is that of the Rural Literacy and Health Programme (RLHP), which focuses on people living in slum areas of the District of Mysore, India. A major element of its methodology is to encourage slum-dwellers to form *sanghas* (local associations) and eventually federations, whose purpose is to seek better housing and educational facilities, higher wages, an improvement in the status of women, and greater participation in local bodies. Looking back on its work since 1984, RLHP staff say that

Slum-dwellers were earlier divided across region, caste, language, and political lines which made it impossible to work with them as a group. Concerted efforts towards social and class solidarity, and intensive awareness programmes, have made them overcome these obstacles to a large extent. RLHP has been able to organise people into sanghas. Federations have been formed to address common issues for mass action involving many slums. ... Earlier, all

Promoting representative organisations

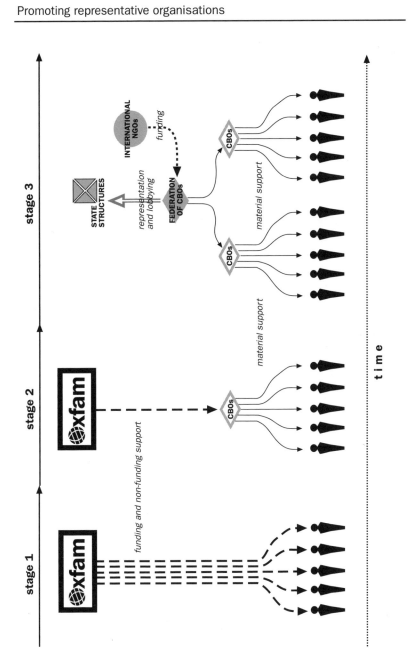

government schemes for slum development were going to non-slum-dwellers. Now, people are confident to demand these from government officials.

Political participation of slum-dwellers in local bodies has increased in the last elections. Eleven sangha *members stood for election, and of these four got elected. Of course, splits and factions continue as political parties are very unhappy about the developments. Earlier, the slum people were dependent on only one category of jobs, namely sweepers. Now they are looking for and demanding entry into occupations other than sweeping... [Before] women were not allowed to come to* sangha *meetings [which has] been addressed by women* sanghas. *Now women come for meetings and invite RHLP staff. Women's participation in local panchayats has improved.*

(Parasuraman and Vimalanathan, 1997:91).

Model 4: Generating independent organisations

Occasionally, projects originally funded by an NGO themselves become independent organisations. This may happen at the local level, as in the case of Kebkabiya in Sudan, where community members and Oxfam staff created an organisation, the Kebkabiya Smallholders' Charitable Society (KSCS), which would eventually take over responsibility for an operational development project:

From the start, Oxfam's approach had been to involve the community. People were consulted, were involved in implementation, were expected to manage aspects of the project. In this way, a sense of ownership was fostered from the outset. ... village committees created a new model of democratic community representation. Through them a sense of community responsibility could be fostered and managerial capacity developed.

A major consideration for Oxfam was how it could relinquish control without sacrificing the social gains ... especially in the field of gender relations. When the KSCS was formed... in preparation for the future handover of the project, the constitution drawn up for the new organisation enshrined the basic principles of democracy and gender equity which were the cornerstones of Oxfam's approach (Strachan, 1997).

Another example of the evolution of an independent organisation is the Arid Lands Information Network (ALIN) based in Senegal, which started life as an Oxford-based Oxfam networking project but is now an independent organisation. Such organisations may continue to receive funding after 'independence', but usually for a limited period only.[3]

Government and non-governmental structures in parallel

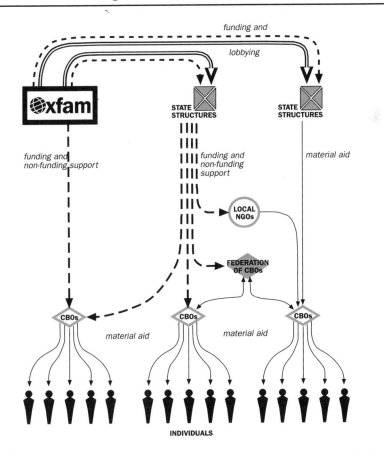

Model 5: Government and non-governmental structures in parallel

On occasion, it may be appropriate to work predominantly through the state, usually through sectors such as the Ministry of Health or the Ministry of Agriculture. Other CBOs or NGOs may be supported to provide training to individuals in both the public and non-governmental sectors. This was, for example, how Oxfam worked in Nicaragua throughout the 1980s; combining support for the popular education programmes run by the regional offices of the Ministry of Health, with funding for complementary health education activities run by Nicaraguan NGOs. Funding of government-run programmes may also be linked with influencing government policy through provision for training and exchange visits.

In 1990, Oxfam in Namibia embarked on what was then the fourth large-scale Primary Health Care (PHC) programme it had supported in the Southern African region within a decade (the others were in Zambia, Malawi, and Zimbabwe). The rationale was to support the integration of the existing People's Clinics (which Oxfam had funded) into a new national health system; one which would reflect SWAPO's commitment to orientation and training. Eventually, the programme was totally financed by the then ODA of the British government, with the Namibia Office administering the funds.

The relative merits of 'working within' or 'alongside' were debated, though in rather technical terms: the *post hoc* internal evaluation laments that for internal reasons 'the "new wave" development debates — good governance, extension of civil society, capacity-building etc — lost the opportunity of being grounded in reality in this newly-emerging state' (Lang, 1996:1). However, the evaluation identified some useful lessons for such an approach, which are summarised below:

- Total financial dependence on official aid can work — if ground-rules are agreed.
- Working with government can work — if there is a relationship of mutual trust; an accepted structure through which to ensure open discussion; a critical mass of stakeholders within the relevant Ministry with the commitment and skills to work for change; and appropriately skilled project staff.
- Community-based activities through a Ministry can take root — if there is a management structure in place that recognises the importance and role of such activities.
- Training can be an entry-point for capacity-building — if the trainers are skilled in facilitation and adult-learning (ibid. ppi–ii).

Model 6: Non-operational emergency programmes

Where local organisations are strong, an international NGO such as Oxfam will usually seek to implement its emergency response through these. This may take the form of supporting the humanitarian wings of rebel armies as in Tigray or Eritrea, or local NGOs such as ADRA in Angola or FASTRAS in El Salvador, or through federations of CBOs as in Burkina Faso. In some circumstances, fostering networking and information-sharing between organisations may help them to develop common strategies and lobby governments or the international community.

This way of working in emergencies is most common in areas where the NGO already has a programme in place, and where its local counterparts may expand their work to cover wider geographical areas, new activities, or greater numbers of people (see, for example, Ardón,1997; and Chapter 8).

Non-operational emergency programmmes

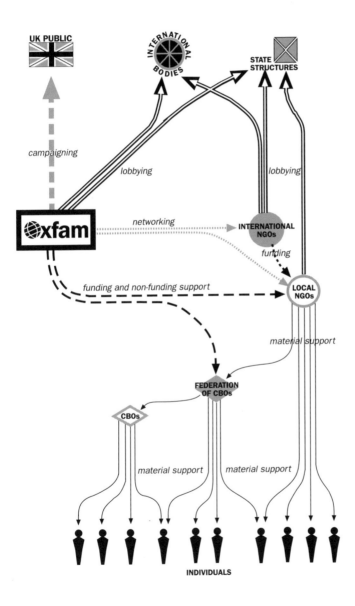

Model 7: Operational emergency relief programmes

Where local organisations and intermediary NGOs are weak, an international NGO like Oxfam may implement an operational programme to provide emergency relief. The overall aid programme may be coordinated by an international body, such as UNHCR. Oxfam may collaborate with or fund other international NGOs to deliver vital services, or take on an operational role in its own right. For instance, in the Rwandan refugee camps in Goma, Oxfam provided water and sanitation facilities to over one million people. Advocacy work is an important element of an emergency response. The focus may be on governments, official donor agencies, or UN bodies. Oxfam may, for example, press host or sending-country governments, as well as the international community, to provide assistance or to protect refugees or displaced persons from further human rights abuses.

An overall aim, even in operational programmes, is to encourage the formation of structures to assist with service-delivery, and to represent the affected population. For instance, in its work with Sudanese refugees in the Ikafe area of Uganda, Oxfam tried to foster community management structures through which to ensure the participation of refugees in decision-making, and to facilitate their integration into Uganda. In practice, however, this has been thwarted by several factors. Firstly, poor communication among the various agencies (including UNHCR and the Ugandan Government) and the Aringa host community meant that 'refugees [were] not informed of Aringa cultural practices and ... violated tradition by using water from sacred water sources' (Neefjes and David, 1996:35). Further, although key technical staff (eg land surveyors) were 'the interface between Oxfam and the refugee and national communities', they proved insensitive. Finally, efforts to mesh the Refugee Council structure promoted by Oxfam, and Ugandan representative systems were frustrated: the former had no legal status, and no right to vote in local Council meetings. So although Oxfam had hoped to hand over 'the management of water points, schools, clinics, grinding mills etc to joint committees, there [was little] dialogue between these two parallel council systems' (ibid. p36).

In a candid participatory review, the Refugee Councils complained that 'the Oxfam structure' was just 'window-dressing', and that without regular meetings they could not participate in decision-making. Oxfam's local representative acknowledged, with hindsight, that it might have been better to have first strengthened the existing Sudanese structures, adding that 'strategies seem to have been decided before we knew more of the culture and social life of the refugees' (ibid. p55).

What this illustrates is the real difficulty in trying to dovetail an operational programme with local representation, particularly in the politicised, fast-moving, and dangerous setting of an emergency. However, the fact that refugees and local people were able to discuss the problems may open the door to more appropriate ways of dealing with these in the future.

Operational emergency programmmes

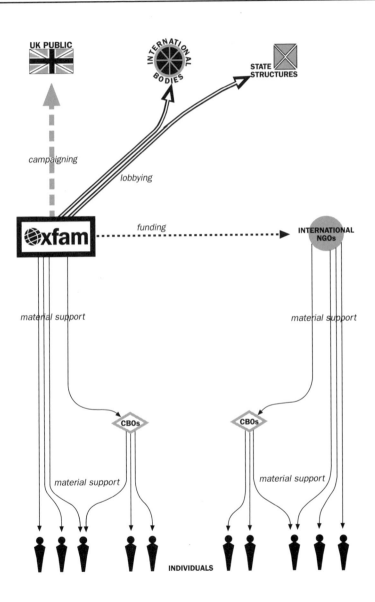

A word about partnership

While Northern NGOs tend to describe their relationships with the Southern organisations whose work they fund as one of 'partnership', the reality is often less clear. Few Southern NGOs spontaneously describe their Northern funders as 'partners'. A true partnership is based on equality, mutuality, and trust. Yet Firoze Manji (Manji, 1997) argues that the relationship between Northern funders and Southern recipients is characterised by inequality and hence by a degree of mistrust: the Southern 'partner' reports to its funder, adapts to its needs, and seeks its approval as the basis for further support. Its survival may depend on doing so. As Mike Edwards observes, 'cooperation is difficult between unequals, and partnership impossible' (Edwards, 1997:7). Northern donors certainly need Southern counterparts — for what World Neighbors describes as 'access to networks, indigenous knowledge, language skills for broader networking, and on the ground opinions about the context within which World Neighbors operates' (CARE, 1994:31 quoted in Hudock, 1996: 17). However, it is rare to find Northern agencies placing such importance on mutuality. For the most part, Northern agencies insist on having the luxury to choose their Southern partners — even if they move on next year.

This asymmetry means that 'it is not uncommon to see Northern NGOs "projecting" or forcing on to the partner the image that the Northern NGO wants to see' (Fowler, 1991:13). The ways in which this happens are varied: explicit and up-front demands for particular reporting and monitoring systems, or conditions on the use to which the funds may be put; or implicitly pushing for certain forms of management or particular agendas. As the leaders of some Salvadoran popular organisations complained, after the end of the 12-year civil war, the sudden obsession among Northern NGOs for 'strategic planning' imposed an unwelcome dynamic which:

.... in a way decapitalised the social organisations, who were thus distracted from attending to our own grassroots membership. But we felt that future assistance to us was implicitly conditional upon our going along with it (Ardón, 1997; my translation).

Of course, some of the demands of Northern NGOs on the organisations it funds are quite legitimate. It is unrealistic to expect a large international agency to accommodate the bureaucratic idiosyncrasies of all the hundreds of organisations it supports; some standardised systems and procedures are necessary both to ensure smooth functioning and public accountability. But the meshing of administrative systems is not the nub of the problem. The real issue is that if the nature of the relationship between two 'partners' is fudged, then the basis for honest negotiation between them is compromised. Since a capacity-building approach is intended to enhance the quality of people's relationships within their societies, and beyond, NGOs can contribute positively only if their own relationships are based on mutual trust and two-way learning, not merely the transfer of money. As one observer says:

There is a reality check for the [funding] agencies, a question simply posed but less easily answered: what would remain of the 'partnership' if one took away the money, that is, took away the aid relationship? (Saxby, J in Sogge et al (eds), 1996:49).

A good start would be to turn the appraisal and monitoring processes on their head. Southern organisations need to have a strong identity of their own 'as a foundation for their negotiating position' (Fowler, ibid, p.14), and need to know as much about their potential donors as the donors insist on knowing about them. And Northern NGOs need to be realistic about who they are, and what they can really offer. Specifically, if a 'partnership' is time-bound, both partners need to know that. If it has to come to an end, the wealthier partner has a duty to ensure a decent 'divorce settlement'.[4] These issues are elaborated in Chapter 6. But here, the last word goes to the development and organisational management expert quoted earlier:

Any Southern NGO contemplating accepting assistance from a Northern NGO, whether there is the prospect of a partnership or not, is advised to draw up an organisational profile of its counterpart. This means ascertaining two things: first, the origins, history and constituency of the Northern NGO [eg its political affiliations, social cultural and religious structures, concern to promote (national) values, ideological identification, issue-focus, purpose, method, and relationship with the market]; secondly, the Southern NGO must determine exactly where the Northern NGO's resources come from and under what conditions. These are a prerequisite for any move towards negotiating a partnership (Fowler, ibid. p10).

4

Whose capacities?

Our key point is that we try to integrate sex, race and class. ...As women, we've become aware that our work is necessary. We can't isolate ourselves or allow problems to isolate us. We want to find better solutions ... We believe we have to search for our own space. Our group is self-financed and many of us are living in poverty. But we're making this project happen. And our group comes out of our own experiences, our own limitations. Interview with Tierra Viva in Smith-Ayala (1991)

Introduction

In all societies and in every social context, men, women, and children experience poverty and exclusion in different, but inter-related, ways. The exercise of power and privilege differ according to gender, cultural, and class identity. Social identities are also shaped by access to resources, including 'power over' others, 'power to' take certain actions, or the 'power within' that gives the inner confidence needed to overcome oppression (Rowlands, 1997). Social identities take on different meanings at different times; they can be a force for cohesion, or for exclusion; they can provide a focal point around which people can mobilise together, or they can be a source of divisive dissent and factionalism.

All societies differentiate between the roles and identities of men and women, boys and girls. People's capacities, needs, and perspectives are also differentiated by age and disability. Cultural, ethnic, and gender identities may crucially affect the rights that are enjoyed by some, and denied to others. Capacity-building is concerned with enabling people to tackle the injustices that derive from discrimination, so that they can realise their full potential, in a society that respects rights and values diversity.

This Chapter introduces those aspects of people's social identities that relate most intimately to their experience of poverty and oppression, and so must underpin any efforts to strengthen their capacity to overcome these constraints and to promote a society that balances its respect for rights and for diversity. This does not imply that the way to address people's particular needs is to focus only on one aspect of their lives. For instance, few people with disabilities define themselves only in relation to these, and it would be wrong to expect them to mobilise around disability rather than any other social or political issue.

The supposed distinction between the practical and strategic interests of such people is also misleading: capacity-building is itself a strategic approach to enhancing the autonomy of those who are excluded, and which is expressed in many practical ways. Social identities profoundly shape people's capacities and their scope for action to change their lives and societies. Their social conditions make them vulnerable in ways that are often overlooked and which may limit what they gain from interventions: development programmes are often designed as though societies were made up mainly of able-bodied men between the ages of 18 and 60 years! But awareness of diversity also means recognising and appreciating difference as enriching analysis and action. An approach to development that does not take into account the diversity of people's experiences also risks failing to build on their many varied capacities. The first part of this Chapter presents ways in which aspects of their social identity may undermine people's capacities. The second part suggests ways in which agencies can ensure that they do not rest with simply recognising diversity, but actually help people to overcome the constraints deriving from it (Goetz, 1995, 7).

Discrimination is not only 'out there'; the structures and behaviour even of 'progressive' CBOs and NGOs often reflect and reproduce the inequalities existing in the societies of which they are a part — even when they consciously aim to eradicate these.[1] Development workers should be aware of their own identities and assumptions about, for instance, gender and age roles. Development agencies should likewise look critically at their own structures and institutional cultures, and tackle the inequalities that may be implicit in these.

Social diversity: discriminating capacities

The values ascribed by a society to gender, class, age, ethnicity, culture, or disability affect people's lives and opportunities. This section sketches out some of the ways in which aspects of social diversity may confer power and privilege on some while denying the rights and access to resources of others. The capacities and vulnerabilities that derive from people's social identities often provide a potent catalyst for change.[2]

51

Gender

The experiences and life chances of women and men involve inequity. Development interventions that ignore gender power relations often worsen the situation of women and girls. However, tackling such discrimination meets with opposition and fear in all societies, because gender power relations lie at the heart of all social behaviour, and to make them more equitable would call into question all other relations of dominance and subordination.

Gender-aware development work is often thought to be concerned only with women's interests, and equated with supporting 'women's projects'. However, women are not a homogenous group any more than men are. Understanding how far women are disadvantaged in relation to men inevitably leads to highlighting their situation. But it does so not by isolating women as a group, but by looking at them in relation to men in society. Women need empowerment in relation to men. But men also need to recognise and understand the need for change, and be prepared to do so.

Gathering information on gender discrimination

An analysis of the roles, attitudes, and control over resources of men and women is vital, at both the 'macro' (country, region and international) and the 'micro' (rural or urban community or project area) level. Categories such as 'family', 'household', and 'community' may well conceal aspects of gender discrimination, while sex-disaggregated data may reveal differences in the status of women and men. For example, sex-disaggregated literacy figures will show any distinction between the educational chances of girls and boys; while health statistics commonly show that boys are better looked after than girls. National statistics may need to be supplemented from other sources, such as women's organisations, or social research institutions.

Although men may claim to speak on behalf of women (and children), if women are not consulted, their interests may be misrepresented, their work-loads increased, and their quality of life and social status undermined. Consultation with women should ideally be done by other women and without men present, and information from other sources cross-checked with them. Critical areas on which information should be sought separately for women and men are:

- legal status with regard to inheritance, land, reproduction and children, labour;
- cultural, religious and ethnic factors;
- access to and control over the use of natural and social resources (including support from NGOs);
- workloads and timetables;
- roles in organisations such as village councils, production and marketing cooperatives, trade unions;

- status and role in the family and household;
- participation in single- and mixed-sex organisations;
- major issues such as violence, lack of employment, rights to land.

Socio-economic conditions

According to UNDP's *1995 Human Development Report,* 70 per cent of the world's 1.3 billion people living in poverty are women. Illiterate women out-number men by two to one, and 60 per cent of the 130 million children not receiving primary education are girls. Women work longer hours than men, but roughly two-thirds of their work is unpaid (compared with one-third of men's working time): women's under- or unpaid labour, claims UNDP, repre-sents some US$11 trillion each year. Women generally lack resources of their own, as well as access to credit. They are also under-represented in public life, since men hold 90 per cent of parliamentary seats worldwide, and 94 per cent of cabinet positions.

Reproductive health rights

Unless women can regulate their own fertility and sexuality, they may have frequent or unwanted pregnancies or resort to unsafe and illegal abortions. Where infant and child mortality are high, and in societies with a strong son-preference, women may be pregnant or breast-feeding for most of their reproductive years, with serious consequences for their health.

Women's bodies are widely considered a commodity for the sexual use and profit of men. Commercial sex workers in particular are exposed to sexually transmitted diseases (including HIV/AIDS), to physical and psycho-logical abuse, and to unwanted pregnancies.

The sexual division of labour

Every society assigns different tasks to men and women, and these tasks are accord-ed different status. Women carry out most household tasks and are respons-ible for most of society's caring work, much of which is unpaid or poorly paid. For comparative purposes, it can be useful to categorise people's work as follows:

- Reproductive: work for the household, such as caring for children and other family members, and the preparation of food.
- Productive: work which is remunerated or has exchange or reciprocal value.
- Social: comprising both management and political roles in the wider community or society, usually on a voluntary basis.

Breaking down what women and men actually do (including seasonal fluctuations) reveals their distinct workloads, capacities, needs, and scope for action. This makes it possible to plan training activities for times and seasons convenient to both sexes, while help with domestic tasks and child care may enable more women to participate.

Violence against women

Violence may be physical, or emotional and psychological, such as sexual harassment and the undermining of women's intellectual and spiritual capacities. Violence and the fear of violence from men are profoundly disabling to women, inhibiting or preventing their full participation in social, cultural, and political life. The UN claims that more than half the world's women routinely experience violence from their husbands and partners in every culture, irrespective of social class, economic status, or occupation. Physical violence and the restrictions placed upon women because of the *threat* of violence, affect every aspect of their lives.

Most domestic abuse goes unreported because of women's well-grounded fear of further violence, their lack of realistic alternatives, and their lack of confidence in the law to protect them. There are many forms of socially sanctioned violence against women: for example, sati, the stoning of women accused of adultery, and female genital mutilation (FGM). The subjugation of women is enshrined in law and custom the world over, and some legal systems overtly discriminate against women.

Rape is often used as a systematic instrument of ethnic oppression. Women are considered as part of the bounty of war, and rape as part of men's reward for overcoming the enemy. The UN Special Rapporteur on Violence Against Women supplements the International Convention on the Elimination of All Forms of Discrimination Against Women (CEDAW), adopted by the UN General Assembly in 1979. Ways to address violence against women, and to challenge the incapacity of social and political institutions to deal with it adequately include:

- legal aid to women who are victims of violence;
- training of para-legal workers to address the issue of violence against women;
- legal education and confidence-building for women who suffer abuse;
- education work to inform health workers, lawyers, the police, the judiciary, government officials, and the wider public through the press, to raise awareness;
- national and international advocacy and networking.

Violence in some form is experienced by some women in every organisational setting and context, including development agencies, NGOs, and CBOs. Taking a capacity-building approach to development necessarily entails efforts to enable women to address this profoundly damaging aspect of their lives.

Addressing gender discrimination

Criteria for measuring women's development have been drawn up by the Zambia Association for Research and Development (ZARD) which can help to measure the impact of efforts to improve women's social, political, and organisational capacities as well as their material status. Any capacity-building approach to development will seek to make progress across several of these indicators.

ZARD women's status criteria

Basic needs: better provision for women of such basic needs as food, water, fuel, housing and health care; proportional distribution of basic needs between men and women.

Leadership roles: proportion of women to men in leadership roles in the community; involvement of women as women's leaders on women's issues.

Consciousness: awareness among women of women's needs and women's issues; awareness of discrimination against women; ability to analyse issues in terms of women's interests and women's rights.

Needs assessment: involvement of women in identifying the priority needs of the community, and in identifying the special needs of women.

Planning: involvement of women in project design, implementation and evaluation.

Sexual division of labour: level of involvement of women in tasks traditionally performed by men; level of involvement of men in tasks traditionally performed by women; number of hours per day worked by the average working woman, in comparison to the number worked by the average working man.

Control over the factors of production: the level of women's access to, and control over land, credit, distribution of income and accumulation of capital.

(Quoted in Eade and Williams, 1995, p.212

Ethnic and cultural identity

Ethnic identity is fluid; it can be dormant or suppressed in some circumstances, and revived in others. It may bring certain entitlements, as in the case of native American Indians claiming ancestral land rights. It can be reasserted in times of competition and conflict, and may be the most fundamental source of identity when other forms of social, cultural, and economic cohesion break down. Since ethnicity is used to define people and groups in relation to others, it can become a focus for discrimination, oppression, and sometimes violence on a massive scale. Though based on long disproven theories of racial distinctions, racism remains a persistent and powerful set of prejudices, which fuels human rights abuses and has profound implications for human development.

Ethnic identity may be experienced differently by women and men, and by old and young, rich and poor. The children of immigrants, for example, may view their cultural background as an obstacle to social acceptance. Women may be regarded as the guardians or symbols of tradition, while men adapt to the dominant culture.

Ethnic difference can be manipulated for political ends: the word 'tribe' was used by colonial rulers in Africa to describe what they imagined to be political entities with a clearly-defined territory, language, and culture; one 'tribe' could then be played off against another. In fact, African people belonged to several social groups, such as the nuclear and extended family, clan, or lineage; and often defined their identity in geographical terms, such as 'people of the valley' or 'people of the mountains'. One legacy of the colonial strategy is the emphasis on 'tribal' identity in the struggle for political and economic power.

In Asia, caste is a 'closed' system, with a set number and hierarchy of castes into which one is born. There are some 40,000 castes and 'sub-castes' (*Varna* and *Jati*) in India, representing both a complex division of labour and a hierarchy built around the concepts of purity and impurity. Many 'polluting' or 'impure' occupations, particularly those dealing with refuse and death, are relegated to the lowest or the below-caste people, the ex-Untouchables. Many see the abolition of caste as the only way to emancipate Untouchables (or Harijans), and have replaced the terms with 'Dalit', meaning 'the oppressed'. Special provision for education and public sector employment has resulted in limited economic mobility for Dalits, but has also caused resentment which has sometimes led to violent protests.

Discrimination and human rights

Race and ethnic relations invariably raise human rights issues. International human rights law provides an arena in which to expose forms of discrimination, including denial of the right to citizenship, to land and resources, to freedom of movement, and to self-determination; and a procedure for holding governments accountable. The legal instruments which deal with ethnic and racial discrimination include:

- The International Convention on the Elimination of All Forms of Racial Discrimination 1966;

- The Convention on the Prevention and Punishment of the Crime of Genocide 1948;
- Declaration on the Elimination of all forms of Intolerance and of Discrimination based on Religion or Belief: UN General Assembly 1981;
- The Indigenous and Tribal Peoples Convention No. 169: ILO 1989.

The following practical criteria may help to balance a commitment to universal human rights with respect for cultural difference:

- No development or relief intervention should strengthen the basis of unequal relationships, whether based on gender, class, ethnicity, religion, or race.
- Development and relief interventions must identify and respect those cultural traditions which protect the enjoyment of basic rights by all members of the collectivity.
- Collective rights to territory and to freedom from oppression should not involve the violation of the rights of individuals within the collectivity.
- Social sectors that are resisting culturally-defined areas of inequality or exploitation may be legitimate and important vehicles for extending the enjoyment of rights and freedoms to all members of the collectivity or wider group, for example organisations such as Women Under Muslim Laws.

Ethnicity and conflict

Ethnicity and race often provide the basis for nationalism and nationalist struggles and conflicts. The term 'ethnic cleansing' describes the systematic persecution and exclusion of certain groups of people in order to establish ethnically-homogenous territories. Disentangling the origins of conflicts where warring parties identify themselves principally according to ethnic, race, or caste identity is complicated and context-specific. Ethnicity and conflict can reinforce each other, and positions harden where they were previously more fluid. The past may be reinterpreted, and new myths, based on prejudice and racial stereotyping, arise to justify the violence meted out by each side.

There is no simple correlation between culture and ethnicity. For example, many indigenous people in Brazil share cultural characteristics, with only small variations of the same language, myths, rituals, and forms of social organisation; yet they distinguish themselves as separate ethnic groups. They emphasise their cultural difference in relation to each other, but their similarities in relation to non-Indian Brazilians and the state. Religion may be a defining attribute; however, different ethnic groups may also share one religion while members of the same ethnic group may have different faiths.

All modern states are culturally plural, and religious or ethnic identity may be the focus of discrimination and conflict in many of them. Ethnic and religious minorities have often been (and continue to be) dispossessed, exploited, oppressed, or subjected to violence. If they are protected, they may also be marginalised from national life; or assimilated through losing aspects of their identity (such as language or dress). Migrants, displaced persons and refugees become minorities, often with little or no right to employment, land, homes, or decent education; cultural differences from the local population often become the focus of intimidation and aggression. There is a strong correlation between low social class, economic insecurity, and ethnic minority status.

Understanding ethnic diversity

To gather information about a given culture or ethnic group, a combination of sources should be consulted, from government statistics and land-use surveys to religious records and archives. Academic or social research may in itself be an important way to strengthen people's cultural identity. In trying to understand people's social and cultural institutions, it is important to be aware of the dangers of using interpreters from a different race, class or sex from the respondents.

Constructing a socio-cultural profile

A socio-cultural 'map' of the region, country or local area would be made up of demographic data, differentiated according to social and cultural variables, as well as gender and age, such as:

- the way people in the region, country or area define themselves in relation to others, and whether this has changed over time;
- whether there is distinct ethnic/race/caste/class classification, and whether people are ranked in social groups accordingly;
- discernible links between ethnic or race identity and political and economic status;
- languages spoken and by whom, and the status of the languages (official, tolerated but not written, forbidden, secret);
- the main religions, who belongs to them, and the status of the religions (as above for languages);
- specific territorial claims by particular groups, the circumstances surrounding these claims, and their history;
- historical conflicts in the area, and how the conflicting groups identify themselves and their opponents.

The political relationships involving ethnic groups and minorities within the region and country:

- the relationship between the state and any ethnic group;
- the activities of NGOs in relation to ethnic groups;
- the political aspirations of the various ethnically-defined sectors of the population;

- whether political control lies with one specific ethnic group and how this came about;
- representative organisations of ethnic groups, and how they relate to each other and the state.

The economic relationships, land use, resource use, and development plans existing in the region or country:
- national policies in relation to land and resources and how these affect minority and indigenous groups;
- national development plans and priorities and how these take the interests of minorities and indigenous groups into account;
- the agents of development and how they relate to minorities and indigenous groups;
- the economic status of different ethnic groups.

(From Eade and Williams, 1995, pp253–254.)

Being aware of false assumptions

Development and relief workers must be aware of their own assumptions and avoid projecting these onto other societies and cultures. Some basic questions are outlined below

---

Understanding the culture

- What is the division of labour among the people in the area? This should be identified by gender, age, ethnic identity, class, caste (if relevant), race, and other relevant cultural factors.
- What is the kinship structure of the people concerned? Is it matrilineal or patrilineal? Are there clans and lineages? Are there other institutions, and how are they constituted? How do such structures relate to each other? (This will often determine the decision-making structures in a group, the work allocation, access to resources, distribution of benefits.)
- What is the form of the (extended) family or household? Who makes what decisions within the household? What obligations and exchanges exist within the household and between households, and who manages these?
- What are people's religious affiliations and beliefs? Do these conflict?
- If the language is different from the official national language, who speaks it exclusively, and who in the group is conversant in the national language? Who is literate and who is not, and in what language(s) (differentiated by gender, age and status)?

- What is the level of education, and how is it differentiated according to gender, class, caste, race, age, etc.?
- What are the illnesses identified as most detrimental by women and men themselves? How do they treat them? Who are the traditional healers and what is their status? What is the belief system concerning the origins and treatment of illness?
- What are the traditional crops and foods consumed and how are these cultivated? What is the full range of peoples' diet, in different seasons?
- How does this particular group of people distinguish itself from others? What are the criteria? Who are classified as allies, who as opponents or enemies?
- What is the relationship of the people to external agents such as the religious authorities, local government, international agencies and so on?

(From Eade and Williams, 1995, pp 256–257.)

Children and older people

Children and elderly people are often ignored in development processes and interventions. Excluding any population group is not only inhumane, but ultimately corrodes society itself. Older people offer the kind of continuity that can sustain rapid social change, while to build for children's future also means enhancing their capacities and life-chances today.

Children comprise about 50 per cent of the world's population, and a higher proportion of refugees and displaced persons. Every week, a quarter of a million children die from preventable diseases such as measles, diarrhoea, pneumonia, polio and tetanus; while many more face a life of chronic malnutrition and ill-health. Babies and young children rely on the protection of adults, but may also need to be protected from adults who may abuse, exploit, or neglect them.

The Declaration of the Rights of the Child was adopted in 1959 by the UN General Assembly, and recognised within legislation covering human rights and International Covenants concerning civil and political rights; and economic, social and cultural rights. The Convention on the Rights of the Child, unanimously adopted in 1989, makes comprehensive and detailed provision for children (defined as all persons under 18 years, unless majority is attained at an earlier age).

Discrepancies between bio-medical and legal or customary definitions of childhood and adolescence may create problems. For example, if there is a difference between the age until which education is compulsory and the minimum age for admission to employment, children falling between the two are vulnerable to exploitation as illegal workers. Adolescents may be sexually active, but denied access to information or facilities to help them to avoid pregnancy or infection until they reach the legal age of consent, or are married.

Children are taught to reproduce their culture, including gender roles. Caring for children is predominantly women's work. Parenting is under-valued, and professional caring is often poorly paid. Men are seldom encouraged to share parenting responsibilities equally with women. The lack of priority given to public childcare provision assumes (and reinforces) this gender bias. Furthermore, child-focused interventions tend to set children apart from their social environment, while most development work with adults is designed as though children did not exist.

Abuse of children

Children may be abused by a range of adults (usually men) whom children trust: parents or relatives, employers, religious authorities, teachers, health workers, security forces, or institutional carers. Incest and child sexual abuse are more prevalent than is generally acknowledged. The abuser relies on his victim's being too frightened to denounce him, not being believed, or not knowing where to go. Child abuse may be an extreme form of social prejudice. For example, the torture and murder by the police of street children, the use of their organs for transplants, or the kidnapping of babies for adoption, is widely condoned by elites in Latin America. The victims are usually poor, and often belong to an ethnic minority group.

Working children

Work may form a positive part of a child's development, or may be harmful either because it interferes with other essential activities (such as play, school, or sleep), or because it is undertaken in exploitative or dangerous condi-tions (such as sex work, working with hazardous chemicals or industrial machinery, or military activities). It is difficult to enforce legislation on child labour: children working in the informal sector or at home are excluded; and the semi-industrial enterprises in which children work are themselves often illegal. However, attempts to abolish child labour, without changing the social and economic environment, can only be short-lived.

Street children

Many children live on the streets of big cities. They may have become separated from their parents or left their families for a variety of reasons. Selling newspapers, handcrafts, flowers or chewing gum, shining shoes, washing or guarding cars, or sorting rubbish, are the usual ways in which street children earn money. They may also survive through begging, stealing, scavenging, sex work, or drug dealing. However resilient and resourceful, street children are also among the most defenceless and vulnerable members of society. They may be injured or robbed, and in some cities, they are raped, tortured, and killed with impunity in so-called 'clean up' operations by police or security forces. Glue-sniffing, drug-taking, and alcoholism are common, along with the usual diseases of poverty.

Children in armed conflict

War is increasingly waged against civilians and social targets, such as health centres and schools. Children often have to assume responsibility for their own survival, and that of other family members. The illegal recruitment of child soldiers (under-15 years of age, particularly boys) in armed conflicts is commonplace. Even if they do not carry arms, small children are used as decoys or couriers, or to detect landmines. Older children have been trained to rape, attack, and kill.

Anti-personnel mines (APMs), used indiscriminately in many recent wars, pose particular threats to children. Their natural curiosity may lead them to pick up an unusual object; they may be unaware of the danger of stepping off a road or footpath; they are often in sole charge of flocks of animals grazing in isolated areas, and may die from their injuries after stepping on mines, before help can reach them. In recent years, many adolescents and young children have been killed or maimed for life by APMs.

The process of ageing

People's experience of ageing depends greatly on their socio-economic and cultural context, both past and present. A well-off healthy man in an industrialised country can expect to outlive his poorer Southern counterpart by 35 years. However, in 1993 some 56 per cent of the world's over-65s (WHO's definition of 'elderly') were living in the South, where they made up 4.6 per cent of the population. Even where life-expectancy at birth is low, as in South Asia, once a person reaches 65 years of age, she or he may well live to be 80, and most very elderly people are women. By 2025, countries with the largest numbers of elderly people will include China, India, Brazil, Indonesia, Pakistan, Mexico, and Bangladesh. But the increase in life expectancy is a hollow gain if people's quality of life remains low. Ageing has become a development issue.

Old age may entail physical or mental decline, such as diminished hearing, memory loss, and impaired sight; or chronic ill-health, such as arthritis, hypertension, diabetes, osteoporosis or depression. Some conditions which appear in old age are the result of occupational injury or long-term exposure to hazards. For example, women who spend many years of their lives cooking food on open stoves in enclosed spaces often develop respiratory malfunctions or eyesight problems in later years. Diseases and infections acquired in youth may become debilitating in later life. Physical disabilities easily result in people becoming more dependent than necessary, especially if these are thought to be inevitable and so are ignored.

Older people may face particular problems as a consequences of stress or rapid changes in social and family structures. For example, over the last ten years many rural Africans have had to care for sons and daughters who are dying of AIDS, as well as for their orphaned grandchildren. Old age may bring additional economic hardship or enforced dependence, especially where people are too frail to fend for themselves. Pensions are only available for those who have been in formal employment, and these are often inadequate to meet needs. Older women are far less likely than to be economically self-reliant than old men, and may have to rely on family support. Widowhood may sometimes confer status or greater social freedom. However, widows may have to hand over any jointly-owned land and other assets to male family members.

Prevalent beliefs about the roles played by older people — whether within the family or broader society — do not always reflect their true situation or needs. Public provision for older people is commonly based on the assumption that their health, economic, and social needs will either be met privately, or within the household or community. Development interventions generally proceed as though older people did not exist. Elderly people form a high percentage of the adults among refugee or displaced populations, but relief programmes frequently adopt patronising and one-dimensional stereotypes about them.

Disability

Disability, poverty, and discrimination are mutually reinforcing. Economic and cultural factors, including social attitudes of prejudice towards disabled people, and public policies on disability, affect how far a specific impairment becomes a constraint on a person's economic capacity and well-being. Assumptions about 'community care' or 'community-based rehabilitation' mask the fact that 80 per cent of home carers for disabled people are women, who take this task on in addition to their existing responsibilities.

Disability is both a development and a human rights issue. The rights and needs of people with disabilities and their carers are seldom explicitly addressed by non-specialist development and relief agencies. WHO makes the following distinctions between impairment, disability and handicap:

Impairment: 'any loss or abnormality of psychological, physiological or anatomical structure or function', for example a wasted limb as a result of polio, the loss of both legs in a landmine explosion.

Disability: 'restriction or lack (resulting from an impairment) of ability to perform an activity in the manner or within the range considered normal for a human being', for example the inability to walk or to see without assistance.

Handicap: 'a function of the relationship between disabled persons and their environment' which occurs when disabled people 'encounter cultural, physical or social barriers which prevent their access to the various systems of society that are available to other citizens', as for example, a man being rejected for a sedentary office job because he cannot walk.[3]

Disability covers a range of physical, mental, sensory and emotional or learning difficulties, the degrees of which vary enormously. This is why aggregated figures — such as the 'one in ten' figure that is still widely quoted — are misleading and now discredited. A disability may be constant or intermittent; visible or hidden; present from early infancy or acquired during a person's life; caused by a chronic condition or brought about by trauma or accident. It may be the result of poverty, or may force people into poverty: an entire household may become impoverished if a person who would otherwise have been the main breadwinner becomes disabled. A disability may affect whole populations as, for example, in the cases of the Bhopal or Chernobyl disasters. In rural communities in landmine-infested areas the proportion of disabled people may be abnormally high. Those whose disabilities are not apparent — such as people with poor hearing — may suffer less overt discrimination than someone whose disability is highly visible, but their needs may also go unnoticed. Such factors all influence how individuals experience disability as well as how society relates to them.

The political, economic and cultural environment is a powerful determinant of how a disability affects an individual. For example, boys enjoy better educational opportunities than girls, as do children of wealthy parents. In a context which also discriminates against disability, the interaction of these biases will further limit the opportunities of a disabled girl from a poor family. Disabled women are vulnerable to sexual violence, but also to efforts to control or deny their sexuality, with more restrictions on their chance to form voluntary sexual relationships than are placed on men. An unmarried disabled woman may face real economic hardship since she is likely (because of prejudice or lack of skills) to be pushed into low-paid jobs.

Women's organisations may share the prevailing social attitudes towards disability, as may other CBOs and NGOs, and so not provide an empowering environment for disabled women. Similarly, institutions for and organisations of people with disabilities are likely to share society's discriminatory attitudes towards women and ethnic minorities.

Capacity-building and diversity: making the links

A capacity-building approach to development concentrates on enabling people to overcome discriminatory practices that limit their life-chances. The following sections detail some of the ways in which this might be done.

Supporting gender equity

Each organisation or group involved in development activities, from large NGOs to small CBOs or international networks, will have its own understandings of gender roles and power relations. Before supporting an organisation's work, it is essential to assess the extent to which it promotes gender equity, and to discuss any concerns openly.

Health and education projects are often assumed to provide an 'entry point' for improving women's position in society (though the women themselves may be unaware of this goal). Rather than forcing an agenda, capacity-building approach encourages deeper analysis. Many people feel threatened by gender analysis and may ignore inequalities, or rationalise their inaction as a wish not to 'interfere with culture'. However, culture has negative as well as positive aspects. Cultural practices which are damaging to women are almost always challenged by some women (and sometimes men) within the culture, though they may be upheld by others. Women must tread very carefully in questioning any aspect of a strongly conservative and patriarchal culture. It is important to respect their own pace, and not to push them into roles which they do not wish to play.

An organisation that is open to examining gender-based discrimination in its work and structures may want to form mixed-sex working groups. Often, however, it is better to work with women separately, especially where is a high degree of social and cultural segregation, or where women are facing acute problems arising from their relationships with men. Just as men do, women need an opportunity to identify their own interests and needs, acquire self-confidence, and work on strategies for change. Genuine empowerment is generated by people's own efforts to increase their capacities, their confidence, and their autonomy. The Southern feminist network, DAWN, puts it like this:

Empowerment of organisations, individuals and movements has certain requisites. These include resources (finance, knowledge, technology), skills training, and leadership formation ... and democratic processes, dialogue, participation in policy and decision-making, and techniques for conflict resolution...

Flexibility of membership requirements can also be helpful, especially to poor working women whose time commitments and work burdens are already severe. Within organisations, open and democratic processes are essential in empowering women to withstand the social and family pressures that result from their participation. Thus the long-term viability of the organisation, and the growing autonomy and control by poor women over their lives, are linked through the organisation's own internal processes of shared responsibility and decision making.[4]

Women's organisations

When mixed organisations do not serve their interests, women may organise around economic activities, campaign for health or community services, work together on issues affecting them, and provide support networks. Women organise in every social context, whether around an aspect of their identity, their occupation, or their interests. Some women's organisations describe themselves as feminist (though there are huge variations in how feminism is interpreted around the world), many do not.

Women's organisations of all kinds often face opposition and hostility, usually from men.[5] Women may be accused of 'dividing the poor', on the one hand, or find that men seek to control their organisations and resources, on the other. As we shall see in Chapter 5, gender power relations are frequently said to underlie the poor success of women's income-generating projects (IGPs). (See also Khan, 1995; Johnson and Rogaly, 1997.)[6] However, it is also true that women's organisations are set up in parallel to men's, with the prime aim of attracting external funding and support. The following criteria may help to distinguish between authentic organisations that represent and will help women, and those that are largely window-dressing.

Supporting women's organisations

- Women should always be consulted directly and encouraged to make their own proposals, and any assets or products generated by the group must be unambiguously controlled by the women themselves.

- Initial inputs required by women's groups are likely to be high, reflecting women's unequal entitlements to resources and benefits. Hence, financial management must be addressed, and relevant training given. Because women are disadvantaged in terms of education, training in literacy, numeracy, accountancy, and project management skills, is a priority even for small-scale enterprises; failure to provide this kind of support can lead to failure, and undermine women (Leach, 1996, DiP).

- Women's organisations may face hostility and harassment from men. NGOs should always be aware of this, and be prepared to provide appropriate support, such as working with men on gender awareness.
- While all poor people struggle with the lack of confidence which comes with poverty and exploitation, women contend with the added dimension of internalised gender oppression. Skills and leadership training for women should be backed up with confidence- and self-awareness building.
- In order to participate effectively, women need support for their domestic work, such as caring for children, and household maintenance tasks. If the organisation is unable to lighten women's productive work, then it must take account of the many demands on women's time.

(From Eade and Williams, 1995, pp 219–220)

Knowledge and networks

Information is vital to participation and empowerment, and hence to capacity-building. Women's access to information, whether through formal education and professional and technical skills or via public meetings or the media, is limited by the many forms of gender discrimination discussed above. Further, many sources of information (including school textbooks) are gender-blind, or depict negative stereotypes of women and girls. The low representation of women in public life adds to women's 'invisibility'. Only recently is gender-specific data being published even by the inter-governmental agencies (for example, UNDP's Gender-related Development Index).

The UN Decade for Women (1975-85) stimulated much research into the lives and condition of women, but much remains to be done. Research and information-sharing networks on issues affecting women have not only promoted international solidarity, but also contributed to policy-related publishing or lobbying work. DAWN, for example, is a Southern network of feminist activists and researchers. Founded in 1984, DAWN now has links with thousands of women and organisations worldwide, demonstrating the growth of women's movements in Asia, Africa, and Latin America and the Caribbean. DAWN publishes material illustrating the variety of Southern women's views on matters such as the debt crisis, population policies, and development ethics.

More modest efforts include the many community radio stations and audio-visual materials that help to bring to the fore the interests of local women and girls.

Supporting the capacities of ethnic and cultural minorities

Ethnic and cultural identity can be a source of solidarity and strength and give people the confidence to resist oppression, and to campaign for their rights to be fully respected. A healthy social fabric can help people to recover from crisis or loss.Where people's basic rights are infringed because of their ethnicity, race, caste, or culture, efforts to tackle this must be based on an understanding of the culture(s) concerned.

Support for human rights work

There are many ways in which human rights work can address the discrimination and deprivation which people face on account of their social and cultural identity. People may be unaware of their rights; much work in this field thus focuses on education, training and awareness-raising. Supporting legal advice and legal aid centres is a practical way to counter discriminatory legal systems. Claims to land rights can be supported through national or international campaigns, and at the local level. Without the right to land, assistance for agricultural production may represent wasted effort — though more productive use of land may strengthen a group's claims to secure tenure.

National or regional organisations, including churches, may take up cases of human rights abuse. Tribal and indigenous peoples' organisations have also formed international networks and coalitions to take human rights issues to the UN system (eg the World Council for Indigenous People), with the support of specialised human rights agencies .

The strengthening of advocacy and campaigning work in the South, to raise awareness and so influence the opinions of policy-makers, competent institutions, and the general public is critical, and can give legitimacy and a strong foundation to 'solidarity' movements in the North.

Health and education

When people lack access to health and education services because of their cultural identity, NGOs may support alternative services to complement state provision, and efforts to lobby for increased state funding. Such interventions should build upon a thorough understanding of traditional health practices and popular culture. The introduction of educational programmes or health-care practices should aim to strengthen, not undermine, the positive aspects of people's traditions. Where traditional practices or beliefs are harmful, these must be tackled with sensitivity.

Reaffirming cultural identity

The discrimination faced by ethnic minorities and indigenous people may erode their confidence and cultural identity. Educational programmes, work with the media, cultural festivals, revival of the language, and setting up resource and documentation centres to record the group's history, are activities which can support the efforts of people to affirm their cultural identity.

Indigenous peoples' organisations may find it helpful to share experience and ideas, in reclaiming cultural identity. For example, in the north-east of Brazil, an Indian group who had lost their own language and rituals visited a neighbouring related group of Indians over a period of time in order to learn theirs. This enabled them to show they were 'real' Indians, in order to support their claims to the land they had occupied for many generations, which had been invaded by other Brazilians.

Peace education and conflict mediation

The ethnic dimension to many civil conflicts has led to a growing interest in conflict mediation or peace education. Its deep-rooted cultural and historical origins, and psycho-social aspects, make ethnic conflict extremely difficult to resolve. Early-warning of impending conflict, efforts at power-sharing, and peace education for groups among whom conflict may erupt, are strategies which are increasingly being used.

Children

All development and relief programmes have an impact on children. This impact may be explicit and deliberate; or indirect, through building the capacities of adults. To focus on children in a social vacuum will achieve little: child-focused programmes and institutions have often been based on a partial understanding of the social and economic context, or on treating the children as deviants or victims. Children might be better helped through programmes to support their parents; and through efforts to bring about far-reaching social change. It is essential to understand and support what people are already doing to care for and improve the life-chances of their children.

Improving physical and social well-being

The health and socio-economic status of mothers affects the welfare of their children. While the empowerment of women is a legitimate objective in itself, UNICEF argues that it is also *the single most effective means* of promoting the healthy development of children.

The need to care for their children is frequently cited as a reason for women's non-participation in development activities, or for their choosing to work in part-time jobs. Since capacity-building concerns the transformation of inequitable social relations, then the question of how society nurtures its children is a mainstream development issue, to be seen from the perspectives of women, men and children. In the immediate term, practical assistance for women with children include arranging timetables to suit working mothers, setting up creches or lobbying for public day-care facilities, and insisting that children and their care are central to development.

Children are extremely vulnerable to physical and sexual abuse by adults. They many not disclose what is happening to them because they are frightened, ashamed, or will not be believed. Health education programmes may offer a forum to discuss reproductive health and sexual abuse. Women's groups may tackle human sexuality from a broader political and social perspective, or run workshops for children and adolescents.

Education

Universal primary education is formally the responsibility of the State and should be compulsory. However, attendance may depend on the economic security and social status of a child's parents..

The reasons for non-attendance include distant or poor schools, lack of money to pay for uniforms or equipment, male preference, or ethnic discrimination. A women's group in India ran pre-school and non-formal education centres for scheduled caste children in order to encourage interest among them and their parents in attending school. Schemes to provide uniforms, books, and stationery where these are beyond the means of low-income households can enable children to attend school. Other effective support for children's education could include provision of special equipment for children with disabilities; funding for a teacher or translator for pupils from ethnic or linguistic minorities; provision of a salary for a female teacher to make it possible for girls in seclusion to go to school; or building a community classroom so that people can demand a salaried teacher.

Non-formal education may provide classes in local languages; night-school for working children; classes for girls where they may not attend mixed schools; environment-awareness programmes; sex education for teenagers; and vocational training. Working children in particular may enjoy structured opportunities for recreation, dance, and creative expression, all vital for their development; an Indian street-girl commented that her greatest pleasure from non-formal literacy classes had been the chance to read poetry.

A host government may be unable or unwilling to provide education services for refugee or displaced children. Teachers from the refugee community can be recruited and trained so that the skills remain with them. Alternatively, responsibilities may be divided between the host government and an NGO or the refugees. For example, Guatemalan refugees in Mexico received their formal education from teachers provided by the Mexican state, and organised their own classes in Guatemalan history and culture with NGO funding.

Social organisation

Children can articulate their needs and anxieties if they are properly encouraged. Effective social organisation of and for children requires some adult involvement, which must imply an asymmetrical relationship between the child and the grown-up. This relationship needs to be kept in balance. Children need a reasonable say in the design and implementation of projects affecting them, but participation is damaging and hollow if adults manipulate the children, or insist that children take more responsibility than they can handle.

Specific forms of organisation range from youth or sports clubs, to congresses to discuss issues such as drug abuse. Legal work to support children's rights, address abuses, or lobby for changes in legal provision, may also be undertaken by human rights organisations, women's groups, or by NGOs that specialise in working with children.

Supporting street children

Street children are an unstable and often mobile group; work with them is generally intended to provide them with alternatives to their situation or to enable them to function better within it.

Allowing for the inevitable setbacks means working to a very long time-scale, with 'results' distant and extremely modest. It is important to ensure that interventions are based on a realistic assessment of why the children are living on the streets, and what their own aspirations are. For example, in the wake of laws banning roadside trading, an Indonesian NGO began offering training in various skills (basic accountancy, sales management, and organisational principles) to young male street vendors, enabling them to upgrade and set up collective sales kiosks in designated areas. Now they can buy in bulk, and they have also established a welfare fund for those who fall ill.

Supporting children in domestic service

Child domestic workers are isolated and shut away from the outside world, and often work in abusive conditions. Existing organisations or unions may be encouraged to extend their network to include children. Other work which can be done includes: raising public awareness about the situation of domestic servants; lobbying to reform the law and its application; establishing refuges or reception centres with legal and counselling services; confidential telephone lines; and recreational facilities.

Supporting the capacities of older people

Development workers seldom have much experience of working with older people, and development projects are rarely designed with them in mind.

Elderly people may also find it difficult to trust young adults from outside their own cultural environment; as a result, their concerns and insights can all too often be ignored.

To promote positive social change means going beyond assumptions, and finding out what women, men and children actually do and think; and how they relate to, and depend on, each other. Research should reveal the roles of elderly people within the household, the community, and society, and how these are changing.

Learning from older people

As people grow older, their security and well-being may depend more on being integrated into a set of social, economic and cultural relationships which provide both meaning and support. Building on their experiences and abilities in the context of social change can provide a sense of purpose and continuity. For example, the Salvadoran refugees in Honduras employed traditional artisans as instructors in skills such as including carpentry, tinsmithing, weaving, and tailoring. Older people were thus fully integrated in the day-to-day functioning of the camps. In Nicaragua, booklets and radio programmes based on information gathered mainly from elderly *campesinas* about medicinal herbs and remedial practices, formed an important part of a national effort to discourage a dependence on imported pharmaceuticals.

Many of the world's most experienced midwives and health workers are older women who have no formal training. They represent a major resource, yet health programmes may disregard them and establish parallel systems; specify skills (such as literacy) that will disqualify the most experienced health workers; or dismiss the beliefs of elderly women as out of date or incorrect. Although some traditional practices are harmful (such as FGM), health programmes should take care not to undermine the positive aspects of traditional healing and systems of health care. In Ghana, a conventional mission hospital works in collaboration with spiritual healers in treating people with HIV/AIDS.[6] Community Health Workers need to be sensitive to the health problems faced by elderly people, and know how to detect and address these.

Organising for change

As populations are ageing, elderly people have begun to form mutual support or pressure groups to lobby for age-related demands and social policies, such as adequate and affordable housing and heating, pensions, health services, and public transport. All these are essential to ensuring that old age should not be synonymous with immobility, dependency, and poverty. These groups and networks can provide support and insights to local organisations, as well as to development agencies attempting to be more age-aware in their work.

Housing and care

People tend to stay in their own homes and familiar surroundings unless there are pressing needs to move. Elderly people are no exception; and there are many simple and practical ways in which their homes can be adapted to suit their changing needs. Organisations that work with disabled people can be useful sources of ideas, equipment, and social networks. Helping the carers of elderly people can also improve the quality of life of the entire household. To avoid the risk of defining people more by their limitations than by their strengths, the overall approach should be to support the capacity of elderly people, their families, and community structures to provide more sustainable forms of care.

Day-care centres provide a social focus as well as a service to monitor people's general well-being or offer out-patient medical treatment. For example, in Zimbabwe, Oxfam funded a community survey to assess the feasibility of giving specialist assistance to the carers of elderly people, in addition to the residential and day-care facilities offered. As a result, a number of health workers began to do outreach work, thus enhancing the impact of the programme in a cost-efficient way.

Residential care may be useful when other caring mechanisms have broken down, or to provide respite for carers; particular kinds of medical treatment or rehabilitation may be provided. All residential institutions tend to restrict certain freedoms, but they should not be run in an authoritarian way, which denies people's basic rights and dignity.

Emergency relief programmes

Older people, alone or accompanied, may form a high percentage of the adults within a displaced or refugee population. Where older people would normally play a role in negotiating with outsiders, their enforced dependency serves to underline their loss of social standing and confidence.

Relief programmes should to take this into account, and avoid treating older people in ways that are degrading or patronising, for example, by selecting literate young men as community health workers because this is simpler than dealing with traditional healers. If refugees are provided with materials to build their own shelters, elderly people may need assistance to do so. Income-earning opportunities may be available to young men, while elderly people (like children) remain dependent on food hand-outs: old people may become malnourished, especially if the food requires extra processing to make it palatable and digestible. Health clinics may be inaccessible to people with limited mobility; and health workers' attention focused on sick children and their mothers rather than elderly or disabled people.

Supporting the capacities of disabled people

A growing disability lobby now exists, particularly in the industrialised North, and in parts of Africa and the Middle East. In Lebanon, for example, a disability coalition worked not only for disability-related rights but also participated in mainstream peace and civil rights movements. But while one person's disability may seem like a defining characteristic to another, most people do not opt to organise around any disabilities they may have. What is important is that disabled people are able to act on their own concerns and priorities without assumptions being made about them.

Three main approaches to disability have been identified:

• The *traditional model* regards disabled people as blemished or flawed, in need of charity or protection. People are defined by their impairment, rather than in terms of themselves or their environment. While much caring work is done within this framework, it has also been associated with patronising and ultimately disabling attitudes.

• The *medical model* is predominant in industrialised countries, in part because of the technical ability and economic resources to correct or treat certain physical impairments. The focus is on individual patients rather than on the wider social issues.

• The *social or political model*, usually adopted by disabled people's organisations, emphasises removing attitudinal and practical barriers to integration at all levels. Without denying the importance of support, it advocates changes in attitudes towards disability, both within society and among health professionals.

Community-based rehabilitation

Community-based rehabilitation (CBR) has often been described as a capacity-building approach to disability. It is based on the assumptions that the greatest resource for helping a disabled person is the immediate family; and that the community around that family can be mobilised in its support. It gives priority to the social integration of disabled people. CBR has been favoured by NGOs, who see it as a cost-effective way of incorporating disability into development; and by health professionals, for whom it is a low-cost mechanism for delivering outreach services.

However, there is mounting criticism that CBR re-affirms the medical model and keeps disability hidden at home. Concerns focus on the limitations of CBR in dealing with fundamental issues: prevention; removal of discriminatory practices; educational and economic integration; and awareness-raising, networking and lobbying. There are also questions about whether

CBR actually works, since without active coordination in policy and practice between the social agencies in health, education and social welfare, neither the CBR worker, the family nor the community can fill the policy vacuum. Further, the term 'community-based' obscures the fact that the burden of caring for disabled people falls principally on women; and that work which addresses the needs of disabled people at the expense of their mothers, wives, and sisters is both unsustainable and self-defeating in terms of empowerment and social justice.

Education, training, and skills development

A disproportionate percentage of disabled people are under- or unemployed, and many NGO programmes have sought to provide opportunities for them to acquire skills or earn an income. Where training is intended to establish or improve earning capacity, whether through providing marketable skills or through a productive activity, realistic economic criteria must be used to assess its long-term feasibility; and steps taken to ensure that the intended participants have the necessary financial, managerial, and administrative capacity to establish independent enterprises.

It is important to distinguish between economic and welfare priorities. In the case of sheltered workshops, such distinctions are often ignored or misunderstood, and participants are misled into thinking that essentially unviable enterprises might become self-financing. It is cruel and self-defeating to encourage people to make products that are neither useful nor marketable: the results will not only be unsuccessful but also reinforce low self-esteem and may also fuel social prejudice.

Lobbying and campaigning work

Supporting the rights of disabled people and pressing for an improvement in their quality of life is a responsibility shared by everyone. Existing anti-discrimination legislation may be a framework within which groups and individuals can challenge customary practice, for example, by raising issues in the workplace with employers and through trades unions. In other cases, the crucial issue might be the need for improved services, such as support for home-carers, or adequate public transport. Internationally, a major disability-related campaign has been spearheaded by ICRC to ban the production, use, sale and export of APMs. In any lobbying work, priorities and strategies for action are most credibly established by those with direct experience of disability.

Networking

National and international networks may develop in the context of practical or lobbying work. For example, the Lebanese Friends of the

Handicapped (FOH) is made up of people with and without disabilities who, seeing lack of transport as fundamental in restricting the mobility of disabled people, set up a taxi service. This met an immediate need, was commercially viable, and also raised awareness about disability.

International networks such as Disabled People International (DPI) are important not only for their lobbying capacity but also because of the information and moral support they provide. The Independent Living Movement or Disability Rights Movement works against discrimination and for more personal and political power for people with disabilities. It concentrates on the practical and political problems relating to self-determination for disabled people; these range from housing and transport to peer-counselling and training for employment.

5

Investing in people

The financial cost of achieving primary education for all has been estimated at an extra $3 billion to $6 billion a year ... a sum representing only about 2 to 3 per cent of the developing world's current annual expenditures on education ...
(UNICEF, *The State of the World's Children*, 1995).

Introduction

Education and training represent an investment in people, and so are important ways to put a capacity-building approach to development into practice. Basic education is a fundamental human right. The lack of access to educational opportunities places a major constraint on people's life chances, as well as on their capacity to participate in the social, economic and political processes affecting them. In a wider sense, education (especially 'non-formal', 'popular' or 'social education') is also a means for marginalised people to develop their critical and organisational capacities, and so contribute to transforming their societies. Indeed, one of the best known training manuals for community workers is entitled *Training for Transformation* (Hope and Timmel, revised 1995).

Yet formal education is in grave crisis, as governments cut back public sector spending. In developing countries, resources have been diverted to debt-servicing, while structural adjustment programmes and neo-liberal policies have resulted in a decline in social welfare services. Spending on education is being cut in some of the world's poorest countries (UNDP, 1997).

[The] strain is being felt particularly in primary schools: miserably paid teachers have had to desert the profession or devote their time to securing other sources of income; and school supplies, especially in the rural areas, are even

scantier than before. In the richer countries, the deterioration in primary education has not been as widespread or as dramatic, but in many of these the ability of public schools to meet minimum standards of instruction seems to be declining' (UNRISD, 1995:132–3).

The decline in overall provision also breaks down along gender lines. In Niger, for example, only 13 per cent of the total adult population is literate, and only six per cent of women. In Afghanistan, Burkina Faso, and Nepal, male literacy in 1993 was three times higher than that of females. In Bangladesh, only 12 per cent of all girls of school age attend school. In 1990, only a tiny handful of the members of a Salvadoran rural women's organisation could read and write, reinforcing their lack of access to agricultural credit. And while countries such as the Dominican Republic, Honduras, and Nicaragua show similar official rates of literacy among women and men, in reality these mask major discrepancies between rural and urban populations, and high levels of illiteracy among ethnic minorities (all figures from *1996 UNDP Human Development Report*).

In a self-fulfilling cycle, since more employment opportunities exist for men than for women, boys' education takes priority over girls' because they are more likely to be able to use it. For instance, in Pakistan, the combined educational rate (primary, secondary, and tertiary) is 24 per cent for women, compared with 49 per cent for men — who then go on to register 81 per cent of earned income in the country. In Yemen, only one-fifth of women benefit from some level of education, and they register a similar percentage of earned income; meanwhile, two-thirds of men receive some formal education, and they register 77 per cent of earned income.

It is important to note, however, that while a negative correlation exists between women's low educational levels and their earning capacity, high female educational levels do not necessarily translate into high income. For while industrialised countries have similar levels of education among men and women, men's share of earned income is often double that of women's. Clearly, education alone is not enough to close the gender gap in life chances enjoyed by women and men.

Social and economic divisions are also exacerbated when a disproportionate investment is made in higher education from which the rich primarily benefit, rather than in universal primary education. Throughout Latin America, over half of public spending on higher education is devoted to students from the richest fifth of the population. Education (like health) is increasingly treated as a commodity for those who can afford it.

Against this background, donor agencies and NGOs are often criticised for viewing capacity-building too narrowly in terms of training; and focusing on its technical dimensions, to the exclusion of other needs (CDRA, 1995). Literacy and numeracy will not alone counteract other factors which cause poverty and disempowerment. Education and training are not capacity-building activities in and of themselves; there is no necessary link between literacy and empowerment, any more than there is between numeracy and wealth. Rather, it is the organisational setting and overall purpose — what is intended, what is being achieved, and by whom — that define them as such. Holding onto this insight enables us to avoid rigid distinctions between formal *versus* non-formal education, or personal development *versus* social organisation, and to focus instead on whether and how effectively a specific activity will strengthen the specific capacities of a specific set of people at a specific point in their history.

This Chapter describes some of the huge range of activities that can be described as education or training. The aim is to indicate the major issues and questions to be addressed in assessing these from a capacity-building perspective; not to give detailed advice on how to go about designing or implementing specific programmes, for which specialised manuals already exist (for example, Fordham et al, 1995; Williams et al, 1994). The first section looks at education, concentrating on the areas in which NGOs are most involved: social education, and literacy and numeracy. The second looks at training, and in particular how it can help people to develop the skills they need, as well as enabling attitudinal change in areas such as race or gender. Donor agencies and NGOs often support skills and vocational training with a view to enhancing the economic and productive capacities of poor people. The final section of this Chapter therefore takes a critical look at what training can offer in this area.

Education for all: a goal or an illusion?

Formal education is generally provided in schools, colleges and universities, with a structured hierarchy of classes, syllabuses or grades. The International Covenant on Economic, Social and Cultural Rights of December 1966 emphasises that primary education must be compulsory and freely available to all. While formal education obviously serves wider social ends, it places the emphasis on the individual's learning and performance; and often does so in a way that fosters competitiveness. *Non-formal* or *social education* is outside the official system. Since it aims to promote social change, it is related to goals such as strengthening the position of marginalised people, in terms of access to land, employment, health care, legal aid, social services, or civil and political rights. It covers a broad spectrum, including literacy and numeracy, awareness-training, agricultural extension, vocational training, health education, legal or human rights education, and organisational skills. The methods use include training courses, workshops, participation in networks or exchange visits, and other informal means.

Much of the work described as social education is inspired by the Freirean method of involving students in dialogue, reflection and action. The 'conscientisation' (consciousness-raising or awareness-creation) process aims to make people aware of the roots of their oppression, and give them confidence to take action for their own liberation (See Chapter 2). Linking the acquisition of knowledge and skills to social needs and mobilisation is the basis of what many NGOs and others call social organisation, or empowerment.

Criticisms of the Freirean method, and disillusion with the outcomes of what has passed for popular education, have generated scepticism among some educationalists and NGOs. Evaluating the impact of social education programmes has proved difficult, to some extent because their goals were over-ambitious, or simply too vague. Ideological commitment alone will not transform unjust social and economic structures, or break down authoritarian or paternalistic patterns of behaviour. Poor men and women may need practical skills to meet their social and cultural needs. The economic crisis faced by millions of people around the world makes it imperative to combine adult education programmes with support for tangible changes in their lives. Adult education researchers in Latin America have concluded that:

... adult education cannot ignore the reality of poverty and the need to satisfy basic, vital needs. The precarious conditions in which many adults live call for more than ideologically oriented activities. People need actions through which they can at least visualise a transformation of their living conditions (Schmelkes, 1997, p.295).

Government cuts in social and educational provision are also forcing NGOs to question their priorities for action in education. NGOs are under increasing pressure to play a role in delivering services to poor people, as official donors turn to NGOs as implementing partners for their aid programmes. Many NGOs are reluctant to compensate directly for cuts in state education. However, the boundaries between the formal and non-formal sector are becoming less relevant when so many people lack access to even the most basic education. NGOs must therefore balance the need to invest in people today with the need to strengthen their capacity to press for better state provision in the future.

Working on all fronts:
the state, NGOs and women's health rights in Brazil

SOF (Sempreviva Organizaçao Feminista) is a Brazilian NGO that works on women's health in poor communities in the south-east of the country.

Ever since it was set up in the context of an authoritarian régime, SOF has provided an alternative organisation for health professionals concerned with public health. The combination of social activism and professional work offered by SOF provided a broad, complex, and innovative experience, involving an immense variety of contributions, and characterised by a collective way of working.

The impact of SOF's work can be measured by the transformations which have occurred in terms of health infrastructure, and by the changes in the region's health policies. SOF participated in the 1983 Parliamentary Commission of Inquiry, where public health policy guidelines for the Sao Paulo City Council were adopted. SOF has also encouraged the participation of women in the region's social movements, trade unions, and political parties. The vigour of the Health Movement shows SOF's input: people living in the south and west of the city have become more and more organised, and made demands which range from the extension of the water supply and sewage disposal, to price freezes on basic items.

One of the reasons for SOF's credibility seems to be the organisation's capacity to connect subjective and gender issues with broader political questions. Maintaining the link between the specific and the macro, SOF aims for progress in its analysis and practice at both ends of the spectrum.

(From Faure 1994 pp 51–54.)

Assessing the needs

Social education may seek to meet a wide variety of needs. It is, therefore, important to identify how a specific programme will enhance the specific capacities of a given set of people. Aims and objectives may include:

- providing education for those excluded from formal schooling;
- challenging the goals of formal education, where this is not responsive to the needs of marginalised people;
- offering alternative forms of education in response to unmet needs — for example, street theatre on reproductive health issues;
- encouraging people to fight for their rights, for example through legal education and support for organisations that represent them;

- providing information in appropriate forms, such as local radio programmes or newsletters.

These goals may reinforce each other. For instance, an Oxfam-funded NGO in Sri Lanka works with Tamil tea-plantation workers and Sinhalese farming communities, in a programme which encompasses pre-schools, health education, savings and credit schemes, vocational training, inter-ethnic leadership training and exchange visits, and documentation on the situation of the plantation workers. The overall aim is to equip these people to fight for a fairer deal in terms of citizenship, employment, and wages. Progress may be more rapid in some areas than others, but each activity makes sense only in the context of the whole picture.

Identifying the agents

The participants in social education should by definition determine the goals of any activity involving them, since enhancing their critical and organisational capacity is central to such programmes. The process of reaching agreement on these goals requires time, and perhaps external support. Participants may be from CBOs, women's groups, religious organisations, unions, NGOs, or other forms of popular organisation. Occasionally, a government department may also have a social education programme, or encourage this approach.

Challenging power structures

Social education is concerned with empowerment, and hence challenges existing power structures. The process may generate unexpected outcomes. Even within an apparently cohesive social group, power structures based on wealth, gender, age, family, religious or ethnic divisions, may affect how individuals participate and how they relate to each other (Kabeer, 1996).

A successful social education programme is likely to meet with conflict at some point, and the maturity to manage such conflict is itself a critical capacity in the development process — a major reason why external agencies should avoid forcing their own pace or agenda.

Assessing achievement

Social education always seeks attitudinal change, and evaluating impact necessarily involves subjective judgement. Outsiders will interpret events differently from those who experienced them, while some participants may attach importance to processes of which others are unaware (see Meyer and Singh, 1997:59–64). Sustainable change may be slow; tangible results may not be seen within the funded period, though many changes may have taken place on a more subjective level.

Participants themselves will have their own ideas about the value of social education programmes. Their indicators are likely to include all or some of the following:

- increased collective and individual confidence in assessing and finding solutions to social and political problems;
- increased participation in decision-making, especially among those who were previously excluded;
- increased ability to make the connections between day-to-day living conditions, and the wider socio-political and economic context;
- greater ability to organise to press the competent authorities for better living conditions or respect for civil rights;
- better knowledge of other relevant organisations (eg NGOs);
- collective acquisition of specific skills together with increased political awareness and skills in social analysis;
- better social relations within the community or organisation, and improved conflict-prevention and conflict-resolution skills;
- higher self-esteem and an ability to challenge negative stereotypes;
- more awareness of each others' needs, and greater willingness to cooperate.

These indicators are no less important for being subjective and not readily susceptible to independent measurement. Changes in how people feel about themselves and relate to those around them often determine whether more concrete changes will be sustainable in the long term.

Building confidence and practical skills

Emerenciana López Martínez describes her participation in a grassroots legal-awareness training workshop organised by the Mexican NGO, SEDEPAC:

I am a single mother and that led me to help other women with problems in my neighbourhood. I think I became a leader because I was angry, and also because at times I felt so impotent, because we women don't speak up. Also I [was angry] because my husband left me with my children... When they invited me to the workshop I just couldn't believe it. I thought it was a miracle, but then I didn't want to come because I was ashamed [because] I have no [education]. But Rose, the lawyer, said: 'Emerenciana, the workshop is for women like you, and besides, you have your experience'. So I attended. I did it because I wanted to know more about things; for example, how can you file a legal complaint? When does a legal case end?

> *What can you do, what can't you do? Also I thought I could meet other people.*
> *Well, many things happened in the workshop: I felt more sure about*
> *myself; I was not ashamed of myself any more, [and] I learned a lot about*
> *the law. ... some women were talking about their experiences and it hit me*
> *that I have to change the way I deal with my children ... the most useful*
> *thing is what I learned about the law and the penal code since we have so*
> *much violence in Chimalhuacan, where I live* (quoted in Rivera, 1995, p47.).

Literacy and numeracy

These skills are always included in formal schooling for children, and often in non-formal education for adults. Effective literacy may vary according to the range of languages used, levels of technology, and forms of economic activity. In most societies, illiteracy is a stigma and a practical handicap. Street signs, official forms, legal contracts, prescriptions, health and danger warnings, operating instructions for machinery, and newspapers, demand the ability to read. To hold a bank account, or to keep accounts or minutes, people must be able to write. However, literacy may be less important where oral communication is the norm, for instance among women and linguistic minorities (Fordham et al, 1995).

Since it is easiest to acquire literacy in the mother-tongue, this can pose problems for multi-lingual countries, or for minority language groups such as migrants or refugees. In Mozambique the colonial language, Portuguese, was chosen as the national language and used in literacy campaigns. This made nationwide communication possible, but disadvantaged those communities who did not speak Portuguese.

Literacy can be lost if it is not used. Functional literacy is more likely to be achieved and sustained if it is linked to people's social and economic interests. Ideally, adult literacy programmes should allow participants to acquire the capacities to use and develop these skills.

Literacy agents

Government-sponsored literacy campaigns may draw on non-formal approaches, and involve existing organisations or mobilise citizens as trainers; partly to reduce costs, but also with a nation-building perspective. In the 1980 National Literacy Crusade (CNA) in Nicaragua, some 95,000 volunteers or *brigadistas* were trained to teach basic adult literacy. These included secondary and college students, factory workers, and civil servants. Within six months, the national illiteracy rate fell from 53 per cent to 13 per cent (though this had risen again to about 35 per cent by 1993).[1]

My children would ask me if I would help with their homework, but I couldn't because I didn't understand the letters. It was hard for me not to be able to help them. But when the Crusade came, I thought this was my opportunity. Before the CNA I couldn't write my name. I didn't even know what letter my name began with. I had to be led by the hand when I began — but the more I learned, the more I could do on my own. When I finished the literacy primer, I could read, and by the second level ... all seemed easy to me ... Slowly I lost the fear. When I saw I could do it on my own, I was thrilled. And in the end I learned.
(Nicaraguan woman, quoted in Peter Sandiford et al (1994:47.)

Effective mass literacy campaigns depend on the political and economic commitment of the state, which must be able to mobilise the population, and to keep up the momentum through a longer-term investment in primary schooling. Teaching materials need to be appropriate for inexperienced literacy teachers, who also need thorough training and in-service support. Well-designed follow-up programmes, through which the newly-literate can practise and extend their skills, are critical.

Many NGOs see literacy as an integral part of social education, and so may incorporate it into a primary health care project, a campaign for land rights, or work to tackle the low status of women. However, NGO efforts are often small-scale and piecemeal. It is generally more efficient to coordinate literacy work within a given area, and share materials and infrastructure.

An integrated approach to literacy also means that educational materials can be developed locally, so that they are relevant to people's lives and experience; and literacy facilitators can be drawn from the community, and so understand specific needs and problems. Sometimes people produce photographs, and audio and video records of their experience, as part of the process of learning to read and write.

REFLECT: An approach to literacy and social change

The British NGO, ACTIONAID has developed the Regenerated Freirean Literacy through Empowering Community Techniques (REFLECT) which build on Freire's theoretical framework and use a methodology drawing on PRA techniques. This was initially piloted in over 100 villages in Uganda, El Salvador, and Bangladesh, covering some 1,550 women and 420 men. The approach proved more effective than conventional methods at teaching adults to read and write, and linking literacy to wider development.

In a REFLECT programme, there is no textbook — no literacy 'primer' — beyond a facilitator's guide. Each literacy circle develops its own materials through constructing maps, matrices, calendars, and diagrams that represent local reality, systematise the learners' existing knowledge, and promote the detailed analysis of local issues.

Eventually, each circle will have produced between 20 or 30 graphics. The graphics are a permanent record for communities, providing a detailed survey of local conditions, needs, and attitudes. As learners construct their own materials, they take ownership of the issues and are more likely to be moved to take local action, and change their behaviour or their attitudes.

Participants noted the following benefits or changes:

- *Self-realisation*: better self-esteem and the increased ability to analyse and solve problems as well as to articulate ideas. These were reflected in better knowledge of the local environment, and improved intra-household and community relations.

- *Public participation:* greater involvement in community organisations, with a majority of learners taking on formal positions of responsibility which they did not hold before the REFLECT literacy programme (eg chair, secretary or treasurer on the Community Council).

- *Community-level action*: efforts to improve local conditions economic activities to health projects. Learners valued having independently arrived at decisions to do something through their own analysis.

- *Resource-management*: women in particular appreciated calendars and matrices to strengthen their analytical skills, enabling them to plan better, develop more effective coping strategies (eg bulk buying and storing goods), and have more control over decisions regarding loan use (previously dominated by men).

- *Health awareness*: as one Bangladeshi woman said, 'We learnt something of health before but it was not very practical and felt like a lot of rules. With making maps, it was a lot more helpful and we understand things a lot better.'

- *Children's education*: local schools experienced a significant increase in enrolment of children of parents in REFLECT; and parents in over one-third of the groups started their own non-formal education centre for primary age children.

Literacy programmes ... have often failed because they have fallen into believing that either literacy in itself is sufficient (so they have ignored other processes and focused on the product); or they have assumed that empowerment in itself is enough (but have in practice tried to 'indoctrinate' people into new ideologies). REFLECT holds these two processes in an effective balance and helps them to build on each other. (Based on Archer and Cottingham, 1997:199–202.)

Literacy *per se* will not guarantee a critical capacity, or improved organisational abilities, though it is often a vital stepping-stone on the way. Literacy
may confer skills which will help people to enhance their quality of life, and
'the empowerment process in turn creates uses for literacy in people's
everyday lives' (ibid, 202). The importance of such 'fusion' is well illustrated
in the example of a rural workers' union supported by Oxfam in Honduras.
This moved away from 'popular education workshops' for its middle-level
cadres, and decided to make a major investment in raising the educational
level of its grassroots membership. As one peasant farmer said, 'if I am the
only one in our group who can read and write, then what kind of organisation
are we? what kind of accountability can the ordinary members exercise?' A
literacy programme was developed in the mid-1980s that earned it
recognition from the Ministry of Education as an educational institution. The
programme's long-term impact was enhanced by developing reading
materials for adults which reinforced other areas of the union's work, such as
sustainable agricultural practices, and primary health care. Its organisers
remarked that:

*What literacy means in this programme is understanding the social, cultural,
economic, and political forces that influence one's life, one's community,
and one's society as a whole. Its goals go far beyond literacy and numeracy, as
participants become actively involved in a life-long process of learning that
develops their critical skills, and empowers them to challenge the social forces
which have kept them passive and dependent for so long. It is education which
aims not to adapt people to the prevailing social order but to transform society;
it thus serves as a tool for liberation* (Mejía, Hernández et al, 1992:199).

The programme's long-term impact was enhanced by developing reading
materials for adults. With a sympathetic local publisher, the union recorded a
traditional village story-teller, and transcribed a simplified version of his tales
in a volume which was sold commercially as well as being distributed through
the literacy programme. This is a clear example of the kind of systemic linkages described in Chapter 3, which help to make the whole much more than
the sum of its parts.

Participation and exclusion

Those who most need literacy training may be the least able to participate in a
long-term programme. Most illiterate adults are female, but women generally
work longer hours than men, and so have less time and energy available for
attending classes. They often have less freedom of movement than men, and
many face hostility from men in their family, or may not join mixed-sex

groups or be taught by a man. People's socially-imposed feelings of inferiority and failure are intensified if humiliated by other students, or if the teaching materials depict them in submissive or demeaning roles. Often, women-only groups (with female literacy workers) provide a more constructive learning environment for women; similarly, in ethnically-divided societies, students may respond better to a teacher from their own ethnic group.

Distance learning

Distance learning is a form of self-tuition using radio, television, or other audio-visual material. It is commonly used to reinforce adult education programmes, especially where it is difficult for people to meet. Radio schools are supported by Oxfam in countries as diverse as India, Namibia, and Peru.

Broadcasting for change

In Mali, Oxfam supports a solar-powered radio station run by a local organisation specifically for isolated populations:

It offers traditional music, played by local musicians, and interviews with local people. These are interspersed with short stories and features about local history, and brief information pieces about improved agricultural and pastoral techniques; about health, environmental matters, and market prices. The radio station also broadcasts summaries of regional, national, and international news in local languages; and information on legal rights and changes in Malian law, especially as these relate to women. The programmes promote the decentralisation process, and aim to equip people to participate in local government.

Possession of radios had long been the privilege of menfolk, but now women began the task of fattening goats for the specific purpose of selling them to raise the money to buy a radio in order to follow the programmes.

Bocoum Koubourou Koita is in charge of programmes for women. She covers issues like health and hygiene. 'We talk about the importance of clean water to women and children. I also interview women about problems during pregnancy, and other things like nutrition, prices in the market, contraception and family planning. Unfortunately, women are very busy and it's a problem for them to find the time to listen. Some men think it is a waste of time for women to listen to the radio. We broadcast women's programmes in the morning, so that they can listen undisturbed while the men are in the fields' (Drisdelle, 1997: 28).

As advances in interactive information technology make communication faster and cheaper, so there is increasing experimentation in electronic methods of distance learning. While this may still be a far cry from serving the needs of peasant farmers in the Bolivian highlands, or fishing communities in the Philippines, it does offer exciting potential for the future (see Chapter 7).

But whether the medium is a wind-up transistor radio, or a personal computer with full Internet capabilities, distance learning works best for those who have some prior experience of studying, and when it is backed up by face-to-face encounters. It is certainly not a 'cheap option'. Good distance-learning programmes, perhaps even more than conventional schools, depend on trained input and on an organisational framework within which learners can apply and review what they have learnt.

Training for social change

Within an organisational context, training conventionally focuses on 'human resource development' — staff training, career paths, management skills, planning and evaluation techniques — that enable the organisation to function better. This is both because the staff are constantly improving and updating their skills, and also because they feel valued and challenged in their work.

Agencies that offer or support training in a development setting may focus on certain groups or social sectors, such as peasant communities, oppressed castes, or lone parents. Though these agencies may specialise — for example, in leadership training, literacy, vocational skills — they usually try to take their lead from the people they aim to serve. Where there is a strong responsive component, this may be called *participatory training*.

Overall, a capacity-building approach is more concerned with enhancing people's capacity to articulate their own interests than with strengthening institutions *per se*. Feminist analysis has revealed how organisations create and reproduce certain structures, 'norms' and 'operating practices' that 'produce incentive systems, formal performance standards, and informal organisational cultures, which direct the behaviour of individual agents' (Goetz, 1996: 4).

Looking at organisations in this way highlights the links, for example, between the attitudes of organisations to racism or to sexual harassment and how their staff think and function on a day-to-day basis. This is very clear in the field of gender, where NGOs and donor agencies often push for standards of equity and equality among their counterparts of which they themselves fall far short. Attitudinal training cannot compensate for discriminatory policies, but it can help to create an organisational environment that is less defensive and more amenable to self-criticism: a first step towards bridging the gap between rhetoric and practice.

Training or skills development supported by Oxfam covers a vast range of activities, including vocational skills for ex-combatants in Angola, organisational management for NGO workers in Eastern Europe, gender analysis for CBOs in Brazil, social survey methods for health workers in Zimbabwe, disaster preparedness for aid volunteers in Bangladesh, small business management for cooperatives in Nicaragua, labour legislation for trades unions in Honduras, agricultural skills for farmers in Haiti, human rights and legal training for para-legal workers in South Africa, and communication technology for networks in the Philippines. 'Extension work' has also been supported in areas such food production, integrated pest management, and community nursing. An important element is the peer-training of local people as trainers. This is a long-term approach to capacity-building that supports people in their efforts to be self-reliant and to shape the processes of change.

Training to build capacity

The main focus of the Oxfam/ODA support for Primary Health Care (PHC) in Namibia was in training to enable the Ministry of Health to implement its PHC policy. It was recognised that it was most important for the Training Unit to develop manuals, modules, and train others to train.

The Unit aimed to develop training and facilitation skills amongst a core of health staff working throughout the four regional health directorates in hospitals, clinics, and management teams. Possible trainees were identified from course participants, and then assisted in developing and practising their skills over a period of time. This gave the facilitators first-hand experience in all aspects of preparing and conducting a training programme. And through this, they learned how to work as a team, and developed an *esprit de corps* that could respond positively to criticism as well as analyse the training session, write reports, use reference material, think critically about the participants' input, and generally facilitate learning (Lang, 1996:23).

Training programmes should first and foremost be based on a clear analysis of the issue they aim to address. Sometimes problems may be better solved in other ways, or require a range of inputs; for instance, changing an organisation's ethos, structure, or management is likely to involve a lengthy negotiation and consensus-building process, backed up with policy changes, before staff training sessions will be appropriate.

Whether it is focused inwards on the organisation, or outwards on the needs of others, training is effective only if it is part of an overall strategy to enable participants to make use of what they have learned. People learn in many ways — seeing and doing, workshops, exchanges, and so on. 'Training is only one avenue to learning' (Smyth, 1997:3), and a combination of training and other forms of learning is often needed.

The lack of certain skills may hinder people's capacity to challenge or change their situation. However, many training programmes supported in the name of capacity-building do not significantly strengthen people's collective or organisational capacities, nor enable them to overcome the forces that oppress them. Training proposals must be analysed in terms of what they offer in the longer term, and to whom. Some skills may be of immediate practical use, others will be strategically important in the longer term. For example, a co-operative may fail to get off the ground unless its members have basic production, marketing, and business skills. But its future sustainability may depend more on knowing how to retain and recruit members, or making links with other businesses.

Planning training: 'The Seven Steps'

1 Aims: why? These must be clear, explicit, and consistent with those of the people or organisation seeking training. Monitoring and evaluation should be part of the process of establishing the aims and objectives. Evaluation indicators should relate to the objectives, and be specified before the training commences.

2 Learners: who? Training is easier if the group is homogeneous, but ice-breaking activities may help to build collective responsibility and identity. This includes gathering information about the different roles, needs, and perspectives of the participants, as well as their various skills, interests, and capacities.

Self-selection of trainees, or selection by 'the community' or other body often discriminates against the less powerful, the illiterate, and women. Selection criteria should be explicit and agreed in advance — such as demanding equal numbers of men and women trainees, or insisting on a mix of literacy levels.

Women tend to participate less in mixed-sex groups, and may prefer women-only courses. Single-sex groups may also be better if there are large gender-related differences in existing knowledge, literacy levels, and social and political status.

3 Access: where and when? This is affected by the different work schedules and the daily and seasonal routines of the trainees. Venues should be convenient and affordable. Provision should be made for those with childcare responsibilities.

People learn better if their knowledge and experience are recognised and valued. 'On-the-job' training, apprenticeships, or extension training are often better than sessions which require long absences. 'Sandwich courses', which combine periods of study with work experience, allow learners to practise what they have learned, and trainers to adapt their courses as required.

4 Trainers: who? Trainers need expertise as well as facilitation skills. Unless there are technical skills to be communicated, formal qualifications may matter less than the ability to communicate well and to establish a good learning environment. Trainers need a good grasp of group dynamics, and sensitivity to all forms of discrimination, in order to encourage mutual respect and understanding.

5 Needs analysis: what for? Only if learning needs have been comprehensively identified can a training programme be drawn up to meet them; this process may itself be a learning exercise. Monitoring helps trainers to keep the course well pitched, and allows participants to give timely feedback. Trainees are often asked to make a post-course assessment. However, this does not measure the long-term impact. Follow-up questionnaires or visits may help, and are vital when periods of training alternate with 'hands-on' practice.

6 Content: what? This relates to the objectives, and may include awareness, knowledge, skills, and behaviour. Training courses should also include time for introductions and group-building sessions, as well as forward planning, monitoring, and evaluation.

7 Methods: how? The chosen methods should meet the learners' specific needs. Participatory methods, based on learners' own experience, are best for adult learning, and are generally more enjoyable.

Materials must be tailored to the educational and linguistic levels of the trainees, and culturally sensitive. Materials should challenge negative stereotypes (from Eade and Williams, 1995: 368–371).

Training for rights

Over and above the practical skills they need, training in their legal and moral rights is often linked to struggles of particular groups, such as homeless squatters threatened with eviction; or fisherpeople trying to fight pollution of their fishing grounds; or domestic workers seeking to unionise; or people facing human rights abuses learning about human rights bodies and legal remedies, such as *habeas corpus*. While it may well have a technical dimension, training in this area is also concerned with giving people the sense that they have rights, as well as the confidence to fight for them.

Training people in their rights is one thing, asserting these rights may be quite another. For example, some Indian women who asserted their legal rights to land, were condemned as witches, stoned and chased away; many human rights workers in Latin America have been the target of death threats or have themselves been assassinated. Such training is nowhere more needed than in areas where human rights are under threat, but it is important that both participants and trainers are aware of the risks they may be running. This may affect the methods and ways of working that can be adopted.

Learning to fight for one's rights

An incident in San José de las Flores illustrates this power in action. The square was full of visitors and journalists, commemorating the anniversary of the repopulation and waiting for the Bishop to celebrate mass. Without warning, the Atlacatl Battalion arrived and began an altercation. Community members told them to leave. In response, the soldiers raised their guns and shot over the heads of the people by the church and then at their feet. In one spontaneous surge, the townspeople rushed the soldiers, who turned and ran, lobbing tear-gas grenades behind them. The unarmed population literally ran them out.

The repopulated communities began to realise their own dignity and power in a process of transformation that was hard to stop. They had some support, but most importantly they had some success. They realised that the powerful did not always win, and that they had important weapons themselves. Their relationship to power was changing (Thompson, 1996: 330).

Training for attitudinal change

Within organisations, norms and procedures tend to validate certain ways of doing things, and to exclude or ignore others. This may not accord with what the organisation says or believes about itself, or may not be logical or defensible on ethical grounds. But where the interests are deeply entrenched, their very existence may be invisible to or simply denied by many people. Challenges to them will be resisted in a variety of ways (Longwe, 1997). Further, people will often participate in marginalising aspects of their own identity. For example, to rise to the top of an organisation, women may adopt 'sociologically male attributes' (Goetz, 1996:7). This illustrates that people who lack power and recognition must assimilate an alien but more powerful culture in order to be rewarded by it.

This has implications for attitudinal training. It is now understood, for example, that in terms of addressing gender inequalities '"technical" approaches to mainstreaming gender, such as the supply of gender-disaggregated information, use of focal points, gender-sensitivity checklists, and the like, are not successful in the absence of efforts to mobilise constituency pressure, and to strengthen women's positions [within] ... bureaucracies' (ibid., p8). Similar problems are faced in areas such as race- or disability-awareness: an organisation develops a policy, ensures that staff are formally aware of it, enjoins its senior managers to ensure that the policy is implemented — and then nothing changes. In-house training is a process of acquiring 'a type of understanding, sets of skills, and expertise which do not "come naturally", but need to be learned, throughout the organisation and beyond' (Smyth, 1997:1). One-off workshops on subjects such as equal opportunities will do little in themselves to change how people behave. Without sustained commitment at all levels of an organisation, rhetoric and techniques may be learnt, but prejudices and discriminatory work practices will persist.

Awareness training addresses attitudes, perceptions and beliefs; unless people are sensitive to gender inequalities, gender analysis training is unlikely in the long run to change planning and practice in development and relief agencies' work. We believe that unless people's emotions are touched, and their practices in their personal lives are brought into the discussion, there is a risk that gender awareness will remain merely an intellectual construct, and will be limited in its power to bring about meaningful social change (Williams et al, 1994: xiv).

Any personal development training, and particularly that which aims to challenge prejudice and discrimination, can arouse strong feelings — anger, fear, hurt or guilt — which may be expressed in the form of denial, rejection, aggressiveness, or self-blame. The issues raised may be deeply challenging to individuals; dearly-held beliefs may be exposed as prejudices or assumptions; or a major rift may be revealed between a person's self-image and how they are perceived by others. People brought up in a very hierarchical culture may find it hard to give and receive criticism, handle power effectively, or respond to conflict. A skilled facilitator will establish an environment in which these negative feelings can be transformed into an impetus for positive change.

Thus, awareness-training cannot be separated from an organisation's policies and procedures, including its formal and informal reward and incentive systems — and the expectations generated by these. For instance, an external gender review of Oxfam found that 63 per cent of employees were women, of whom 60 per cent were clustered in lower-graded positions (grades 5 to 9). Of the 37 per cent male employees, 40 per cent were in senior positions (grades 11 to 15). Fewer than 30 per cent of women were in these high-level managerial posts. The author observed:

High workload and working styles were two contributing factors toward the imbalance observed between women and men in senior positions ... High workload was problematic for both men and women. For those individuals who are the principle carers and unpaid workers in the home, tackling more senior positions ... often becomes highly undesirable and unfeasible. Those who do work a double shift are often considered, whether directly or indirectly, [to be] less committed .. [H]igh workload, especially when coupled with a second shift in the home, was often linked to feelings of inadequacy, powerlessness, and stress levels leading to inefficiency and ineffectiveness (Carson, n.d., 17).

Oxfam's own experience in trying to implement its gender policy shows that it is far from easy to change an institutional culture when this is itself a reflection of wider society. Training, we have stressed, is only a small part of the answer. For example, assertiveness-training may help women to acquire the necessary skills to compete *on the same terms* as men; but it does not question the implications of having a 'masculine' organisational management style. To bring about fundamental change in women's status within an organisation, and so alter the institutional culture for men as well as women, would need a range of actions such as:

• encouraging support networks for women bureaucrats, for sharing ideas and experiences;
• adjusting the working day and making provision for no-penalty 'career breaks' or flexible working patterns for staff with small children, or dependents;

- providing paternity leave, nursery facilities and/or making a contribution to childcare costs;
- keeping the travel demands of all jobs down to a realistic minimum, and allowing for under-5s to accompany their parent(s) where possible;
- actively drawing on critical support from women's groups and other organisations;
- aiming for a 'strategic mass' of women in senior posts and at every level throughout the organisation, and investing in making this happen.

When Oxfam (India) Trust surveyed staff on what *they* thought would make a difference to women's job satisfaction and career prospects, respondents suggested mechanisms such as job-swaps, affirmative action (including encouraging men to apply for lower-grade jobs), and skills-development. The survey also revealed that women staff worked in fear of sexual harassment both from male colleagues and from men in local counterpart organisations, particularly while travelling alone or at night. Pregnant women were especially concerned about the heavy travel schedule. And most women felt a burden of responsibility for Oxfam's gender policy; but lacked contact with senior staff who could affirm their efforts (Gwynn and Sehgal, 1996:30–32). However, this survey conveyed an important message that senior managers were prepared to listen, take action, and commit resources to issues that had hitherto been regarded as non-existent or unimportant.

Enhancing economic capacity

Small businesses and micro-enterprises are a major source of employment for poor people worldwide, producing goods and services for local consumption or for export. Low-capital, low-technology, and labour-intensive enterprises must, however, survive within an increasingly harsh economic context. Trade liberalisation and deregulation have forced fragile national economies to compete in the world market, often reducing the security of poor producers in the process. Small enterprises are highly vulnerable to a flood of cheap imports, or competition with mass-produced goods. Further, they are often constrained by lack of credit facilities, training opportunities, access to technology, legal protection and regulation, and marketing outlets.

Many such enterprises are in fact part of a long production chain controlled by large businesses, who contract out the riskier and less lucrative parts of the production process to home-workers and small firms. For them, the 'free market' may mean in practice that they must compete with enterprises that flout the law, and pay desperately low wages in order to keep prices down. For workers, rising unemployment means that any job, however badly paid, may be better than none at all. In such a cut-throat context, poor producers have only very limited scope to establish economically viable — and ethical — alternatives:

... deregulation has affected women's workday. The tariffs of the 1980s protected production cooperatives, allowing them to offer significant benefits, standard hours and more flexible conditions of work. After 1990, with open economy policies ... the Women's United Textile Cooperative encountered stiff competition from large garment factories such as the maquiladoras *in Managua's free trade zone which paid sub-minimum wages to women working 60 and 70 hour weeks... Imports of used clothing from the United States flooded the market. The Textile Cooperative went from 68 members in 1982 to 29 members in 1991, and the store folded in 1993. The only women who continued to produce clothing were ones that were able to work long hours and travel farther, terms of work that not all members were capable of meeting* (Kidder, 1996:43).

The 'informal' economy is the only means of survival for millions of people. Many of these are self-employed, working for small or family enterprises, or are contracted as out-workers (or home-workers) by big businesses. Such small enterprises are often unregistered, and hence may not qualify for access to certain facilities, such as subsidies and credit. Exempt from protective legislation, they may offer exploitative pay and conditions. Employees in such businesses, often women and children, have no legal redress in the event of abuse by their employer, and are seldom unionised.

Gender or caste-based divisions of labour may also lead to or reinforce inequalities in ownership and control of productive resources and income. Women are often confined to unskilled activities, and denied training and promotion to better-paid work. Even in the same jobs, they may be paid less and have less employment security than men. Male tasks are generally assigned a higher social and economic value than female tasks; and when the latter are upgraded, for example through access to improved technology or credit, they may be taken over by men. Labour-intensive 'traditional' female skills usually equip women only for low-paid work, and provide limited marketing opportunities.

Small-scale economic enterprise: some lessons

• Many small-scale economic projects make no or only minimal profit. Often they simply increase workload and stress. The more successful projects are those that include elements of consciousness-raising. An analysis of gender relations should be an integral part of any income-generation project.

- Many economic projects are based on inaccurate conceptions of people's work and use of time. This severely limits their chances of success and long-term sustainability. NGOs must appraise women's and men's situation both at the micro and macro level, and gather appropriate and disaggregated base-line data.
- NGOs should look closely at what services women as well as men require in order to support their reproductive and social roles and thus allow them to participate in economic enterprises more easily and effectively. Indicators for planning, appraisal, and evaluation should reflect the perspectives of both sexes.
- NGOs should not fund projects in isolation. Economic enterprises should strengthen social organisation and aim to empower people and communities. NGOs should look beyond the immediate project towards back-up services such as consumer or production co-operatives.
- Training is essential, and sound management is crucial. Women in particular need access to leadership and organisational skills because of their more limited experience in this area. Training in better production techniques, marketing, and so on, is also vital.

(Based on Piza-López and March, 1991)

Oxfam's experience has largely been in the informal sector, through the provision of vocational and other forms of training, organisational support, help in marketing, and access to credit and other types of micro-finance assistance either directly to organisations such as producer groups, co-operatives, unions, associations of self-employed people, and small businesses; or via intermediary NGOs that specialise in providing such services. The aim is to help people to escape from insecurity and the cycle of low productivity and low income; and to support the efforts of poor producers and workers to deepen their understanding of economic forces, and to defend their social and economic rights.

Strategies may involve helping people to improve incomes, conditions, and security in existing enterprises; to set up new enterprises to take existing products into a new market, perhaps by serving a different area or clientele; to set up new enterprises for new products that build on existing skills and technology, such as new kinds of processed foods; or to undertake market feasibility assessments prior to setting up new industries or developing new products.

We shall look very schematically at some typical interventions: training, organisational support (including marketing), and microfinance. (For a more detailed and specialised account of Oxfam's thinking and practice in the area of economics, productive enterprises, and micro-finance, see for example Piza-López and March,1991; Kidder, 1996; Millard, 1996;, Coote, 1996; and Johnson and Rogaly, 1997.) The Chapter concludes with a critical discussion of women's income-generation projects (IGPs), since these are a major component of many NGO and donor interventions in the economic sphere.

Vocational and skills training

Vocational and other forms of training are often designed to raise the incomes of poor people, on the assumption that with new and marketable skills they will be able to find work or set up enterprises of their own. But training will not create jobs or markets, or turn poor and uncredit-worthy people into entrepreneurs. Nor does the economic success of an enterprise imply either that gains are fairly shared, or that the workers are empowered! Raising the economic capacities of poor women and men in a way that is both equitable and sustainable demands a range of technical and organisational skills.

Vocational training for women often revolves around upgrading skills such as tailoring, weaving, embroidery, and knitting; or domestic activities such as laundering, hairdressing, or cooking. The assumption is that these are 'traditional' female activities, and that they therefore constitute the best 'entry point' for raising women's incomes. Yet such assumptions have often been incorrect. The gender biases of aid agencies have been detrimental to women, fostering their 'domestication' by privileging reproductive labour over women's other economic activities — such as farming. Sewing machines may be as alien to women as anvils or lawn-mowers; and though women may make, alter, and repair their children's clothes, tailoring may be a male occupation within their particular culture. There are also problems in 'scaling-up' activities from the domestic to the semi-industrial level. A Guatemalan woman may spend several months weaving a traditional blouse, or *huipil,* for herself. To make a *huipil* for sale that was based on full input costings, and rewarded her labour well enough to make the effort worthwhile, would price it out of all but the specialised international market (Millard, 1996).

Vocational and technical training focuses on the trainees' real or potential work opportunities. Whether these are commercially viable and sustainable must be assessed *before* embarking on training. Equally important are organisational and management skills, which range from leadership, knowing how to hold and minute meetings, negotiate contracts, or keep accounts, to personnel, financial and business management, information and stock control systems, and marketing expertise. (For guidance on the skills required in financial management and export marketing, see Cammack,

1992; Elliot, 1996; Millard, 1996). As an enterprise expands or becomes more complex, skills in conflict-prevention and resolution, and in group dynamics and organisational decision-making, are also valuable.

The technology used in an enterprise may affect access to government facilities such as credit, training, and marketing. New technology may change production methods. Training in the use of new technology, maintenance of new machines, and appropriate business skills, is indispensable. As changes in the production process occur, it is important to ensure that women do not lose out as new gender divisions of labour arise.

Small businesses are as likely to fail through mutual mistrust, or poor personal or business management, as from lack of production skills. Since needs are constantly evolving, training should be treated as an essential part of business development, whatever the scale or nature of the enterprise — both upgrading existing skills, and learning new ones. It often pays, therefore, to re-invest some of the profits into a programme of training and skills-development.

Support for producers

Producers and workers can gain many benefits from belonging to some kind of local group, cooperative or union. These can, for example, cut the cost of raw materials by buying in bulk; facilitate storage, transport, and marketing of goods; give producers more power in negotiations with larger organisations, including local authorities and merchants; provide organisational skills-training and educational services; and represent producers in wider movements for change. At their best, these not only offer poor people better control over the means of production, but also strengthen their forms of social organisation and their capacity to work towards an equitable economic system. (See also Chapter 3 and Chapter 6).

Producer groups are not, however, automatically based on democratic participation and fair access to resources. They may well be hierarchical or based on systems of patronage or exclusion, with unfair distribution of profits, and low levels of participation. The kind of support and training they need is likely to include financial and management skills.

Sometimes skills are 'upgraded' in the hope of earning higher incomes, though there may be only a limited market for the improved product, and one which is unfamiliar to small producers. Product or market diversification gives producers greater security. An analysis of the risks and benefits of different markets will in turn determine the producers' short and medium-term needs for training, credit, and other inputs.

Marketing problems often arise because producers have failed to under-take adequate market research and to develop marketing strategies (Millard,

1996). Alternative trading organisations (ATOs) may assist producer groups both in assessing the marketability of their products, and in gaining access to international markets; such advice can represent a major contribution to capacity-building.

Credit and microfinance

Difficulty in getting access to credit and related services is often the major problem faced by small producers and artisans, and by women in general.For instance, in Latin America and the Caribbean, only one in ten beneficiaries of credit programmes is female (UNDP, 1996:4). Many development interventions in the production sector therefore focus on credit: well known examples are the Self-employed Women's Association (SEWA) in India, which has a woman-run and fully independent bank; Grameen Bank in Bangladesh, which also concentrates on lending for women's micro-enterprises; and Banco Sol in Bolivia. Growth has enabled these organisations to deal with micro-credit while also covering much of their costs through income from interest and fees on loans. SEWA has also been successful in its efforts to improve the situation of self-employed workers, through mobilising its members in public campaigns.

Repayment rates in credit schemes are not unequivocally an indicator of sustainable success: in Bangladesh, for example, poor women were repaying their loans promptly, but in some cases it was their husbands who were primarily benefiting from the borrowed money (Goetz and Sen Gupta, 1996). Increases in household incomes through access to a loan may be very modest, while economic security for micro-enterprises usually depends on a range of other back-up services over and above credit. It may well be beyond the scope and expertise of one NGO to offer the required range of services.

[An] NGO should carefully and honestly assess whether it has the appropriate skills and resources before beginning work. Acquiring or developing the specialist skills is a long-term commitment which itself requires substantial investment of funds. Poor people's needs for financial services are enduring and long-term. An NGO considering whether to provide services must understand the need for a commitment to do so for a considerable length of time: the 30 years or more of a bank's existence, rather than the three to five years of donor funding arrangements (Johnson and Rogaly, 1997:119).

External intervention in local financial markets thus requires a detailed knowledge of how those markets function, of the social context, and of the existing options for and constraints on small borrowers. This includes an awareness of informal or self-run savings and credit schemes, such as 'chit clubs' or ROSCAs; links (or potential links) between the informal sector and the formal banking system; and of the different practices and needs of men and women. Lack of such knowledge can result in interventions that are damaging for the very poorest, exposing them to high risks (Johnson and Rogaly, 1997:11). For most NGOs, the most appropriate intervention may be to encourage people's economic capacities through village banks or credit unions; to support training in financial management; and to enable them to link up with specialised providers.

Access to credit may be needed over a long period as small businesses grow, and to cover fluctuations in the profitability of small and micro-enterprises. It may be used not only for income generation, but also to enable poor people to protect their livelihoods against 'unforeseens' and so increase their overall security: 'the poorest are likely to need to build up a degree of security before investment and growth become possible' (Johnson and Rogaly, 1997:118). In particular, microfinance services may support people's willingness and capacity to save.

Examining financial sustainability

Financial sustainability is only one component of ensuring that schemes are able to provide services in the long term; aspects of management and organisational structure are equally critical. The organisational form may be the most significant design element in relation to long-term sustainability. Some NGOs have turned themselves into banks, but this is not likely to be an option for most NGOs.

Pressures for financial self-sustainability are likely to produce dilemmas for the organisation. An institution which increases loan size may lose its focus on poor people; the strategy of deliberately including better-off people in order to subsidise lending to the very poor requires a clear organisational vision if it is to succeed.

• The monitoring and management of financial information is a specialist area and should be recognised as such by building the necessary skills among NGO staff or using outside specialists.

• Considerations of sustainability in both organisational and financial terms need to be made from the outset; but even when a project is already underway prospects for financial and organisational sustainability should be addressed.

• In order to develop a sustainable organisation within the national regulatory framework it may be necessary to undertake advocacy work to change existing government policies.

- The progress of the institution towards financial and organisational sustainability is not the sole indicator of achievement. For organisations with an agenda for poverty reduction, assessing the impact of the services on users is essential (Johnson and Rogaly, 1997:71).

Income generation projects (IGPs)

Efforts to enhance the earning capacity of self-employed people or informal sector micro-enterprises are known as income-generation projects (IGPs). This type of project has been predominantly associated with women. A vast amount of official and NGO funding has focused on IGPs supposedly to 'enhance the status of women', or to enable women to 'become economically active'. Such projects

... need many resources to be viable and sustainable, including time (women's labour), leadership, financial capital, physical assets, technology, skills, raw materials, and marketing channels. Women first need access to these resources. Next, women need to be able to acquire or use them at prices that are comparable to those faced by other (men's) enterprises. Prices include both the cash exchange value and the often unquantifiable transaction costs such as the time, stress, uncertainty or travel required to obtain or use resources (Kidder, 1996:23).

Proponents of IGPs argue that, unlike jobs in the formal sector, productive activities can be carried out alongside women's normal household work. They claim that the extra income can increase women's autonomy and change intra-household relations; may enable women to challenge male domestic violence; and can help in awareness-raising and collective strategising. Women's IGPs may also offer an opportunity to expand women's existing skills and organisational experience. There have certainly been cases, for instance among Dalit women in Southern India, where the economic security afforded by an IGP given them the confidence to participate in social and political life.

The success of IGPs is, however, patchy, for various reasons (Piza-López and March, 1992). In general, IGPs for women:

- are often seen not as a serious economic activity, but a way for women to earn 'pin money'. Hence, they are not scrutinised in terms of viability and sustainability: how much capital is needed? How much income will be generated? Over what period? How will assets be distributed? Nor are they based on solid market research.

- are often based on women's traditional activities (such as weaving) that are themselves labour-intensive, gender-segregated, and geared to survival needs rather than to growth or profit. Further, these activities may normally exist within relationships and networks of reciprocity that provide an in-kind insurance policy or welfare provision.

• tend to cast women solely as self-employed entrepreneurs rather than wage workers within the formal and regulated sector: this further locks them into a fragmented informal sector (that is assumed to be homogeneous and benign), rather than enabling them to enter the (unionised) job market.

• are often supported by donors and NGOs not primarily for economic reasons, but as welfare interventions, or to meet other objectives (eg to provide an 'entry point' for awareness-raising or social mobilisation). Different objectives require different strategies and timeframes; further, donors and participants may judge success or failure against different criteria.

• have tended to rely on a limited awareness of women's existing work burden as well as other social relations and obligations, or have been super-imposed upon these, on the assumption that cash income is better for women than the non-cash support they may derive from such networks.

• have usually been based on a superficial understanding either of the wider economic (policy, market and industrial) context, or of the micro-economy of the area or sector in which they must function: being seen in isolation rather than as part of a dynamic (global) system.

• have failed to meet the full range of training needs and skills (including leadership and organisational management), or to help women to alter the policy environment in which they are functioning by offering opportunities for education and advocacy.

• are often seen as short-term projects rather than a long-term strategy, with the result that women are disappointed and drop out when the expected benefits do not materialise rapidly.

In addition, women commonly say that they fear making a success out of a business enterprise lest their husbands demand the profits: one reason for the popularity of women's banking services, and for collective savings and credit schemes controlled by women.

For these and other reasons, women's IGPs often fail to survive the withdrawal of external funding, and so are neither profitable nor sustainable, and further undermine people's capacities and confidence. A group whose activities increase its members' workload without offering material or other benefits, is damaging to them. Far better to support women producers in gaining access to resources such as land, credit, training, or representation within existing producer groups, than to invent schemes that are of questionable benefit. Indeed, supporting women's entry into the formal economy may provide them with as much income, security, and opportunity to organise as they would gain within a fragile and isolated micro-enterprise in the informal sector. Such an approach would place the stress on education and training, to ensure that women enter the job market on favourable terms; and on support for workers' representation.

Finally, it is vital that the donors' objectives coincide with those of the people involved in a funded activity. It is indefensible to encourage poor women to invest their time and energy in activities that are doomed to failure, on the grounds that this will somehow 'empower' them, or give them useful organisational experience. The problem is not in having objectives that include both economic and empowerment goals; but in ensuring that all parties agree on the relationship between them, and on how progress towards them will be assessed.

6

Investing in organisations

*Civil society in the form of a multitude of vibrant and variegated
organisations can continue the process of development towards
integration, towards a more conscious society and a more conscious
individual, capable of redressing division and imbalance, experimenting
with new forms of meaning, creating new productive structures and
possibilities... This is 'people-centred development', as opposed to the
provision of services or the struggle for power* (Kaplan, 1996:62–63).

*There is truth in the old adage that there is strength in unity. If political
participation ... is uncoordinated it is unlikely to lead to change... it must
be coordinated into a constituency pushing certain concerns into policy
decisions and implementation mechanisms*
(Butegwa in Reardon (ed), 1995: 60–61).

Introduction

Freedom of association is a fundamental right. Further, without the capacity
to mobilise, poor people have little influence on the social, economic, and
political processes affecting them. Overcoming oppression ultimately
depends on action by those whose interests are at stake: organising, gathering support for their cause, and defending their rights. Outside agents, such
as NGOs, may stimulate action and encourage positive change, but cannot
themselves sustain it.

However, organising instead of depending on patronage — whether of
government officials, landowners, employers, money-lenders, elders, or male
relatives — also involves dangers. The risks are greatest for those who are
most vulnerable. For marginalised people to organise protests or resistance
requires great courage and self-confidence. Any such threat to existing power

structures may meet with covert or even violent repression. Where the known risks outweigh the potential benefits, it is not surprising that many people prefer just to survive as best they can.

Strengthening people's ability to create or maintain organisations that can represent and be accountable to them, is the essence of a capacity-building approach. Forms of organisation are immensely varied; some are informal and operate at a micro-level, others are concerned with shaping public policy, or have international dimensions. People need support to build their capacity to relate to each other in ways that enable them to tackle the causes of their vulnerability; to enhance the *quality* of their participation in the processes of social change.

People may set up organisations which relate to where they live, work, or worship — or to what they believe, feel, care about, or need. In relatively homogeneous settings in which resources are bounded (such as paddy rice systems), cooperation may relate to production; in more diverse settings, such as pastoralist or fishing communities, people's relationships with each other may focus instead on forms of mutual insurance. An organisation may offer cultural or occupational identity and peer support. Or it may be a channel for action on issues as varied as wages, domestic violence, the rights of asylum-seekers, land reform, public transport, or cruelty to animals. Some have a representational mandate, such as labour unions which negotiate through collective bargaining. Others, such as consciousness-raising groups, may be more fluid in terms of their membership, and have a loose hierarchical or organisational structure. Some forms of association may be traditional, based around religion, ethnicity, kinship, marital status, or age: in this sense, membership is not voluntary, but part of social identity. Others, such as professional bodies, provide services to those meeting their membership criteria.

Organisations can also be socially exclusive, or serve to reinforce power and privilege. Access and influence may be controlled by visible markers — such as sex, age, or skin colour. Often, however, exclusion is indirect and based on factors such as social class, upbringing, or religious faith. These forms of exclusion may be deeply ingrained, so that to challenge them, for example, through affirmative action policies or quotas, is seen as perverse or interfering with 'nature'. Since they are embedded in and reflect their societies, institutions, including NGOs, may well reproduce in their norms and practices the very prejudices they seek to challenge (see Longwe, 1997; Goetz, 1995; Goetz, 1996). Civil society organisations are not inherently benign: movements based on racial, religious, ethnic, sexual, or political intolerance and bigotry exist to a greater or lesser degree in most societies.

Since people organise for different reasons and in different ways, it may not be feasible to transfer forms of organisation from one situation to another.

It is essential for an NGO to understand the role(s) and objectives of an organisation before deciding whether, how, and for what purpose to strengthen it. To have a lasting impact, an organisation needs to be able to adapt; organisational development is concerned with promoting and responding to change, not with institutional stagnation.

Good practical, analytical, and managerial skills are essential if organisations are to function effectively and democratically. A capacity-building approach focuses on what is right for the organisation and its constituency; the methods and approaches preferred by donors may not always help its counterpart to become autonomous. As we have stressed elsewhere, in any relationship that is mediated by power and money, achieving such autonomy is easier said than done: a donor may impose its views unwittingly; an organisation that needs funds will naturally try to optimise its chances of support, and so seek to accommodate the wishes of its benefactor. But if NGOs adopt the planning and management tools favoured by their own donors (many of which were developed in the corporate sector), this in turn places demands on their 'partners' or 'users' to conform with the bureaucratic requirements and priorities that arise — however superfluous, top-down, or distorting these might be.

[o]nce such procedures become the norm, then not only are the much vaunted flexibility and cultural appropriateness of the NGOs denied expression but they are vulnerable to strong pressure that NGOs should now recognise the desirability of competing for development contracts with other organisations, including private sector consultancy companies (Powell and Seddon, 1997:8).

The onus is on those who provide or channel funds to Southern counterparts to foster a range of approaches to organisational development that matches the range of organisations they support. Above all, they must avoid equating their counterparts' compliance with their *own* management systems and cultures with capacity-building.

This Chapter is divided into three main parts. The first describes four major types of civil society organisation with which NGOs and donors work: traditional or informal associations; membership-based bodies; those that are sponsored by third parties (such as governments or NGOs); and NGOs. The emphasis is on common approaches to strengthening organisations, whatever their particular purposes and potential. This is followed by an account of factors that affect all organisations, such as governance, representational legitimacy, and growth. This second part also describes problems which often occur in relationships between donors, NGOs, and local organisations and sets out ways in which to measure organisational health.

The third part covers aspects that are associated with effective management, such as planning, monitoring, evaluation, and financial procedures.

These are presented under separate headings, though they are intimately linked. The way in which an organisation handles its resources is affected by its values and structures. Since organisations evolve in response to their environment, it is wrong to think in linear terms: appraisal, planning, monitoring and evaluation should be continuous processes, with considerable movement between them. Rather than advocating specific methods, we refer readers to more specialised publications[1] that address how to choose appropriate methods for particular contexts.

Organisational forms: similarities, differences, and pitfalls

Whatever their precise form or purpose, organisations which represent poor people can be a means to:

- offer mutual support and solidarity
- enhance self-esteem and collective confidence
- improve people's ability to combat injustice, through collective action
- be a forum for learning
- promote discussion and analysis of common concerns
- increase citizens' participation in the political process
- lobby on issues of direct interest
- demand access to government and other powerful officials
- negotiate with élites, official bodies, NGOs, and donors.

How they do these things depends on their origins, and the role(s) they play within the wider social context. The legitimacy of an organisation lies in its purpose, performance, and representational capacity. It may be counterproductive to demand of a local parent-teachers' association the same structures and controls (such as ballots, elections, bank accounts, and formal procedures) that would suit a large membership organisation, such as a federation of trades unions. The relationships between an organisation's identity, values, and purpose, and its performance, systems, and structure are usefully depicted in the diagrams overleaf.

An Organisational Framework – Model I

(From Fowler et al, 1995:4)

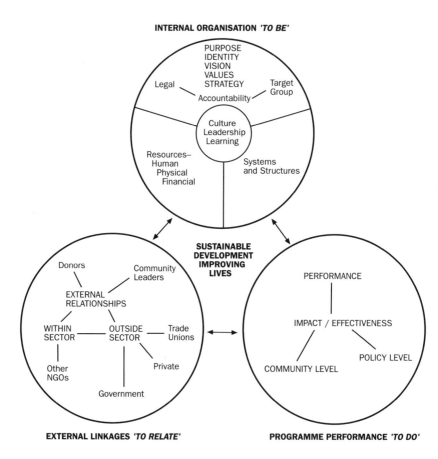

Model 1 divides the organisation into three key areas — Being, Doing, and Relating — and emphasises 'the importance of seeing an organisation in terms of what it does and who it relates to, not just in terms of its internal life' (ibid.).

Model 2 prioritises the various attributes of a healthy organisation. Each needs to fit with the other for the whole to be fully functional; in other words, 'form follows function' (ibid.).

An Organisational Framework – Model II

(From Fowler et al, 1995:5)

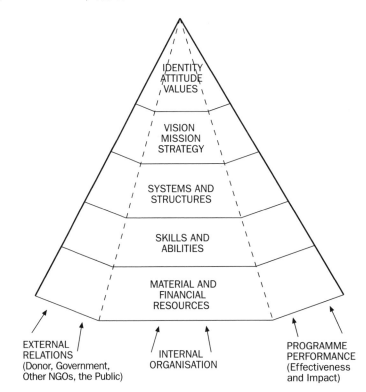

What each of these models shows, however, is that how an organisation splits up these factors 'is less important than having a good reason for [making] the choice' and then being fully consistent with it.

There are major differences between the representational roles, political identities, and relationship with their constituency, of membership organisations and NGOs. Yet donors often blur these distinctions, expecting them to behave similarly, and conform to the same bureaucratic requirements. Referring to all grant recipients as 'partners' and to all funded activities as 'projects' further distorts the various relationships between those who raise and give money, those who receive it, and those who are intended to benefit from it.

The following paragraphs describe some of the distinctive features of civil society organisations that NGOs or donors often support. It is not suggested that all these characteristics are always present, or that others are not. What is important is to recognise the nature of an organisation before seeking to strengthen it; and to analyse *how* it is accountable to its members or its constituencies, before accepting its claims to 'represent' them.

Traditional organisations

Existing or traditional organisations may strengthen and be strengthened by the development process; or frustrate and perhaps be damaged by it. Such organisations may have the authority and capacity to mobilise along village, clan, religious, ethnic, age or gender lines. They may be a powerful force for social cohesion and a focus for collective identity. However, while conferring privileges on some, they may also severely constrain the rights of others. A traditional organisation may co-exist with others, or be in conflict with them. Traditional or religious leaders may also play a role in formal political bodies and official institutions. This may confer legitimacy on the organisation, or be a means through which outsiders can manipulate or co-opt it.

The legitimacy of these organisations may be recognised throughout the community, though appearances can be deceptive. For instance, Chamula communities in southern Mexico violently 'expelled' those who joined Protestant Christian sects, even going to the lengths of destroying their few possessions. Government and church authorities alike explained this by invoking 'traditionalism'. However, Oxfam-funded anthropological research showed that such expulsions were generally motivated by the traditional leaders' refusal to tolerate any challenge to their own authority. Tradition was invoked by them as a means to retain tight control over major economic resources — and also provided a convenient pretext for the civil and religious authorities not to intervene on behalf of the 'expelled'.

Even where traditional organisations are concerned mainly with cultural issues, such as religion, kinship, and marriage, these significantly affect the social, political and economic status of individuals, households, and social groups. Certain beliefs and practices may be irreconcilable with the agendas of development NGOs, particularly with regard to the civil and political rights of women and girls, or of ethnic and religious minorities. 'Tradition' (often in combination with revolutionary or fundamentalist ideologies) may be invoked as a form of resistance to external forces which are seen as morally decadent or culturally threatening. This was argued by religious leaders of the Iranian Revolution in the 1970s, and more recently by the FAS in Algeria or by the Taliban in Afghanistan. When the Taliban took control of Kabul in September 1996, they announced that women would no longer be permitted to work outside their homes, nor girls to attend school. At that time, Oxfam was employing local female staff in its relief and development programme in Afghanistan, and had to suspend some of its operations which depended on women workers. In Kabul and other towns, huge numbers of women worked in schools and universities, in the health services, factories, and family businesses. Many of them were the sole bread-winners for their families. One women, prevented from earning a living, said 'The international community need to do something... They need to put pressure, any pressure they can, to demonstrate for the women in Afghanistan. Other women need to know what is happening to us, we need their support' (Johnson, 1997).

Like any other social structure, however, traditional organisations evolve by adapting to external changes or in response to challenges from within. For instance, in the 23 countries in which it is represented, the Inter-African Committee on Traditional Practices Affecting the Health of Women and Children takes an active and critical stand on many practices (such as Female Genital Mutilation and scarification) that are justified by some in the name of tradition. This shows the importance of gathering a range of views on cultural practices, not only those of traditional 'leaders'.

Membership organisations

Examples of membership organisations include labour unions, sports clubs, political parties, research networks, professional guilds, and consumer cooperatives. They are generally based either on functions or identities, or on issues and interests. Most membership organisations exist to provide some benefit to their members, though some — such as Amnesty International — exist in order to support others. The common characteristic is that their membership is voluntary. An organisation's ideological agenda does not always determine how it functions or the quality of its work. It may profess commitment to equality and participation, but itself be run on rigid, doctrinaire, or patriarchal lines. A mismatch between an organisation's purpose, and its ways of working, makes for instability.

People become members of organisations or networks either to gain some benefit, or to show solidarity. Membership organisations may also have a formal or *de facto* representative function. For instance, a union may represent members who have a grievance, as well as acting as a negotiating body for members' collective rights; a political party should aim to represent the views of its members. A membership organisation needs adequate mechanisms for two-way communication between leadership and members. Some — co-operatives or mortgage societies, for instance — may need a legal constitution, elected officers, formal assemblies, and audited accounts. Others may not be legally constituted or recognised. However, features of internal democracy generally include regular consultative mechanisms, such as assemblies or newsletters; open elections for officers and representatives; and some method of approving the accounts.

Revenue may be raised from membership dues, fund-raising activities, donations, and grants. Many organisations also seek external support for activities such as training programmes, welfare services, legal advice, cultural centres, and publications. If support is given to such activities, their status needs to be clear: if managed within the elected structures, their direction may be vulnerable to political interests; if semi-autonomous (run, for instance, by paid staff), they may be more isolated from the formal structures, but relatively immune from political 'in-fighting'.

NGOs and membership organisations often complement each other. An NGO may do preparatory work with people who are not yet organised, or it may offer training for membership organisations. In both cases, the NGO seeks funds for work it does on behalf of others. The important distinction between such 'brokerage' and representation is often blurred by NGOs and donors alike. Membership organisations may in fact see NGOs as rivals for funds and contacts, or a demobilising influence. For example, Honduran peasant farmers' unions who were lobbying for land reform felt undermined by a well-connected and prosperous local NGO which purchased land for families enrolled in its social welfare and food-aid schemes.

Trades unions, a particular form of membership organisation, may be legally prevented from receiving foreign funding. While the right of workers to organise is internationally recognised, union leaders, members, and labour lawyers, may well face harassment at local or national level. Millions of workers, in particular young female employees of transnational companies, are forbidden to unionise; and women and part-time workers are vastly under-unionised worldwide. Companies in the so-called 'free trade zones' are usually exempt from certain national labour laws, as are small companies. Workers may be dissuaded from unionising either through fear of reprisals, or through the offer of financial inducements by their employers. Others are unable to join a union because of the nature of their employment contract. For example, home-based workers who are sub-contracted by large manufacturers, are largely unprotected by legislation or by membership of a union. There are no reliable estimates for the millions who work in the informal sector, or who are employed illegally.

A union's legitimacy depends on its representative function. However, unions are commonly criticised for being over-bureaucratic, over-centralised, and poorly managed. It is also clear that, like other institutions, in defending the interests of certain people, they may jeopardise those of others. For instance, low levels of unionisation among women are commonly attributed by them to the fact that unions do not take their concerns seriously, and that union leadership is male and its ethos patriarchal (though such charges are not exclusive to unions). The extent to which a union actively encourages internal debate on such issues is one measure of its health.

If union activity is subject to harassment or repression, a union may not be able to hold open elections or mass meetings, or publish its views through normal democratic means. In addition, if a union cannot deduct subscription dues at source, it may be hard for it to cover its core activities. If its officers are not allowed to undertake union activities in working hours, it is less likely that women will participate — either because of their family responsibilities, or because their husbands will not allow them to (Kassey Garba, 1997).

Educational programmes can help to build up capable and confident middle and lower cadre representatives, and so strengthen the internal democracy that is so vital to the health of any membership organisation. Training in financial management, and in leadership and organisational skills, such as knowing how to run meetings and workshops, or communicate and negotiate effectively, is vital. Trades unions may also be well placed to undertake research, for example in the field of occupational health and safety. The findings may be relevant not only to its members, but for other workers, NGOs and policy-makers.

Organisations sponsored by external agencies

Many local organisations were set up by an external agency, often the state, a religious body, or an NGO. State-sponsored co-operative and 'community-development' initiatives, for example, have in some countries created a structure of co-operatives or local councils (such as *panchayats* in India or *patronatos* in Latin America).

Initially, these structures were often under firm state control, and their ways of working and structures were considered alien, complex, and unresponsive. They were seldom run by or able to represent poor or disadvantaged people. However, in combination with strong, independent organisations which can lobby for change, they can become a vehicle for significant advances for disadvantaged groups. Systems of quotas for Dalit women in Southern India, as for women in several European countries, have brought women into public life in ways that have both enhanced the representational capacity of public and formal structures, and benefited women in general. Similar 'power-sharing' processes have taken place in relation to black representation in post-apartheid South Africa, as in other multi-ethnic communities.

NGOs often encourage their intended beneficiaries to organise together, sometimes to press for their own rights, sometimes for purposes defined by the NGO. Sometimes these organisations may assume a life of their own. However, unless they are linked to wider independent movements, they can easily become preoccupied with local activities and remain isolated and limited. The range of NGO-sponsored organisations is as wide as that of NGOs themselves. However, four main types are:

Ad hoc groups with short-term membership to carry out a specific activity. Examples include literacy projects, savings and loan funds, immunisation programmes, and social forestry schemes. Given their limited or short-term focus, such groups are often not legally constituted, and may not outlive their immediate purpose.

Open-ended groups pursuing various social and economic issues may originate in some form of local action, but develop in response to new needs and challenges. For example, a squatters' union may become involved in urban health and low-cost housing. These organisations may hold regular meetings, and have a fixed membership, and an established programme, or they may be semi-dormant, mobilising only when necessary.

Producer and consumer co-operatives are formally constituted and their internal functioning may be subject to legal obligations. Formal registration may bring a range of benefits, such as access to training, credit or marketing facilities. Co-operatives are often organised into regional or national federations.

Issue-based groups are active on concerns such as women's rights or campaigns to regulate the sale of pharmaceuticals. Organisational structures may take the form of loose coalitions, or more formal affiliation to national or international networks (see Chapter 7).

Development (non-profit) NGOs

These may be service-providing agencies, solidarity organisations, technical assistance programmes, or confessional bodies: the size and diversity of the NGO sector makes it difficult to produce universal typologies.[2] The following profile will help to situate a given NGO within its context, and indicate its potential to catalyse or reinforce the capacities of poor people:

- ideological inspiration, eg, religious or non-confessional, political affiliation, humanitarian, feminist
- institutional origin, eg religious body, union, political party, social movement, educational establishment, professional body, international agency or movement, 'parent' NGO
- field(s) of action, eg human rights, health, micro-enterprise
- social focus, eg disabled children, landless farmers, refugees
- scope, eg local, national, regional, international
- activities, eg adult literacy, farming, networking

NGOs can also be characterised by their organisational form and ways of working:

- formal identity, eg charity, federation, association, co-operative, collective
- source of funding, eg government or official donors, international or national NGOs, own income and/or income in kind, membership fees, fundraising efforts, local donations;
- scale of budgets, eg small annual grants, multi-million long-term commitments
- staffing arrangements, eg volunteer support, professional staff; fixed-term or tenured posts; social benefits (such as maternity leave, pension fund, social security, in-kind benefits)
- staffing profile, eg proportion of women and men, and average age and ethnic composition of staff at all levels; recruitment policies
- decision-making structure, eg elected trustees, supporter assemblies, executive line management
- institutional culture, eg associational, consultative, or hierarchical management.

An NGO's way of working is affected largely by its relationships with the various stakeholders indicated in these organisational profiles. According to John Saxby (in Sogge et al, 1996, pp 42–43) the main types of NGO that are involved in the aid chain are:

- Non-profit non-governmental enterprises largely financed by and account-able to an official aid body.
- Agencies whose funding is largely from the state and from religious or political constituencies, but not from the general public.
- Agencies funded by public and private donations, but with a disparate formal constituency.
- Agencies that receive public and private donations, and also have a well-defined constituency.
- Membership-based organisations, such as co-operatives, that also use their own resources to reach out to non-members.
- Agencies that exist solely to raise funds to be disbursed via other organisations.
- Privately endowed foundations, in which the endowment managers are accountable to the trustees.

While no one model or type of agency is *intrinsically* likely to be a better vehicle for capacity-building activities than another, Saxby argues that the 'combination of sectoral expertise and secure membership/funding base' of the solidarity-based activities of membership organisations may 'make the "traditional" agency passé' (ibid. p45).

Many claims are made about (and by) NGOs, for example, that they are more efficient and cost-effective, that they are flexible and can adapt to change, that they are unbureaucratic and favour participatory, democratic approaches, and that they are accountable to and legitimate advocates of 'the poor' by virtue of their proximity to them. Such claims are more easily invoked than proven, and obviously gloss over the major differences among NGOs, as well as some of the less welcome features of their ways of working (Powell and Seddon, 1997).

Social organisation and NGOs

If their resources are to catalyse poor people's autonomy — their capacity to organise around their own life options without undue physical, political or socio-economic constraints upon them (Barrig and Wehkamp, 1995) — NGOs must listen to what the women and men concerned have to say, rather than rushing in to identify and solve their problems for them. They should make themselves familiar with a situation before intervening in it, and remember that there is no 'right' answer, and that people's needs and perspectives differ, and also evolve. Above all, they should be patient; capacity-building for development is not a race against the clock, and sustainable change requires time and effort.

As formal institutions, NGOs may have qualified staff, and be legally accountable to a Board or to their funders. Many NGOs offer their services disinterestedly. Others are motivated by religious or ideological persuasions. Most NGOs depend on raising funds via the public, the state, official donors — or combinations of these.

While mechanisms for accountability to their donors may be inadequate, NGOs' accountability to their beneficiaries is generally far worse (Edwards and Hulme, 1995a, 1995b). This asymmetry can result in donors providing local NGOs with resources (vehicles, equipment, staff) to build their capacity, while being unaware of how these NGOs are viewed by the people on whose behalf they work. Donors may judge NGOs in terms of their efficiency and cost-effectiveness in complying with reporting requirements and managing budgets. Yet these bureaucratic demands also exert a pressure that may ultimately compromise an NGO's priorities and existing relationships with local groups.

The following paragraphs outline some common 'mis-matches' between NGOs and various forms of social organisation. They indicate the need for *critical self-appraisal* on the part of the intervening NGO and the organisation it aims to assist.

Autonomy or dependence?

Representative organisations have a natural interest in being independent of external support. However, assistance may be crucial in helping them to get started, to expand into new areas, or develop new skills and ideas. Funding NGOs usually make a time-bound commitment, and aim to reduce their inputs over time. However, many organisations never evolve beyond this dependence on external funding. This may be because initial support was given without clear agreements being reached about when it would cease; or because progress is slower than expected, so that plans to phase out funding are suspended, in order to prevent the organisation collapsing. In addition, if a funding NGO has to justify its existence to its own donors, it may be reluctant to 'release' the groups with which it works since their dependence shows that its services are needed. There is an important distinction between supporting people's own efforts, and trying to solve their problems for them. If NGOs make themselves indispensable, by intervening on behalf of funded groups, joining in their activities, or even becoming part of the internal management structure, this can weaken people's capacity to act for themselves.

Many NGOs and donors distinguish between supporting an organisation's activities, and funding its core functions (such as an office, salaries, and communications). This may allow the funding agency to feel that it can withdraw from the relationship relatively easily. However, as we shall see below, this artificial distinction may perpetuate the counterpart's dependency.

Linking or blocking?

Very few villagers or slum-dwellers can choose which NGO will work with them! They may be interested in what it offers, but indifferent to its beliefs and motives; being funded by an NGO does not imply any wider identification with what it represents.

An individual may belong to several organisations, and expect different things of each. Sometimes, loyalties may conflict. For example, the union may promote action (such as a land takeover) of which the church disapproves. Or, as happened in Honduras, the church may strongly encourage educational and activities among peasant women which the union considers 'divisive' (described in Rowlands, 1997). An NGO may be involved on both sides of such conflicts, and torn between competing loyalties. As an interested party, however, an NGO should beware of trying to mediate; and ensure that its practice conforms to its stated principles and values.

NGOs may aim to promote social organisation, but in fact keep close control of 'their' beneficiaries, sometimes even blocking their contact with those of 'rival' agencies. The reasons given may be that the other NGO has inappropriate working methods, is aligned with a different political faction, or that the beneficiaries themselves lack the maturity to handle relations with it.[3] But if NGOs cannot relinquish control over those whose interests they claim to serve, it is unlikely that their impact on them is empowering.

Processes or projects?

Social organisation and capacity-building are long-term processes. Problems can occur if NGOs try to speed up the process by focusing on projects rather than long-term strategies. In their anxiety to see quick results, NGOs may rely on limited contacts or unrepresentative leaders; fail to invest in preparing new or middle-level leaders; neglect people's practical and organisational skills; overlook the need for a reliable resource base; or disregard the need for the organisation to establish political independence through relationships with government bodies (see Parasuraman and Vimalanathan, 1997).

Prime responsibility for assessment, decision-making, planning and evaluating activities should rest with local people, even if this takes more time. If an NGO dominates these processes, it not only disempowers, but may also generate a dynamic in which people become involved chiefly to obtain the benefits it appears to offer. However, the enthusiasm even of the most committed may flag if anticipated benefits do not materialise. Problems may be precipitated by the failure of a specific project, or by internal differences. Any setback may generate a crisis: a split, an exodus, and a loss of legitimacy and confidence. Some groups dissolve, while others re-emerge or re-structure with a clearer sense of purpose — perhaps months or years later. Such evolution is a natural part of organisational life. It is at such difficult junctures that 'critical accompaniment' (with or without funding) is most needed. The temptation, however, is for Northern NGOs and donors to regard such crises as a sign of failure and to abandon their 'partners' to their fate.

Real achievements can generate collective self-confidence, though without clear overall objectives it is easy to get lost in a mass of micro-actions. Different inputs are needed at various stages in an organisation's evolution, just as members' needs will also differ. For example, younger members may need to practise public speaking; or it may be an urgent priority for all members to learn about human rights legislation. Often lacking the skills and organisational experience on which full participation depends, women's forums may foster the collective strength which will ensure that their concerns become organisational priorities.

Effective leadership is essential. Good leaders can inspire confidence, articulate concerns, and forge links with relevant bodies such as banks, government departments, NGOs or funders. However, those with the skills may not be ideal representatives, and it is unwise for any group to rely on one or two individuals. An organisation can only represent people if they have confidence in it, and access to its decision-makers. The organisation's leaders must be chosen in ways that are considered fair. New or potential leaders need time to gain confidence and practical experience in order to become effective. Training a wide range of women and men in leadership skills may be the best strategic contribution to strengthening the capacity of an organisation. Similarly, disputes over money are best pre-empted by ensuring financial probity; and extensive training in money matters is a critical input in organisational capacity-building.

The integrity of an organisation depends to some extent on whether its members can hold leaders accountable, and remove them if necessary. Open systems for sharing information, consulting members, and electing officers are critical; and a strong regulatory framework can help to prevent corruption. This is as true of a food distribution committee in a refugee camp as it is of an organisation as complex as the World Bank. However, it is not enough for an organisation to be answerable only to those who are inside the system, be they committee members or governments; it should also be accountable to the wider constituency of 'stakeholders'.

Expansion or enhancement?

In the 1980s, the term 'scaling-up' described the efforts of NGOs to increase their impact, and ensure sustainability. The term implied that NGOs might best enhance their impact through establishing effective 'synergistic' links, whether through complementary activities or through confrontation (Clarke, 1991). Much of the advocacy work undertaken by NGOs is justified precisely in terms of trying to shape the policy environment within with local-level initiatives might flourish.

However, the term became fashionable just when official donors were turning to NGOs as channels for their own development aid. Today, as much as 25 per cent of official development assistance from some countries is channelled through NGOs; and about one-third of NGO resources actually stem from government sources (Powell and Seddon, 1997:5). For NGOs, the opportunity to expand by handling rapidly increasing budgets also encouraged them to 'scale-up' by filling the gaps in social provision resulting from cuts in government spending.

The term has since been discarded by several NGOs, because 'scaling-up' had come to be seen as another term for rapidly increasing staffing and budgets, the size or number of projects funded, or the areas covered. Instead, many NGOs today use phrases such as 'added value', or speak of 'widening', 'deepening' or 'enhancing impact' in order to convey the sense that expansion is only one way of doing this. Indeed, with stagnating or declining revenues, some NGOs have concluded that the way to maximise their impact is to 'scale down' their activities and become more focused.

Planned organisational growth can enhance efficiency and effectiveness. However, expansion always exacts a price, and organisations can be overwhelmed if they grow too fast, or if their members' expectations exceed their capacity to respond. Even carefully planned growth can profoundly alter an organisation's ethos and direction. As organisations become larger, there is a need to formalise policies and procedures. Informality is replaced by minuted meetings, circulars, and committees. Spontaneity is constrained by hierarchies, job descriptions, schedules, and workplans. Leaders or directors require detailed and up-to-date financial information and reports, upon which renewed funding depends. Old forms of consultation are replaced by line management, specialised departments, and compartmentalised information. This in turn leads to the need for recruitment policies, salary structures, and disciplinary procedures, along with induction, training, and negotiation.[4] If values and 'commitment' take second place to formal qualifications and skills, it may seem as if the organisation has lost more than it has gained. However, the 'professionalisation' that growth demands may also protect individuals and groups from discrimination, and ensure that people are fairly appointed and promoted.

Instead of assuming that expansion will necessarily strengthen an organisation's capacities, it is important to ask:

- What exactly is the problem which growth will address?
- Is growth the only way of addressing it?
- How will the negative consequences of growth be avoided?
- What would happen if no growth took place?

Solidarity or salaries?

Membership organisations may pay their non-elected personnel a formal wage, and offer a stipend plus expenses for their elected officers. When donors decide to fund such organisations, conflicts of interest may arise. If elected officers are paid from donated funds, their accountability is distorted, especially if they are also responsible for negotiating grant renewals.

Some aid agencies believe that community-based workers should be voluntary or paid only in-kind, believing that to earn an income from this work may compromise their relationship with the community. Others argue that without remuneration, only those with material and social support can afford to volunteer — and that volunteers cannot easily be held accountable for their performance. Ethical as well as practical questions arise in expecting poor people to work for nothing, especially when aid agency workers are themselves paid. On the other hand, serious problems can arise if community-based workers become dependent on an income which itself depends on decisions of foreign funding agencies, which provide no security or insurance against job loss (Parasuraman and Vimalanathan, 1997:ii).

There are no easy answers to these problems. Agencies need to be aware of potential difficulties, and ensure that funding decisions do not undermine existing forms of solidarity by raising expectations that cannot be met, or by distorting existing forms of internal accountability.

Capital assets: consolidation or distraction?

Computers

All organisations have communication needs. Computers are invaluable where large quantities of data need to be stored, retrieved, and analysed. They are also essential for organisations involved in networking.

Rapid growth in information technology (IT) means that many Southern organisations have already by-passed some of the older and costlier forms of telecommunication. For instance, the Latin American Social Science Council (CLACSO) in Buenos Aires is ahead of its European counterparts in its use of electronic scholarly networks. (But see also Chapter 7 for a more critical account).

However, IT equipment is often purchased or donated by Northern agencies without proper consideration of how, where, why, and by whom it will be used; whether it is compatible with existing systems; and whether local support is available. Conversely, opportunities for using IT are not taken up by local organisations because they lack advice on how it could help their work; or because the donor does not appreciate its relevance, or views it as inappropriately 'high-tech' for its Southern counterpart.

The cost of installing and running IT should not as a rule exceed 10 per cent of an organisation's total start-up costs (unless it needs desk-top publishing software and high quality printers). Running costs over three years are about the same as the purchase price. Software can comprise one-third of the IT investment. If a donor is funding the purchase and installation of computer equipment, it should also include provision for the essential software packages as well as maintenance costs, and initial and follow-up training.

Vehicles

For many organisations, the cost of purchasing and running vehicles is the single biggest item in their budget after salaries. A vehicle can contribute to an organisation's capacity by making it more efficient or by expanding the geographical area in which it works.

Before investing in some form of transport, an organisation must consider what has to be carried, where, by whom, and how often? What are the alternatives: public transport, taxis, vehicle hire, motor cycles, bicycles, animals? A reciprocal arrangement or vehicle share? Three examples, all from Oxfam's experience in Honduras, illustrate some creative, low-cost responses to these questions:

• A parish committee wanted to buy a pick-up truck to reduce the hours which community workers spent walking from one hamlet to another. On reflection, however, they decided that instead of a vehicle, which only one person could use at a time and which would bind them into long-term dependence on aid, they would seek money for the purchase and veterinary costs for six mules — cheaper to buy and to sustain, and less ostentatious than a vehicle.

• The co-ordinating committee of a women's organisation spent several days each month travelling in uncomfortable buses across the country. They could have worked far more efficiently had they owned a vehicle. But this idea had never occurred to them, because none could drive or had considered learning. A practical (and transferable) contribution to capacity-building was the offer to pay for driving lessons.

• An alternative to repeated requests for vehicles from local organisations was to purchase a 'pool car'. This was administered by a reliable local NGO, which undertook to ensure that it was properly maintained and fairly allocated, and used only for agreed purposes. Users paid a small contribution to the cost of maintenance and depreciation. Thus one vehicle served a wide range of organisations for many years. This arrangement not only met a practical need, but also served to establish trust where none had previously existed: a spin-off was the collective responsibility and solidarity thus generated.

A vehicle takes time, money, and effort to maintain, and an organisation's ability to provide these should be carefully assessed. While simple maintenance may be easily absorbed in a core budget, major servicing and repairs require spare parts, workshop equipment and a trained motor mechanic. A financial commitment must be made for several years to cover running and maintenance costs and depreciation. Even if a vehicle costs only 10 cents per kilometre to run, this amounts to US$2,000 a year for an average of 20,000 kilometres. A well-maintained vehicle may give good service for about seven years, after which it is generally cheaper to sell it.

Unlike other capital investments, owning a vehicle brings legal obligations — it must be taxed, licensed, and insured; and every driver must hold a valid licence. Legal arrangements are needed against the possibility that the organisation might dispose of its assets: sometimes an NGO has folded, and its vehicle and other assets have simply been inherited by individual workers.

Access to its vehicle can be a remarkably divisive issue within an organisation. It is a mark of status and privilege, and so may exacerbate rather than reduce any existing tensions concerning the abuse of power. The private use of an office vehicle is often seen as a 'perk' for favoured staff members. Once such informal benefits become institutionalised, it is difficult to remove them. For this reason, many organisations prohibit or regulate private use.

It is also common for men to monopolise office vehicles, either because of their place in the hierarchy, or because women have not learned to drive, or because of prejudices about female drivers. Donor agencies may redress this by facilitating lessons for women in driving and vehicle maintenance.

Organisational knowledge: assessment and self-appraisal

A constructive relationship between a Northern agency and its Southern counterpart depends, among other things, on both having a clear vision of what each has to offer and can expect. In the past, assessment and evaluation were seen as 'snapshots' that Northern agencies took of their partners before, during, and after disbursing funds to them. Today, they are increasingly seen as two-way processes:

> ... *organisational assessment should not be seen as a one-off exercise but as an ongoing process in the life of a healthy NGO with structured periods of review and reflection. It is then more likely that the organisation will learn more effectively and be able to monitor and manage change and development over time* (Fowler et al, 1995:3).

Five approaches to such assessment are briefly described below.

Stakeholder analysis

This became fashionable in the early 1990s, particularly among Northern NGOs that adopted the strategic planning (SP) model. It involves an examination of the motives of the various stakeholders in an organisation, the external pressures upon them, and the ways in which accountability to them is exercised. A stakeholder analysis can indicate whether the interests of the stakeholders are compatible, and if there is a need to negotiate on competing expectations and priorities.

In an NGO context, the stakeholders are likely to include all or some of the following (Moore et al, 1995):

- *owner*: shareholders, members, Trustees
- *financier*: investors, official and individual donors
- *user*: customers, owner-users, counterparts, direct or indirect beneficiaries
- *regulator*: responsible for ensuring that an organisation meets its legal obligations
- *political superior*: within a hierarchy, or in terms of providing the overall regulatory framework for the organisation's actions (usually the government)
- *'Mafia'*: people who can push for an organisation to act in different, sometimes illegal, ways
- *staff*: paid and volunteer.

Some NGOs have formal mechanisms for meeting certain stakeholder interests — such as staff assemblies, trustee committees, unions or other negotiating structures, or regular dialogue with the formal regulatory bodies. Relatively few international NGOs, however, have structures which allow their Southern counterparts or beneficiaries to exert pressure on *them*. Some observers regard this asymmetry as a fatal ethical flaw, and one that gravely compromises the legitimacy of NGOs (see, for instance, Sogge et al, 1996).

Social audit

This is a tool for assessing the performance of an organisation, rather like a financial audit of its accounts. In a social audit, an organisation reports on its social impact and ethical behaviour in relation to its own aims and from the perspectives of its stakeholders. The audit is public, regular, and externally validated. The New Economics Foundation (NEF), which promotes this process in the voluntary as well as the private sector, finds that the closer the link between an organisation's values and its actual behaviour, the better its performance.[5]

Social relations analysis

This has developed furthest in the field of gender studies, where feminist research has shown some of the mechanisms whereby an organisation reproduces prevailing social values even when it claims to do otherwise. Tracing the differential impacts of an organisation's work on women and on men can reveal the structures, practices, and agents that embody and promote gender interests. These are often 'embedded in the structures and hierarchies of institutions, in the conditions and requirements for access and participation, in their incentive and accountability structures' (Goetz, 1996:3). A similar approach could be taken with respect to race, ethnicity, socio-economic class, or age. The following table summarises the types of questions to ask.

A gender profile of institutions

(Drawn up by Chris Roche, to summarise Goetz, 1996:5–7.)

Institutional and organisational history	Who was involved in establishing the organisation? Who was not? How was this done?
Ideology	What are the academic disciplines and ideologies that animate the organisation? What are the underlying assumptions these tend to make about gender roles?
Participants	Who makes up the organisation? What is the gender division of labour? What is the gender and hierarchy profile in the organisation?
Space and time	Are working hours conducive to women employees? Are meetings or social activities held at times which might hinder women's participation? Is provision made for career breaks, childcare, etc? Does the organisation demand travel away from home as part of the job?
Authority structures	Can women command authority for their approaches and views within the organisation? Do women have to take on 'male attributes' to be heard? What achievements are valued in the organisation?
Incentives, accountability, and organisational resourcing	On what do performance targets tend to focus: more on quantitative than qualitative targets? To whom is accountability mainly oriented: upwards, downwards, or horizontally?

Appreciative Inquiry (AI)

This represents an alternative to the conventional problem-solving approach, regarding a healthy organisation not so much a well-oiled machine as a living thing that will respond positively to affirmation. Through Listening Workshops, AI seeks to affirm those moments ('peak experiences') during which stakeholders felt satisfaction or a sense of worth and belonging through their participation in the organisation's activities, and to envision a future based on these values. Instead of identifying and analysing problems, causes, and possible solutions, AI aims 'to appreciate and value the best of what there is, envision what might be, dialogue what should be, and innovate what will be'. Beyond the staple ingredients of 'transparent management systems, clear communication, participatory work approaches', other elements will vary considerably from one organisation and culture to another (Postma, 1997).

Historic analysis

Since organisations are constantly evolving, it is important to establish their history, and what experiences and values will shape their future. This includes looking at the prevailing intellectual and political climate during major phases in an organisation's development; the formal and informal structures and divisions within it; the background behind the organisation's identity, values, rules, and norms and its management of accountability; and how it codifies and learns from its experience.

Further ways to build up an organisational picture may include an examination of its own literature (both public and 'grey' literature, such as unpublished reports, policy documents, grants lists), financial accounts, and discussions with staff, former staff, and representatives of those supported by its work (Roche, 1998).

The five approaches outlined above can be used in combination with each other, and with other methods. Self-appraisal processes are often facilitated by an outside expert who can hold 'a critical mirror' to it by helping its members to ask 'the right question at the right time, the one question which will elicit further self-reflection and growing awareness..' (Kaplan, 1996:114). The question of organisational learning will be considered in Chapter 9.

Organisational skills: planning, monitoring, evaluation, and financial management

However modest an organisation's scope and objectives, its work must be planned and properly resourced, and lessons drawn from its successes and setbacks. If these skills are firmly rooted within the organisation, they will make a sustained contribution to its wider capacities. If organisations adopt rigid approaches to planning, monitoring, and evaluation, or see these simply as technical procedures, it is likely that they will become a burden rather than a tool for self-reliance. Northern funding agencies often export their own preferred methods, sometimes as an actual or perceived condition of funding (Powell and Seddon, 1997; Riddell, 1997; Ardón, 1997). It is doubtful that techniques that are imposed on the recipients of aid, especially if these are culturally or politically alien, contribute to building organisational capacity.

Interest in capacity-building has produced a gradual move from the focus on *project* management, towards more general management training. The following sections sketch out some areas in which organisational capacities are needed, and in which outsiders may assist. These include planning, monitoring, evaluation, financial management, and fund-raising.

Planning

One of the most important lessons for me following the genocide in Rwanda was that in certain situations, the planning and preparation process completely fails. In such situations, it is not only necessary to improvise but, above all, **to be capable of improvising***... The sad lesson for me was that we are at times overwhelmed, that we must have the flexibility, the imagination, and the creativity to adapt for the unforeseeable*
(Esther Mujawayo, Oxfam's Deputy Country Representative for Rwanda, Central Africa, quoted in Buell, 1996:3).

Planning is closely linked to self-appraisal, and provides a framework within which an organisation and its constituency can affirm what it wants to do, and how it will do it. Monitoring and evaluation are feedback mechanisms to ensure that problems are identified and dealt with, and that lessons can be learned and applied in future planning. However, plans and realities are not the same thing. Strategic planning should offer scope for flexibility and creativity. A strategy gives the agreed parameters within which staff can improvise. The confidence this gives is itself empowering.

Sadly, planning is often seen as a technical and top-down exercise that focuses more on the elaboration of written documents than on the processes to which these relate.[6] Essentially, a plan is a 'to do' list, in which performance can be measured in terms of how many items have been achieved. Strategic planning, however, aims to bring together the kind of self-appraisal described in the preceding section, with an analysis of the wider environment, in order to set the broad directions for the future. As its proponents argue, SP is about management, not about planning systems *per se*. No amount of planning will compensate for weak analysis, poor management, or low morale.

Whatever its limitations, the SP process may help to create consensus around a shared sense of purpose, as well as prompting an organisation to look beyond itself in order to:

- define what it is and wants to be
- identify external trends relevant to its success or failure

- identify strategic issues and how to address them
- establish its priorities
- identify its strengths and weaknesses
- be more effective
- agree monitoring and evaluation criteria
- allocate resources, including for training and personnel development
- achieve standards of excellence.

All organisations experience tensions between what they have done before, what they are doing now, and what they would like to do. Their success will depend on a combination of factors, of which planning is but one. These include: participation by the ultimate beneficiaries of the organisation's work; strong and effective leadership and management; committed and appropriately rewarded staff; a favourable external environment, including good relations with government; and decentralised decision-making.

Much NGO planning activity revolves around project management. But development does not depend on projects, however well planned and managed, unless these are geared to strengthening participants' existing capacities as well as developing new ones. Effectiveness and sustainability depend on 'bottom-up' participation in the design and management of projects.

Questions might include:

- What is the problem (or set of problems) to be addressed?
- What are the power relations in terms of class, race, gender or age giving rise to (or intersecting with) this problem?
- Who defined the problem, and who experiences it?
- What capacity to address the problem do women and men already possess?
- How does the planned activity strengthen (or weaken) this?
- What capacities exists (or are needed) to sustain the project, in terms of organisational ability, labour, time, material resources, and commitment?

Short-term objectives (or targets) enable an organisation to review progress towards its long-term aims; and these targets are often related to projects or programmes. For example, an NGO might aim to enhance the economic well-being and autonomy of women-maintained households in a low-income neighbourhood. The objectives of its education project are to provide vocational training, child-care facilities, and employment opportunities for x number of women over x years. It will monitor progress against these targets, and evaluate results against the central aims.

However, reaching such targets should not become an artificial imperative. Targets and indicators of progress change over time. Social processes are uneven and unpredictable, and projects are only a microscopic part of the wider environment: they cannot prevent the devastation of an earthquake, stop a massacre, or reverse the impact of economic structural adjustment; and gains achieved at an earlier time may subsequently be lost, or become inappropriate.

Monitoring

This is an internal checking mechanism to enable adjustments to be made in a methodical way. Monitoring systems should be simple and efficient, so that they can be readily incorporated in day-to-day routines. Ideally, monitoring should be done by 'front-line' teams who will restrict the collection of data to what is relevant and useful.

Monitoring helps to:

- check assumptions and hypotheses against performance
- chart progress and achievements
- detect unintended results, both positive and negative
- identify difficulties
- plot trends
- account for resources
- indicate where and how the plan should be adjusted
- improve future practice.

Appropriate monitoring indicators relate to the aims, objectives and specific activities of the planned work, and must reflect the evolving concerns of intended beneficiaries. Quantitative indicators are easier to handle, but qualitative indicators are always needed to reveal the full picture. For example, attendance rates in an adult literacy project will not provide much insight into the quality of people's participation, what this meant to them, or how to remove the constraints on them. Further exploration might show that women's family responsibilities prohibit them from attending regularly; that they cannot concentrate because their children are always with them; that men undermine women's participation in mixed sessions; or that the teaching materials use negative gender stereotypes or are focused on 'male' topics. Such qualitative information gives the organisation far greater insight into how to improve its work.

Assessing impact: a multi-faceted task

Oxfam's Health Policy Adviser visited a women's health project working in both the Albanian and Serbian sides of Kosovo, and elicited the range of indicators or parameters that activists and medical staff were using to measure impact in the population and changes in themselves.

131

Activists' parameters for changes in their lives:
- They listen more to people.
- There is a sense of solidarity and increased self-esteem.
- Activists apply what they learn.

Activists' parameters for impact on women's lives:
- The women come and talk; they are interested, and ask questions.
- There are more visits to gynaecologists.

Doctors' indicators of success:
- Women are interested: they come back, ask questions, ask for more sessions on the same topic, talk about topics for the next meeting, are more confident talking to doctors especially as compared with private medical consultations. Changes in women's behaviour when talking to doctors may also reflect the differences in doctors' attitudes between the friendly equal terms of the health meetings and their more authoritarian approach during consultancies.
- More children from the target villages taken for vaccination.
- Women attend clinics for gynaecological check-ups. Some of these women may never have talked to a doctor before.
- Young girls have the courage to seek medical help for neglected problems, eg a girl went to check a lump in her breast which had been ignored for a long time.

Coordinators' indicators of change and impact:
- Her mother communicated to her all the health messages from one session because a play had been used: 'No way my mother would remember all this through lecturing'.
- Women are interested. For example, a young mother left her 6-week old baby at home, telling her husband, 'if you tie me up, I will still go to these meetings'.
- When a woman misses a meeting, she asks others what they learned.

Changes in the lives of activists and village women:
- Activists are free to talk, though the village women still feel inhibited.
- Initially, the activists were afraid that people would laugh at them behind their backs, but now they have more confidence.
- There is a girls' volleyball team who are planning to play in other villages to demonstrate girls' capabilities and to encourage other girls to join sports activities.
- The activists feel connected to each other and they like spending time together as friends.

- 'At the beginning, I did the work because of my concern for the village, now I do it also because I value the work itself and value working with other women'.
- 'I used to dislike to talk or listen to women, especially the uneducated ones. Now I love talking with them. When women used to come to my house, I used to go and watch TV and did not like listening to their problems. Now I am closer to them'.
- 'After a disability-awareness session with the Oxfam disability adviser, I visited a house with a disabled child. The woman was very happy because she has no contacts to help her with her disabled child, has no information about where to get help, and kept the child closed up for seven years!' (Kamal Smith, 1996)

Monitoring may be done by routinely gathering information, or by methods such as spot-checks, visits, meetings, audits or reports. The following questions give some insight into what makes a good monitoring system (following Roche, personal communication):

- Does it focus on what is important?
- Is it simple? How many key indicators is each manager monitoring?
- Who participates in, uses, and understands the system? (Beneficiaries, staff members, trustees?)
- Does the system 'reward' people for the quantity of data collected, or for its usefulness to front-line staff?
- Are the data easily assimilated?
- Do all staff (and particularly front-line staff) actually use the monitoring system?
- Are the data disaggregated by sex, age, etc.?
- Does the system allow evolution to be measured according to the different priorities of different interest groups?
- Does it reveal progress towards or deviation from overall goals?
- Is there more than one channel for monitoring information, ie are there checks and balances to verify information?
- What mechanisms exist for ensuring feedback into new programming phases?
- Who is responsible for the monitoring system? Who is monitoring the monitoring system? On what basis are changes made?

Evaluation

The capacity of an organisation critically to evaluate its own work is a measure of its maturity. The processes and methods by which it does so may vary, but should be appropriate for the organisation and its overall aims. Evaluation is concerned as much with the future as with the past: assessing the results of past actions, in order to incorporate the lessons in future planning. By evaluating its performance, an organisation can:

• determine how far the various aims and objectives have been met;
• assess the relevance, effectiveness, efficiency, impact, and sustainability of what has been achieved;
• reconsider, in the light of experience, the validity of the assumptions behind the original plan;
• indicate what insights can be offered to improve broader development policy and practice;
• improve its capacity.

Evaluation is not a one-off exercise, or something which can be 'tacked on' as an afterthought. Like monitoring, it is part of the way in which an organisation ensures that its work is constantly under critical review. However, while monitoring is focused on progress towards a set of goals, evaluation may question the goals themselves. Evaluation should enable an organisation to assess achievement as well as failure, and to learn from mistakes.

However, formal evaluations are sometimes depend also on the wishes of its donors, who may insist on a particular methodology, or on choosing the evaluators. An evaluation process depends on trust, which requires a frank acknowledgement of the distribution of power, between donor and recipient, decision-makers and those affected by their decisions, the agency calling for an evaluation and the organisation that is being evaluated. Each of these is accountable to different constituencies, whose needs and interests may not coincide. If an evaluation is linked to funding decisions or some hidden agenda, those on the receiving end are likely to find the process undermining rather than affirmatory.

On the receiving end of evaluation

The Movimento de Organizaçao Comunitaria (MOC) is a multi-disciplinary advisory centre that has worked in north-east Brazil for some 30 years. Oxfam began funding MOC's work in 1972, and in 1990 it commissioned another Brazilian NGO to evaluate it. Here, MOC reflects on this experience, and draws out some basic principles for good practice.

NGOs, including MOC, usually include evaluation in their on-going activities. Often, however, donor agencies insist on evaluations with very specific and detailed objectives, to involve or be coordinated by outsiders. This was what Oxfam proposed. How did we feel about it?

The first question was whether we could realistically say 'No' to the proposal. After all, we were dealing with our funders. In the end, we felt we couldn't very well refuse... Another issue worried us: who would carry out the evaluation? What would their connections be? What ideological positions would they represent? And who would see the final report? ... The possible repercussions arising from the evaluation were a real worry for us. This has a lot to do with how the funding agencies behave and pool information among themselves. For example, some were asking us to share the report with them, even before the information-gathering phase had been completed.

Another issue was that, since we were being evaluated, our own competence was implicitly on the line. To an extent, the survival of the organisation was in the balance. But who is to say what competence means in the context of social organisation? Oxfam always claimed that the evaluation had nothing to do with whether funding would continue or not. Our own feeling, however, was that any new grants would depend crucially on a positive outcome from the evaluation ...

Because of what it represented, the evaluation was in fact a burden, whatever the good intentions of the evaluators. Not everyone felt like going along with it. Sometimes, we got the feeling that we were under surveillance ... While we had seen evaluation as a process and not as a document, what predominated was the fixation on the report. Since this was one with which we did not agree, the gap between ourselves and the evaluators grew wider ...

We believe that there are some useful lessons to come out of this process, which can help everyone involved in evaluations.

- An evaluation proposal must be discussed fully and clearly, allowing everyone to explain their particular way of seeing things, express their expectations, and explore their concerns, in order to reduce the scope for misunderstandings.

- We Southern NGOs must develop the capacity to reflect on our work and be clear about when and under what conditions we think evaluations should take place. In this way, we can also be straightforward and open with Northern donor agencies in deciding, on a more objective basis, whether it is appropriate to embark on any particular evaluation process. In our opinion, we are rarely free to do

> this. And what would the Northern NGOs think of the idea? What is
> certain is that, at the moment, we get involved in one evaluation after
> another, without any of them really helping us to be more effective in
> achieving our aims.

- It is imperative to ensure a proper match between the nature of the
  work to be evaluated and the expertise of the evaluators, especially in
  the area of social organisation. Only then will an appropriate
  methodology be agreed.

- In our view, it is crucial that evaluation should be a collective process,
  not one in which we are treated or made to feel as though we are just
  an object. The main thing is that evaluation should help us to think
  more deeply about what we are doing, drawing the lessons and
  redirecting our work, if necessary. We have no wish to be objects of
  studies and research.

- Donor agencies and local organisations need to learn how to deal with
  the question of evaluation more calmly, more self-critically, and more
  honestly. Of course, evaluation is absolutely fundamental: it has to
  happen and should never be ignored. But decisions cannot be made
  unilaterally, because so much depends on timing, practicalities, the
  choice of evaluators, and so on. Everyone involved needs to
  understand the objectives and agree with the choice of evaluation
  methods. For the most part, academic research methodologies are
  inappropriate for evaluating social organisation work (Movimento de
  Organização Comunitaria, 1993: 209–212).

Approaches to evaluation

In a development and relief context, the aim of evaluation is to enhance
efforts to overcome poverty and injustice. Except in the case of highly technical interventions, it focuses on correlating the activities being undertaken
and wider impacts, since causation can seldom be proved, and people may
be affected in different ways by the activities. Evaluations can be informal or
formal, or a mixture of the two. What matters is that the organisation
concerned is clear about the role of evaluation in its work. Where several
parties are involved (eg a donor agency, a local NGO, and a community
group) it is also important to be open about how any findings will inform their
respective decisions.

Evaluation is often informal and self-managed: self- or auto-evaluation,
participatory evaluation, and user evaluation. (The characteristics of each are
described in Eade and Williams, 1995; and Rubin, 1995.) Informal does not

mean unplanned, and regular or occasional 'stock-taking' exercises may complement routine monitoring. Nor does it necessarily mean low-cost, though it is invariably cheaper and more efficient to deal with problems as they arise than to wait for a major formal exercise.

Informal evaluation is a measure of an organisation's own self-critical capacity. However, major issues may be avoided because to tackle them involves challenging individuals, hierarchies, or prejudices. Where certain individuals or groups are marginalised from decision-making, or where internal accountability and policy review are deficient, self-evaluation is more likely to confirm the status quo than to alter it (see, for instance, Goetz, 1996). External facilitation may enable critical issues to be dealt with in a more constructive way.

User evaluation goes one step further in seeking feedback from everyone involved in a given activity, in order to agree on practical and immediate solutions to any shortcomings. A simple example is that of workshop participants being asked to state their expectations at the start of each session, and to share their evaluations with a steering committee, so that the programme can be modified. As social auditing does on a more public scale, user evaluation can foster mutual accountability, in particular to those who are intended to benefit from the intervention. If NGOs and donor agencies are committed to capacity-building, they should actively seek this kind of critical feedback from beneficiaries, and act on it.

Formal evaluations are major exercises with agreed Terms of Reference (TOR), usually led by external evaluators. They can be expensive and time-consuming, and are justified only if major policy issues are at stake, or when it is important for political or financial reasons to subject the programme or organisation to external scrutiny.

Formal evaluations are classified according to when they are conducted. An '*ex-ante* evaluation' is the initial planning stage. A 'mid-term evaluation' is conducted during implementation, to review progress and make any major adjustments. 'Final' or '*ex-post* evaluation' takes place at the end of a project's activities.

While informal evaluation may require a few days per month for compiling and reviewing data, a major formal exercise takes months of preparation, some weeks of concentrated fieldwork, and lengthy negotiation on the recommendations. The opportunity cost for the people who will be interviewed may be considerable. Formal evaluations usually report in the language of the donor agency, though some way should be found of sharing the findings locally, for instance through workshops or discussions, audio-visual presentations, or summaries in local languages.

Whatever the form of an evaluation, its purpose is to strengthen the capacities of the organisation. The following paragraphs focus on ways to integrate the interests of donor agencies and those whose work is being evaluated.

Priorities: The interests to be reconciled include those of the intended beneficiaries, intermediaries, funders, and constituencies. Without a process for negotiating between these stakeholders, the most powerful is likely to predominate. The priorities for evaluation should reflect the values that shape the work. They are also influenced by how the evaluation is to be used. For example, an NGO may conduct a thematic evaluation to make comparisons among different areas, and so may look at the cost-effectiveness of each operation. But if it wishes simply to improve what it is doing in one location, then an evaluation might analyse the main areas of difficulty and come up with alternatives.

Criteria: Initial monitoring and evaluation indicators should be agreed among stakeholders, particularly beneficiaries. However, these indicators may change over time, perhaps as a result of the intervention. It is as important to record any such evolution as to measure achievements against the initial indicators.

There needs also be to a sensitive balance between quantitative and qualitative indicators, reflecting the relationship between long-term aims and short-term objectives. For example, the aim of an HIV/AIDS education programme might be to change people's sexual behaviour: something which will take years to promote, is hard to prove, and must be sustained after the programme is over. Methods might include various awareness-raising approaches: public conferences, radio slots, poster campaigns, public health education, AIDS support groups, and lobbying of local health professionals; as well as on-demand condom distribution. It may be viable to quantify the specific activities undertaken. But it would be unrealistic to measure long-term impact within the lifetime of the programme; or to attribute a simple cause and effect relationship between the services provided and changes in personal behaviour. The absence of 'hard proof' does not mean, however, that no conclusions can be drawn about the likely relationship between the programme and its wider impacts.

Scope: Evaluation may be comprehensive or focused. For example, an NGO may have several programmes, each funded by a different donor. A global evaluation would be a better measure of effectiveness than focusing narrowly on the activities funded by a single donor. Certain aspects may need to be more fully examined than others. Impact, effectiveness, efficiency, relevance, and sustainability are context-specific and must be appropriately interpreted within the broader environment, by examining the perspectives of different interest groups.

People may not reveal their views and feelings when responding to outsiders' questionnaires or structured interviews. Some of the techniques of Participatory Rural Appraisal (PRA) and its many derivatives may be more appropriate. Listening Workshops, Listening Theatre, role-play, drawing, and video have all been used to help people to express things they find hard to put into words. It may be precisely these things that need to be understood by intervening agencies.

Cost: A benchmark figure for evaluation costs is between two and five per cent of the cost of what is being evaluated. This figure should enable a judgement to be made about whether more is called for than routine monitoring and evaluation.

Handling difference: The process of agreeing a formal evaluation report should provide an opportunity for comment to those affected by it. Evaluation may reveal differences between the parties involved. For example, an agricultural project may have worsened the relative condition of women by making credit available only for crops which are the monopoly of men. If everyone agrees that this is undesirable, then the evaluation has highlighted a problem to which solutions can be sought. However, one set of people may accept the data but disagree on the need for corrective action. If stakeholders do not share the same basic criteria, it may be necessary to end the relationship.[7]

Financial management

An organisation can only budget realistically if it can predict its resources. An organisation that cannot make long-term plans must rely on raising funds for short-term needs. This prevents it from consolidating or developing further: the resource-poor organisation becomes resource-led. Lacking a clear direction, it finds it even harder to attract the support of donors. Dependent on external funding, it may be kept in financial suspense, unable to plan from one year to the next. It may become both ineffectual and unsustainable — which is the reverse of what its donors intended.

Why might this be? First, donor agencies like to protect their own revenue from disruptions which might threaten *their* core activities. So, they negotiate grants annually, seldom committing funds for more than three years. Second, most donor agencies prefer the flexibility that project-funding gives: their outstanding commitments will be minimised if their own income falls; and they can adapt their project portfolio if their priorities change. Third, many Northern NGOs raise money by appealing to individuals, who seem more willing to support individual projects than more flexible programme grants, within which the recipient exercises discretion over the allocation of funds.

Fourth, almost all donor agencies disburse their grants in instalments, perhaps to retain control over how the money is spent. But this prevents recipients from establishing reserve funds or depositing the money in a high-interest account. Finally, grants are often negotiated in weak local currencies but approved in hard currencies: this allows the donor agencies rather than their Southern counterparts to take advantage of exchange rate fluctuations. *Hence, the very mechanisms which donor agencies use to protect their own resources are thereby denied to those whose independent capacity or autonomy they want to promote.*

Here, we focus on practical ways to break the vicious cycle described above, so that local organisations can develop into healthy and accountable institutions.

Core budgets

The recurrent administration costs essential to the running of an organisation (salaries, travel expenses, purchase and maintenance of equipment, office space, communications) make up its core budget. Donors often dislike funding administration, or treat these costs as projects, picking and choosing as they please. This can lead to absurd double standards. For instance, the Director of an Indian NGO was amazed to find that in the head offices of the Northern NGO that was its major funder, there were photocopiers in every department and computers in each office. Yet his own NGO's repeated requests for such standard office equipment had been rejected, on the grounds that these were 'luxury items'. An organisation whose basic running costs are not guaranteed can neither think nor work strategically; and its efficiency and effectiveness will be undermined.

A more constructive approach may be for donor agencies to provide flexible programme grants that allow Southern counterparts to make their own decisions about priorities. Assistance may include providing information about organisations involved in alternative financing, such as providing guarantee funds or access to the formal banking system.

Experts on sustainable financing strategies for Southern NGOs and CBOs stress the need to have enough funds to survive temporary cash-flow crises (for example, when a grant payment is delayed) and to cover the annual budget, even without programme grants. It is also important to keep core costs to the minimum. Their advice is as follows:

Cut down administrative expenditures: check the unnecessary use of vehicles, monitor the use of telephones and photocopiers, and limit the number of staff on establishment rather than programme-related contracts.

Minimise the administrative budget by putting 'support' programme activities under programme budgets: define the organisation's function under main headings (Information, Training, Relief, Development, Administration, including management and fundraising) so that resources required for non-administrative work appear in programme budgets.

Ask donors for an 'overhead' for administration on all project grants: as a benchmark, UN agencies add 14 per cent on projects they administer, though NGO overhead charges range from 8 per cent to 20 per cent. (The smaller the budget, the higher the overhead costs as a percentage of this: a vehicle costs the same to buy and run, whether it belongs to a small organisation or a large national NGO!)

If no overhead is available, debit the project accounts for all services rendered by the organisation: calculate a reasonable percentage of all items in the annual budget that, directly or indirectly, support each project (personnel, transport, equipment, office maintenance, including rentals and depreciation, auditors' fees) so that the true project costs are explicit.

Negotiate institution-building grants from donors: seek a commitment to meet salaries and other essential starting-up or running costs over a reasonable period of time. (It may be more economical to purchase than to rent or hire office space and equipment, but calculate maintenance and depreciation costs realistically!)

Increase the sources of income and use this to cover administration: existing activities or resources could be used to generate an income to offset basic costs. (Check that these are economically feasible and compatible with the organisation's aims and priorities.)
(Adapted from Vincent and Campbell, 1989, pp 86–95.)

Salaries and related benefits (such as social security payments, pension or savings funds, or life assurance) are often the largest single component of core budgets, accounting for up to 65 per cent of an organisation's total revenue. These may form an even higher proportion of individual project costs. Some organisations have a universal salary rate, with allowances for dependents, or other forms of in-kind support, such as food tokens, transport or housing subsidies. Some fix ratios for salary differentials: for instance, that the highest paid person should not earn more than three times the salary of the lowest paid. Some determine their salaries in relation to legal minimum wages, while others aim to remunerate their staff equitably, even if this means offering above market rates. Others opt instead to pay salaries that are below commercial market rates. Not uncommonly, the salaries actually paid depend on how successful the organisation has been at negotiating grant funding.[8]

The right salary structure depends on many factors, including the organisation's ethos, as well as its resources. However, it should respect any minimum legislation concerning salaries and other terms and conditions of employment (donor agencies should remember this when deciding the level of their input).

External funding: a mixed blessing

There is no one answer to the question of how long an organisation and its work should rely on external support. International cooperation is not necessarily a bad thing in itself, provided that the relationship is sound. However, most organisations fear excessive reliance on a single source of funds just as many donors also seek to avoid becoming the sole sponsor.

In order to retain their own flexibility and to discourage dependence, many donors limit the length of time they will fund the same organisations. These limits can be rather arbitrary: for instance, a major US foundation told a Guatemalan human rights organisation that funding would not continue beyond three years, because it was 'doing nothing new' in continuing to document and denounce the worst record for human rights abuses in the Western hemisphere! If they are serious about capacity-building, donors should help their 'partners' either to diversify their sources of funding or to generate an income of their own.

Where the grant-funded activities are very specific (such as an event), or can be expected to show tangible results within a defined period, the point at which to review continued funding may be self-evident. However, once a donor takes on the core costs of an organisation, the criteria for its support must be unambiguous. Otherwise, organisations may outlive their natural lifespan; or, as often happens if their funding stops without warning, be faced with premature extinction.

Breaking the dependency cycle

There are two main ways to break the dependency cycle: either spreading the risk across a number of funders, or generating an independent income.

Diversifying their support base

One writer suggests that Southern organisations need enough donors to have 'exit options' if their conditions prove too onerous (Hudock, 1996:3). Before any organisation approaches a new donor, it needs to be well-informed about its policies and practices. One way to find out is to consult other recipients. Donor agencies should also expect to be subject to the same kind of scrutiny that they themselves apply to their 'partners'. What are their strategic agendas? How do they raise their money? What strings are attached? How are their counterparts depicted in their fundraising and publicity material? While a large grant might be tempting, the conditions accompanying it may not.

However difficult the cash-flow problems, organisations should avoid 'chasing the money', or expanding too rapidly. An increase in the budget of more than 25 per cent per year above inflation is likely to create serious tensions, though it is not uncommon for Southern NGOs to grow by far more than this. The demands generated by uncoordinated reporting and accounting obligations, and frequent meetings and visits, can also be self-defeating. Organisations should ask donors to coordinate their visiting and payment schedules and reporting requirements, and accept consolidated global reports. Funding by a donor consortium may prevent individual funding agencies supporting only innovative projects, leaving others to cover administration costs. On the other hand, the collective strength of a consortium may leave the Southern organisation more vulnerable to Northern pressure than if it dealt with each donor agency individually. To be able to cope with these problems is exactly what organisational capacity means.

Maintaining organisational integrity

While dependency is most obviously seen in terms of resource flows, other forms of dependency can be associated with funding. Three practical ideas for protecting the integrity of the Southern organisations have emerged from Ann Hudock's work on 'institutional inter-dependence'. The first is that they might be encouraged to establish their own boards of advisers or trustees. These enable Southern organisations to 'remain accountable to their donors while preserving their integrity in carrying out their work with beneficiary groups' (Hudock, 1996:31). They also enable the organisations better to undertake the self-appraisal processes described earlier in this Chapter, and decrease their 'vulnerability to external control by anchoring the organisation and guarding against co-optation' (ibid.)

The second is that donor agencies might finance the position of a grants compliance officer 'charged with the task of acquiring resources and reporting on their use' (ibid.). This would enable them better to manage their relationships with various donors, while also releasing 'managers and project staff from these responsibilities, which means they can concentrate on roles they are better equipped to fill' (ibid.).

The third suggestion is that donor agencies assist their Southern counterparts to train in fund-raising and public relations, much as they do themselves. The possibility of staff exchanges between Northern and Southern NGOs, for instance, would permit 'SNGOs [to] learn from NNGOs' technical skills and media knowledge, while NNGOs could learn from SNGOs about development issues, and thus present them more accurately to donor publics' (op.cit., p30).

Generating income

Self-financing activities can generate some income or in-kind support which gives an organisation at least a symbolic measure of autonomy and demonstrates that it is providing a valued service. However, NGOs seldom charge

143

for their services. For registered charities or non-profit organisations, it may be illegal to do so. Few believe that the supplier-client relationship can fittingly apply in a humanitarian relief context, and many development agencies also feel that to treat their beneficiaries as paying customers would be wrong, since it would amount to taking money directly from the poor.[9]

Other ways to recover costs include various forms of in-kind payment, such as board and lodging for community workers. Consumer co-operatives may buy in bulk and sell at a rate that allows them to cover their own costs. Credit unions may charge interest on loans, in order to offset their own administration costs. Some organisations can use their existing activities to raise money: for example, a rural workers' union might pool a percentage of the income from selling agricultural produce, to offset the costs of building a warehouse. Where exchange and barter arrangements are common, these can also provide the basis for some form of in-kind cost-recovery.

Generating an institutional income may require NGOs and other civil society organisations to think in a more entrepreneurial fashion, but can also encourage them better to value their skills and assets. For example, organisations might hire out equipment, such as tape-recorders or projectors; or charge for photocopying or fax facilities; or let offices or meeting rooms. Documentation centres could charge a subscription fee for external users, sell news cuttings services, or provide a sales outlet for publishers. Publications should never be distributed free without good reason, and should at least aim to recover the cost of production and distribution. In addition, most people set greater value on material for which they have paid.

Organisations with skilled personnel might provide commercial services, for instance, typing, wordprocessing, translation, desktop publishing, or printing. For instance, a research and documentation centre in Mexico recuperated some of the costs of its computer equipment by offering training for other NGOs and popular organisations. NGO staff might undertake consultancy work, such as feasibility studies or evaluations for government or international agencies; the accountant in one Honduran NGO was commissioned by local agencies as an experienced and trustworthy auditor, thus earning a small income for his own organisation.

Fundraising activities may also be possible, and Northern NGOs may be able to suggest ideas or assess proposals. No self-financing scheme will work, however, unless it is commercially viable; and if it can realistically be combined with the aims, priorities and values of the organisation undertaking them. If not, as the following textbox argues, it may prove a costly distraction.

Sustainability is not just about money!

Pursuing so-called 'money-making' ventures can prove a dangerous distraction for many development agencies which are ill-equipped to do so... [B]oth success and failure can have negative consequences. Success of an ancillary activity encourages programme managers to expand that activity and, in the process, to devote more time and resources to what, initially, was intended to be merely a secondary 'money-spinner'. Similarly, failure prompts programme managers to switch attention to the secondary activity in order to ensure its success. Because there are often sunk costs and deep emotional commitment to the income-earning activity, it is difficult to withdraw from it once started. In either case, it is the original developmental objective that suffers.

Donors' insistence on sustainability in the purely financial sense must, therefore, be tempered by a recognition that desirable developmental activities — particularly those that cater to 'the poorest' — will never be(come) sustainable in that sense as their capacity for revenue-generation is weak or non-existent ... it is time for donors to 'dispel the sustainability myth' by acknowledging the reality that, in most developing countries, there are constraints in local financing capacity which threaten sustainability.

On the recipient side, the overwhelming lesson is that sustainability is emphatically not a financial issue. There seems to be a common path down which recipient institutions travel. Having defined the problem posed by the termination of donor funding as a financial one, they logically seek financial solutions. Halfway down that path, however, they find that they must confront the reality that sustainability means much more than simply finding a way to raise sufficient revenue to meet their recurrent costs. If the definition of the problem is wrong, the solution must be equally wrong ...

Recipient institutions are thus well advised to work out from the outset an appropriate definition of sustainability that applies to their specific programmes and contexts, as well as a detailed plan for achieving it. A strategy for sustainability ought to be built into the programme design from inception and the modalities for achieving it settled early in its life and not left to the final year (or worse, the dying months) of funding (Brown, 1997:188–189).

7

Investing in networks

Not even the most repressive régime can stop human beings from finding ways of communicating and obtaining access to information. This applies in equal measure to the information revolution sweeping the globe. No one can roll it back. It has the potential to open communications across all geographical and cultural divides... But... the technology gap between the developed and developing nations is actually widening. Most of the world has no experience of what readily accessible communications can do for society and economy (Nelson Mandela). [1]

Introduction

In a capacity-building context, there are two main reasons for promoting networks. First, to share new ideas and information in order to learn from others with similar interests. And second, to pool participants' experience and energy in order to enhance their collective and individual impact. Participation in international networks can enable people to make the links between the global level and what is going on in their own lives. And networks can help to facilitate the practical 'action by citizens and social movements in both South and North, coming together to put pressure on governments to act' which 'provides the best hope of securing rights and ending poverty' (Watkins, 1995: 315).

Not all networks result in tangible gains for their members, or lead to practical action or change. But belonging to a network, or making informal links with other like-minded people, can significantly strengthen the position of those who are thus inspired and enabled to work for change. Whether this happens depends largely on *who* belongs to a network, and *how* they use it. And people may make creative use of what a network offers, in ways that were not originally intended.

A network may serve its members in different ways, each of them equally valid. For instance, during the 1980s, several international NGOs in Central America used their institutions' membership of the NGO-umbrella group, ICVA, to convene high-level meetings and engage support for region-wide policy initiatives that none could have achieved individually. For many other Southern NGOs, membership of ICVA was important mainly in facilitating their access to international policy-making fora. In both cases, belonging to an international network enabled its members to maximise their impact within their own spheres of activity.

The term networking covers the informal linking and communication that goes on between people and organisations, at a local, national, or international level. Support for these connections and alliances among pro-poor activists is an essential part of a development strategy for NGOs. This Chapter looks in turn at the kinds of linking activities that allow people and organisations to find common ground, and then discusses the role that more formal networks can play in capacity-building. The final section looks specifically at the potential and pitfalls of electronic networking.

Linking

Linking and networking are more usefully seen as development strategies than as tools; they therefore require an investment of time — and usually money — before the full impact can be felt. They enable people and organisations to learn from each other, exchange resources, and become more independent as a result.

In 1992, Oxfam launched two ambitious global linking projects. These brought together Southern counterparts, outside experts, and Oxfam's own programme staff to consider issues of gender and development, and environmental problems respectively.

The external evaluation of the Women's Linking Project (WLP) made several observations on the ingredients for successful linking:

* *Respectful partnership and equal access to resources*: participants must be willing to respect others' learning processes and cultures, prepared to learn from each other, and openly to discuss their own values and difficulties. Resources include power, money, and information.
* *Mutual interests in linking*: linking will happen if and when people and organisations recognise their mutual interest in it. It does not have to be a continuing process in order to be valuable.
* *Management of linking*: a central agency, such as an NGO, may facilitate initial linkages, but linking is ultimately self-managed: everyone can start or continue a linking process, and everyone can stop it. The centre is no longer fixed, but can move about (de Wit, 1995: 54–55).

147

Effective Networking

(From Nelson, 1955, p.80)

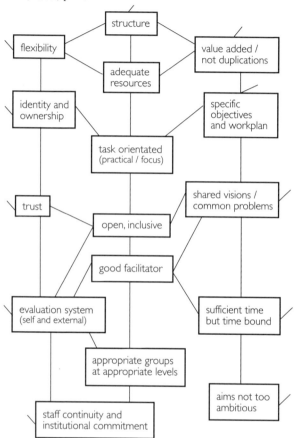

The evaluation also highlighted how hard it is for the participants in a linking process — in this case, Oxfam and women from Southern organisations — to change the terms of their existing relationships. To dedicate resources to linking people is an active and value-driven intervention. To move from this into a purely facilitating role is extremely difficult: some people may want and expect the agency that took the initiative to continue to take the lead (what has been called 'trained incompetence'); others may be resentful if the agency tries to direct the linking process in any way. As one participant in the WLP put it:

*If you say that we are partners, equals, and that the South is going to decide
things, then you have to be willing to go with that, because it's not acceptable
in the end to say that what you came up with is no longer okay*
(quoted in de Wit, 1995:35).

The cost-effectiveness of linking processes or activities need to be assessed.
Transport, translation, management and administration, are expensive; linking across countries and cultures requires considerable financial and organisational investment. One-off linking events may achieve an impact, but an
organisation will only sustain the links it values. The objectives of linking, and
how the linking process will improve the situation of people who are poor
and excluded, need to be clear.

The evaluation of linking work is complex. Lessons from the reviews of
Oxfam's two linking projects include:

• The facilitating agency should avoid having too many criteria of its own,
since this can 'narrow the field of vision'. Rather, it should look at the different
criteria of those directly involved in the linking process.

• Linking represents an investment and should be seen as a starting point.
Quantitative and qualitative assessments of the participants from what they
identify as their starting points are required, and these indicators used to
measure the progress they have made over time.

• Participants may find they are at different stages; and their needs and
interests may evolve. Early gains may be fragile, and depend heavily on
'people and casual coalitions'. Different skills may be needed to consolidate
these gains.

• Linking is ultimately a political process. Such processes do not follow a
logical progression, but show 'leaps, gaps, and backlashes'. The effects of the
process are often internalised and may be under-valued by external agencies,
though highly valued by participants: benefits of linking include feelings of
solidarity and connectedness, confidence, and awareness.

In particular, the evaluations of both Linking Projects stressed that since
linking and networking are not themselves linear processes, conventional
linear approaches to impact assessment are inappropriate. An open, flexible
approach in which objectives are constantly evolving 'requires a creative learning system to chart what happens in such a diffuse programme, to understand
the processes at work, and to assess the spin-offs of these processes, and any
long-term impact' (Nelson, 1995:2) (see opposite page for characteristics of
effective networking). Evaluating this should be firmly based on the participants' own assessment.

Building capacities through linking

Linking between stakeholders in development in the North and South, is a method of working which is increasingly being adopted by Northern NGOs in an attempt to break through the communication barriers. Women's organisations are agents for change, and their capacity is enhanced by links with like-minded organisations, both feminist and mainstream, regionally and globally. Links need not be permanent, and they need not be all-encompassing. They can be part of a short-term strategy to reach a particular goal, or a long-term strategy for information exchange...

[F]or many smaller NGOs working on gender issues in the North and South, North-South linking has been an important way of developing policy, and for building international solidarity. South-South linking, unmediated and uncensored by Northern funders or by head office, is also an essential means of capacity-building in the South. Funding is needed to facilitate such networking (Reardon, 1995: 160–161).

In the remainder of this section, we shall explore in turn three kinds of linking activity: exchange visits, workshops, and conferences.

Exchange visits

Networking may start with no more than a visit between one group and another, within the same country or between countries. An advantage of such visits is that people learn more readily from their peers than from an outside expert who comes along to lecture them. Visits may not just be bilateral, and not all 'exchange' visits are reciprocated. But hosts to a visiting group may then meet up with another organisation, and so the networking begins. An effective network will evolve, however, only when the potential members wish to invest the time and resources, and when they have built up enough trust to work together.

There can be any number of reasons for an exchange visit: to learn about innovatory practices; to see the work of more experienced groups; or to discuss different ways of dealing with a particular problem. To make the exchange worthwhile, hosts and visitors should share similar objectives, and be mutually committed to making good use of the visit. Ideally, the learning should be two-way: the visitors should also have something to offer to their hosts. It is often better that at least two people come from the visiting group, so that one person is not solely responsible for assimilating and communicating what they have seen and experienced, and how this could be relevant their own organisation.

Exchange visits can be expensive, especially when international travel is involved, and the expected benefits must therefore bear a reasonable relationship to the cost. Travel arrangements, visa requirements, access to foreign currency, language difficulties, and an unfamiliar cultural environment can all mar a visit, and undermine people's confidence. It may help to ensure that at least one of the visiting delegation has travelled before. Within Oxfam, for example, a staff member from the Middle East has visited India to share experiences on gender and disability; a Ugandan has been to Zambia to find out more about poverty assessment work and research on Structural Adjustment Policies; two Zambians have visited Burkina Faso to look at cereal banks.The primary benefit from these exercises accrues to the individual visitors from their direct exposure to different programmes, approaches and ideas. The degree to which others have gained has varied considerably. Some visitors have proved quite adept at distilling and disseminating relevant insights on their return, whilst others have been less successful. Similarly, whilst certain individuals have managed to contribute fresh insights and ideas to their hosts, this does not happen consistently. To some extent, these difficulties could be overcome if visits were organised upon a reciprocal basis. A key constraint is the cost per participant, which is already quite high (Howes and Roche, 1996).

To avoid participation in a visit being seen simply as a prize or privilege, criteria for selecting the visitors should be established as part of defining the objectives. Like any other resource, the opportunity to travel may serve to reinforce existing power structures and gender power imbalances. For example, women may not be offered the chance to participate, or be unable to benefit from an exchange, because they do not read and write. Other constraints on women may include lack of childcare arrangements, opposition from men, not being able to attend mixed events, or not speaking the national language. A solution may be to organise women-only exchanges, to enable them to benefit fully both as participants and through the debriefing and follow-up. Oxfam's experience in fostering South-South links between people from very different cultural backgrounds is that enough time must be built into the programme to allow the visitors and hosts to establish their own common ground — without which there is little likelihood of lasting results.

Debriefings need not be formal or in writing in order to communicate what has been learned. Instead, feedback might include meetings and discussions, and audio-visual or dramatic representation. 'Information and knowledge may flow along many different channels', such as kinship, geographical location, friendships, political or religious affiliations, and so on (Nelson, 1995:79). If an exchange visit is to be successful in terms of capacity-building, the benefits must be shared with all members of the organisation or group.

Bringing people together

An Oxfam worker who was involved in arranging an exchange between Filipino and Latin American fisherfolk commented:

If we did such an exchange again, we would focus more on similarities in concerns, contexts, and be less ambitious...Exchanges can be a very important way to start empowering people. The international component can be very important in taking people out of their limited national perspective ... but the thing to avoid is supporting globe-trotting representatives who have no contact with their community any more and so links are broken in taking back that experience outside the area and in sharing the information and learning on return. Taking the community experience from one area to another is very important with regard to ... solidarity, especially for fisherfolk who are often very isolated
(quoted in Nelson, 1995:68).

Workshops

Workshops enable people to work together on a common concern in a structured but informal and participatory setting. This is why they are often used for training or to assist in 'brain-storming' on a given topic. Preparation is all-important: defining themes, aims, objectives and methods; inviting resource people and facilitators; making practical arrangements; obtaining funding and keeping the accounts. In terms of selecting the participants, it should not be assumed that the mere fact of working in the same sector or on the same issues, or being funded by the same donor, will mean that people will automatically trust each other, or be able to work well together.

Workshops may bring together people from disparate backgrounds or levels of experience. This, as well as language difficulties, can sometimes impede communication. It takes time to establish confidence, especially if people have only just met, or are not used to operating in a participatory environment. Creating a constructive workshop atmosphere, so that everyone can participate fully, depends on good facilitation.

Workshops that are well-planned, but flexible enough to respond to new concerns that arise, are an exciting and creative way for adults to learn from each other, and to develop new ideas. Often, the informal discussions are as valuable as the official sessions. For example, in 1987 Oxfam funded a one-week workshop on Feminism and Popular Movements organised by a Mexican NGO, which convened women from the entire Central American region. The value was not just in exploring a complex issue in a supportive environment, but also in forging links between various national organisations, for whom bilateral contact was otherwise impossible. Five years after that seminal workshop, half a dozen new regional and bilateral initiatives had developed — outcomes which were not part of the original objectives, but which doubtless grew out of creative discussions after workshop sessions, that went on long into the night!

Some kind of workshop report is vital to record the proceedings, to share the results with others, and to suggest future activities. It need not be a conventional written document. For example, a workshop in Kenya brought together largely non-literate pastoralist women, and used visual and drama techniques to share experiences; the resulting report was an informative photographic composition to which everyone had contributed.

Conferences

No capacity will be built by sending delegates to a conference simply to collect copies of the papers. Where the conference is part of a process of shaping development policy and practice (such as the 1996 World Food Summit or the 1997 Micro-Credit Summit) it may be more important to participate in the preparations than in the event itself.

All the UN world conferences and summits since UNCED in 1992 have had a large parallel NGO forum. This has offered major opportunities for North-South networking, coalition-building, and lobbying; and also allowed NGOs to organise around themes or regional interests. In practice, however, the NGO presence, both in the main conferences and in the NGO sections, has been heavily dominated by the North. Southern NGOs lack the resources to attend, this often not being considered a priority by their donors; and Northern NGOs are often better linked into the preparatory processes, and have influential contacts within the relevant official and multilateral agencies and the journalists covering the event. Southern NGOs may rightly ask, however, how Northern NGOs are helping to build the capacities of their Southern counterparts in sending only their own delegates and lobbyists.

While such large conferences are generally exclusive and unparticipative, the opportunity simply to observe the formal proceedings gives a unique insight into how such events are managed. Southern delegates whom Oxfam sponsored to attend the NGO Forum at the 1995 World Summit for Social Development argued vehemently for their right to gain access to the main conference, rather than being stuck on the NGO sidelines.

Participating in the conference process

The women's caucus at the World Conference on Human Rights (WCHR) [in Vienna 1993] was organised to promote communication between members of UN agencies, official government delegates, the press, and others attending the conference.

During the first week, the caucus met daily to strategise about how to incorporate women's concerns into the draft declaration. Recommendations made by women's groups, who held a separate caucus, were used as a basis for discussions. The dialogue between NGOs and official delegates was crucial to ensuring that the women's recommendations were incorporated into the final document, since the drafting committee was closed to NGOs.

In the second week, the caucus shifted its focus to the implementation of the paragraphs already incorporated into the document. The caucus met with key players responsible for the follow-up to the WCHR...to discuss and share their thoughts on how they would concretely address the gender components in their implementation steps.

After the conference ended many of the networks formed through the women's caucus continued. Women's groups are working closely with the UN Centre for Human Rights to assist them in monitoring and addressing acts of gender violence. Government officials concerned with women's issues are now in close contact with NGOs working in this area (UNIFEM/UN-NGLS,1995).

Networks and networking

The major difference between a formal network, and the informal linking activities described above, is that the former starts out with a clear purpose while the latter are essentially open-ended. Networks — associations, movements and coalitions — are semi-formal groupings in which each participant remains autonomous, but where enough common ground exists to establish shared concerns. They are seldom rigid or hierarchical, and so implicitly challenge possessive attitudes towards information and power. International networks draw strength from diversity. For example, the Southern feminist network DAWN (Development Alternatives with Women for a New Era) aims to generate a global support network for 'a world where inequality based on class, gender and race, is absent from every country and from the relationships among countries. Where basic needs become basic rights and where poverty and all forms of violence are eliminated' (Sen and Grown, 1987, quoted in Antrobus, 1991:315).

Networks may be primarily literature-based (for example, via newsletters or journals), topic-focused, or revolve around exchanges, training workshops, and other encounters. Their members may meet or communicate with each other bilaterally, or through a central coordination point. International networking has been revolutionised by the recent advances in information technology, which have enabled organisations around the world to share information, build common strategies, and interact in many other ways.

One of the most famous, and most successful, single-issue citizens' networks was the International Baby Food Action Network (IBFAN). Starting out in the 1970s, IBFAN orchestrated an international boycott of Nestle, the company identified as the worst offender in promoting artificial baby foods; and developed an international code to govern their promotion (see overleaf).

Networks originate in various ways. They may start because an external agent, such as an NGO, puts people in touch with each other, or provides funds for them to get together. They may grow spontaneously out of the contacts made at a conference or other event, or because one group or individual takes the initiative to convene others to work on a shared concern. Establishing a formal network may not be the most efficient or cost-effective way to meet specific aims. Members of a potential network need to be clear about its purpose, objectives, structure, method of communication, and membership criteria, and these must all be kept under constant review. Feedback from members — and potential members — is critical. Thus a network needs good systems of internal communication and accountability, as well as the capacity to attract new members.

Networks come in many different shapes and sizes. Some typical structures are:

- *Bicycle wheel or star networks:* members communicate with each other through the centre, through which information also passes
- *Family tree networks:* information begins at the top, and works its way down to each successive level, with little communication among members or across 'generations'
- *Spiders' web networks:* a clear centre which sets the direction, but with many sub-networks and webs of communications among members
- *Fishing-net or loose weaving networks:* the 'centre' can shift according to need, with many 'nodes' of communication throughout the network

Some major pitfalls are being resource-led rather than inspired by purpose and vision; a mis-match between formal structures and purpose; unclear or inappropriate membership criteria; a weak, outdated, or inappropriate system for communicating with and between members; and over-dependence on, or domination by, individual members or leaders.

The world of politics, power and people: The IBFAN Network

(From Carmen, 1996)

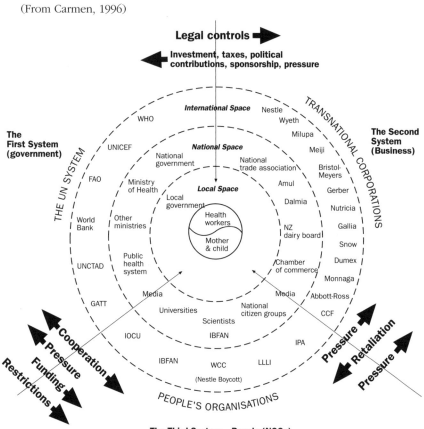

The Third System – People (NGOs)

The benefits and pitfalls of networks

The review of Oxfam's South-South Environment Linking Programme offered the following reflections on the benefits of networking, and the problems and pitfalls that can arise:

At their best, networks can:

- link isolated groups or people who would not otherwise interact
- raise awareness of specific issues

- build confidence among members or participants
- strengthen the capacities of NGOs and CBOs
- create a critical mass for action leading to policy change and other improvements
- bring greater weight to advocacy and lobbying
- reduce duplication and share skills
- increase cooperation and regional coordination
- 'scale up' activities and create synergy
- motivate and generate solidarity with people who confront seemingly overwhelming problems at the local level
- validate local and indigenous practices and culture
- broaden contacts with NGOs and others
- coordinate support and funding from donors.

But things may go wrong if networks:

- have unclear objectives
- are dominated by certain groups
- are centralised and bureaucratic
- are competing with or duplicating what other networks do
- have participants from very diverse backgrounds and realities
- face communication problems due to language, culture, or distance
- have concentrations of power, or unequal power relations
- are interfered with by donors
- lack human and financial resources, and organisational capacity
- cannot move from theory to practical action, since this requires additional resources
- face serious contextual problems, such as political constraints
- are unable to assess their own impact (Nelson, 1995, Appendix 8).

Since networks necessarily evolve, and must always be prepared to respond to new challenges and changing needs, a useful way to assess how well their forms and functions are matched is to use a 'lines of dynamic analysis' developed by Novib (quoted in Nelson, ibid.):

Time line: What is the history of the network, how has it evolved to its present situation, what future challenges lie ahead?

Vertical line: How has the leadership developed, what is the inter-connection between the 'top' and 'bottom' of the network? And between a central office and other members or involved participants? How do information and opinions travel — top down, or bottom up? What gets through and what gets blocked? Why?

Horizontal line: How do various people and activities of the network relate to each other? Is there an integral view? Are there tensions and contradictions between activities or people?

External line: How does the network articulate with other networks and organisations? For example, how does the network relate to governmental institutions and the media?

General context line: What is happening socially and politically around the network? How is that affecting the work? What new challenges are emerging?

International networks have occasionally been censured for excessive spending on travel, which could not be justified in terms of benefit to the organisation (though the same criticism could well be made in respect of the huge amounts of money that aid agencies spend each year on flying their staff around the globe). When such apparent distortions arise, the underlying problem is often one either of the network's over-dependence on certain individuals, or of unplanned, often resource-led, growth. A secretariat-style structure can easily produce a bureaucracy which consumes more than is spent on the network's central function. Networks may also try to diversify and take on activities, such as lobbying, for which they were not set up and are poorly qualified.

Networking is not an end in itself, nor does it necessarily contribute either to capacity-building or to development. The questions to be asked are not whether a network should spend less on foreign travel and more on its newsletter — these are choices for the members to make — but how effective the network and its activities are in shifting the overall balance of forces in favour of the poor; and how these could be more effective.

Belonging to a network only makes sense if the benefits outweigh the demands that membership will make. An organisation or group planning to join an existing network should first assess its own networking needs and priorities, and then decide how joining a given network will help to meet them. It may opt to join various networks, each for different purpose: for example, Oxfam UK and Ireland is an Affiliate of Oxfam International as well as being a member of the European NGO coalition (Eurostep), the Steering Committee for Humanitarian Response (SCHR), and scholarly networks such as the European Association of Development Research Institutes (EADI). Some of these are primarily for lobbying and policy debate; others provide access to new thinking on development issues.

Resources are critical. Networks need to meet their core costs (salaries, rents, infrastructure, and communication) and activities (workshops, publications, conferences). They may need access to contacts or information, or marketing or organisational assistance (See Chapter 5). Survival may mean embarking on membership drives, updating the membership package, or charging for some services. Networks that depend on members' dues may take this route: if their members are not satisfied with what they get, they will 'defect' to a more dynamic network. Others may opt to restrict the membership or scope, and to specialise their services. For example, the Arid Lands Information Network (ALIN) in Senegal has members from countries in arid and semi-arid areas of Africa who work in pastoralism, soil and water conservation, and dryland agriculture. Its members chose not to expand to a broader geographical area in order not to dilute ALIN's effectiveness. Recruitment to the network is done mostly by personal contact, and ALIN has a policy of insisting that the individual write a letter to the ALIN office to request membership. ALIN staff have been content to let the network grow at its own rate, rather than sending out publicity to recruit members. The aim has been to build up an active and committed membership, rather than simply to establish a large mailing list. It is easy to join the network, as long as a genuine interest is demonstrated (Graham, 1993).

Electronic networks

The number and scope of computer-based electronic networks is growing very rapidly, especially with the advent of the World Wide Web ('the Web') and Internet ('the Net') — a global 'network of networks' that links networks in academic and government institutes, libraries, businesses, and others. Electronic networks can provide access to information and contacts on an unprecedented scale, and add a global dimension to communication. The number of Internet users doubles every year, and the amount of traffic per user is growing even faster. The sheer speed of developments, and volume of what is available, underline the need to analyse the likely benefits of spending time and resources on electronic networking.[2]

Electronic networking — contacts or content?

The Cedar Centre is just one mile geographically but many miles economically from the smart shops of Canary Wharf [in London]. There was real excitement at the prospect of being given access to the Internet. Its global links could, it was claimed, help the area's broad mix of ethnic groups, including Bangladeshi, Chinese, Vietnamese and Somali, keep in touch with developments back home. But the excitement faded as staff and volunteers wrestled with slow and cumbersome software, finding little information on the Net of direct use.

> 'Some people thought we would immediately start swapping experiences via the Internet with a village in Bangladesh, but people in poor countries often don't have access to a telephone let alone a computer', says Helen Menezes.
>
> The Cedar Centre was chosen by Channel Four and the Scarman Trust for a Get Netted! project. On the theory that deprived communities are disempowered by lack of access to information, the project provided a computer and free Internet connection to see how information-poor communities would benefit from the technology.
>
> '[T]hese groups came with fresh eyes to the Internet and discovered a major weakness: that it is about contacts rather than content', says Matthew Pyke of the Scarman Trust. In response, the Trust ... has set up its own site, the Hive, aimed at providing indexed news and information relevant to people involved in community regeneration (Searle, 1996).

Electronic communication has enabled — even compelled — some existing networks to review their functions and revamp their ways of working. One such example is the long-standing Society for International Development (SID) which opted to use new information technology to facilitate 'living links' between its various national Chapters, and across several programme areas; and to bring on-line debate into the pages of its printed journal, *Development*.

But for all the appeal of the 'information super-highway', there is also the danger that it may exacerbate inequalities between North and South, introducing new forms of exclusion and poverty. For despite claims for their universality and openness, electronic and conventional telecommunications together represent only a tiny fragment of human communication.

Who is communicating with whom?

Percentage of the population with a mainline telephone:

- In Sweden, 69% of a population of 8.7 million
- In Poland, 9% of a population of 38.3 million
- In Peru, Botswana, and Paraguay, 2.7% of populations totalling 29 million.
- In China, India, Indonesia, and Sri Lanka, 0.7% of populations totalling 2,307.5 million.
- In Cambodia, Chad, Mali, Niger, Vietnam, and Zaire(now the Democratic Congo Republic), 0.1% of populations totalling 146.9 million.

- The USA has some 142 million phones — the equivalent of one for every two people. The USA and China are countries of comparable size. But although there are four times as many Chinese, the USA has 76 times as many mainline telephones.
- Both Switzerland and Bolivia have a population of 7.1 million. Yet there are about 4.3 million mainline telephones in Switzerland, compared with 178,000 in Bolivia, ie 24 times as many mainline telephones in Switzerland than in a country that is 26 times larger.
- In Finland, 7% have a mobile cellular phone; in Australia, 3%; in The Netherlands, 1%. In most developing countries, numbers are too small to register.
- There are two radios per head in the USA. But in Angola, Burkina Faso, Nepal, and Tanzania, there are fewer than 30 radios for every 1,000 people.
- There is only one television for every 100 people in Afghanistan, Angola, Bangladesh, Benin, Burundi, Central African Republic, Haiti, Laos, Mali, or DCR. This compares with 53 sets per 100 Danes.
- There are more televisions per person in Oman than in Canada, in Qatar than in the UK, in Barbados than in Bulgaria.

Dirt-track or super-highway?

The subversive potential of electronic communication was dramatically seen when the Mexican guerrilla leader, Sub-Cte Marcos, sent declarations to the 1995 World Summit for Social Development in Copenhagen direct from his secret headquarters in the Chiapas jungle. Elsewhere in Latin America, Amazonian indians and Peruvian peasant farmers also communicate with each other by cellular mobile phone. Spectacular exceptions aside, however, an assessment of the impact of electronic communication to 'democratise' the power relationships between people or countries, is less encouraging.[3] The terms 'information-rich' and 'information-poor' are now part of the development vocabulary; and, as Nelson Mandela stressed in the opening quotation to this Chapter, the gulf between them is becoming broader and deeper.

What does it mean to be 'information-rich' or 'information-poor'? We can gain an idea by asking who has the basic hardware, whose interests are served, and who is actually doing the electronic networking.

Who has computers? Electronic communication depends on access to basic hardware. In a period of only 10 years, PCs have become standard office and domestic equipment in the North; 96 per cent of the world's computers are in industrialised countries, which represent only 30 per cent of the world's population. The remaining 70 per cent are still on 'the information dirt-track' (Panos, 1995).

Further, since computer hardware and software are designed, developed and controlled by manufacturers in the USA, Japan, and Western Europe (Hamelink, 1995:3), as poorer countries modernise their communications systems, they will become more dependent on importing the technology and know-how. This is likely to be prohibitively expensive for most CBOs and many NGOs in the South.

Who has telephones? Electronic networks depend on access to a telephone line or another connection to computer networks (such as satellite or microwave links). As the figures quoted earlier show, such access is highly concentrated in the industrialised North. Many millions of people in the South have never used a telephone.

Who is communicating? Given the concentration of communication technology in the North, it is not surprising that information flows mainly among OECD countries. South-South communication accounts for only 10 per cent of all telephone, telex and fax traffic. Since March 1995, there have been more commercial servers on the Internet than all other types combined — including educational and government servers.

And with whom? Electronic networking is a complex literate medium that also requires 'computer literacy' and the ability to deal with instruction manuals and software that are poorly translated, or available only in English. Even experienced users require expert assistance from time to time. Such skills and back-up facilities are widely available in industrialised countries, where basic computer skills are now part of the primary school curriculum.

Equal access does not imply equal use. A 1995 survey of the Internet by the US Matrix Information and Directory Services found that male users outnumbered women by two to one. Further, while the democratic nature of electronic communication can be seen as a positive attribute, it also allows those who care little about human rights to disseminate their ideas. There is increasing concern about the use of the Internet to evade national legislation concerning pornography, the depiction of violence and sexual abuse, or the promotion of paedophile and other criminal networks. The issue of censorship is now being debated in the context of global electronic networks: the right to associate and to freedom of expression, on the one hand, and the right for individuals to be shielded from abuse, or for governments to protect the national interest, on the other.

To be 'information-poor' is, then, to be excluded from access to major existing knowledge systems, and from information and ideas that relate to global processes of social, cultural, and economic change. Such exclusion may derive from, and reinforce, material and other forms of poverty. It may be deepened by commercial interests that control access to and provision of information for private profit rather than the public good. Or it may be the result of deliberate efforts by governments or corporations to disinform or withhold information, or to restrict access to it. This exclusion systematically deprives poor countries, and poor or marginalised sectors within all countries, of the opportunity to participate fully and effectively in the process both of creating knowledge, and of shaping change in a way that will benefit them. Since information-poverty is a relative as well as an absolute condition, if the 'information-rich' become richer, the 'information-poor' will become correspondingly poorer.

The consumers of information and culture are seldom organised in associations to protect their interests. Concerns about how information and the related technology and know-how are controlled, and particularly the roles of states and private commercial interests, have been taken up by Third World Network (TWN) in Malaysia, the Centre for Communication and Human Rights in the Netherlands, the US-based Cultural Environment Movement, and the AMARC-World Association of Community Radio Broadcasters in Canada/Peru. These organisations hold the view that 'people should be active and critical participants in their social reality and capable of governing themselves' (Hamelink, 1996). The People's Communication Charter: An International Covenant of Standards and Rights[4] has been drawn up in order to provide a framework for reviewing the quality of the cultural environment in its widest sense.

Extravagant claims about global communications in the 'information age' must, therefore, be set against the material poverty in which most human beings live. Ease and speed of communication with someone on the other side of the planet can be a powerful resource in the defence of human rights. It will not, in and of itself, eradicate the poverty and oppression that constitute the daily abuse of those rights.

Global village or feudal estate?

We live in the information age, so we are always told, in which information is apparently as vital as agriculture and industry once were, an age of infinite possibilities in education and scholarship, teaching and research, economic growth and political freedom; a brave new world blessed with the open intimacies of the village, where the boundaries of national isolation and intellectual provincialism are withering away as knowledge explodes in its relentless march towards human

163

enlightenment. Extravagant claims, no doubt. Knowledge, as creed and commodity, as a proprietary privilege, reflects and reproduces the spatial and social divisions of power, old and new, material and ideological, between and within societies. The 'information highway' is a dangerous place for those on foot or riding ricketty bicycles. It is designed for, and dominated by, those driving courtesy of powerful and prestigious publishing systems and academic enterprises of the industrialised North, who churn out the bulk of the world's books, journals, databases, computers and software and other information technologies, and dictate international copyright and intellectual property laws to the information-poor world. A harmonious global village, it is not. A feudal estate, hierarchical and unequal, it may be.

...We need to unravel the content, the value, of the information. What social good has it generated? To what extent has the explosion of information led to more enlightened human relations within and among nations? Is the 'information highway' all speed, noise, and fury leading nowhere, and leaving behind only data-glut and confusion? In short, we must interrogate the ethics of information, the social and political morality of knowledge creation, consumption and content, and assess its record in bettering the human condition, not just materially, but in ennobling social relations, in uplifting the human spirit (Zeleza, 1996, p293).

But in spite of serious reservations both about the exaggerated claims that have been made, and about the growing gap between the information haves and have-nots, electronic networks have already significantly increased the potential for horizontal interaction and collaboration among thousands of civil society organisations worldwide. Simultaneous global communication allows individuals in several countries to work together on the same document, sharing comments, and reaching a consensus in far less time (and more cheaply) than via conventional means. Information, documents, and audio-visual material can be transmitted cheaply and quickly to anyone who has access to a compatible networking system. Databases and documents that are easily accessible electronically are often either unavailable in-country, or are prohibitively expensive. Further, there are no limitations on how long a document may be held, or restricted opening hours, as with a library or documentation centre. Users are not limited to a physical location, but can communicate whenever they like and from wherever they happen to be.

Many organisations also have a 'site' or 'Homepage' that enables them to display and update information and materials very easily. For instance, the UN agencies all have sites for press releases, databases, catalogues and publication samples, and news of developments in their respective fields. Since electronic communication is user-based, individuals decide whether to visit a site: this process of self-selection, in theory, ensures a good fit between the user and the provider of information, and avoids the expense and delay of printing and sending possibly unwanted written material by post.

Electronic conferencing enables users to 'post' information on a bulletin board (also called a 'Usenet newsgroup', a 'forum', or an 'e-mail mailing list') at a host computer, for exchanges on specific issues. 'Discussions' may not be systematic, and there is no mechanism to control the quality (or quantity) of what is contributed. But the process allows users to organise events or campaigns, to make direct 'on-line' contact, or to share information instead of or prior to face-to-face meetings. Many people prefer the perceived 'user-friendliness' of a more casual style of communication than is used in formal correspondence.

Many publications are available electronically, as well as or instead of the printed form. This offers readers different ways to use the same material. For instance, Oxfam's journals, *Development in Practice* and *Gender and Development* are also available 'on-line': this not only allows several people to read a single issue simultaneously, but also enables them to assemble their own selection of material and to conduct rapid bibliographic searches. Many reference books are now on CD-Rom, such as the annual publication *The World: A Third World Guide* published by the Third World Institute (ITeM) in Uruguay.

Handbooks and manuals abound, but there are also a number of handbooks for NGOs which cover everything from which basic equipment to instal through to critical descriptions of what benefits and problems to expect, and listings of important contacts.[5] Good advice is vital. As the Cedar Centre found, it can be demoralising and wasteful to invest in expensive equipment without also having adequate training and back-up in how to make best use of it.

Networking for change

A dynamic network is not just a cosy club. Its participants are active and keen not merely to reinforce their existing knowledge and beliefs, but also be introduced to new ideas. The ability of civil society organisations to 'scale-up' or enhance their impact depends on optimising the effectiveness and efficiency with which they influence change for the benefit of the poor — at a local, national, regional and, increasingly, global level. Whether those who are isolated and powerless can do this depends largely on their capacity to cross boundaries and collaborate with each other. Many people and organisations draw real strength and confidence just from knowing that they are not alone in their struggles.

8

Building capacity in crisis

The way to avoid 'dependency' is to maximise the area within which people are able to make decisions for themselves. This means emphasising their strengths rather than their needs. It means, for a refugee population, giving them as much control as possible over the allocation of scarce resources, including food, rather than 'putting them to productive work' and asking them what they would like others to do for, or to, them (Turton, 1993).

Introduction

For people who are living in poverty and on the margins of society, the difference between normal life and what outsiders define as a crisis may be marginal. Poverty and exclusion are themselves a kind of chronic emergency. Even very modest changes in their situation may enable poor people either to increase their toe-hold on survival; or plunge them into deeper crisis. It thus becomes meaningless to maintain rigid distinctions between relief and development assistance, or to define people's experience in terms of a linear progression along a 'relief-rehabilitation-development continuum'. For 'with the terrible exception of genocide, most deaths from war are not the direct result of violence and battle... it is a sad irony that the safest place to be in many of today's wars is probably the army'.[1] The biggest killers even in chronic conflicts are the malnutrition and diseases that arise from the poverty that may well have contributed to the conflict in the first place — but which are invariably exacerbated by it (Ardón, 1997).

To enable men and women not just to survive a critical situation, but also to transform it, aid interventions should support what people and their organisations are already doing themselves, and respect their priorities for change. For 'development' — in the sense of participation in political life, economic production, social organisation, the creation of alternative education and health services, forms of cultural expression, and international communication — continues even in situations of acute or chronic insecurity.

... many of the 1980s generation of [Salvadorean] NGOs are essentially the institutional expression of sectors of the urban and rural poor who organised to defend themselves from violence and repression... a concrete manifestation of the energy, creativity, and organisational and negotiating capacity developed by poor people, simply in order to survive
(Alvarez Solís and Martin, in Eade 1996b:52–53).

The need for relief aid thus co-exists with the need for other forms of support. Investment in capacity-building can enable poor people to respond to crisis more effectively in both the short and long term.

Crisis may be experienced on various levels, and in different ways. Conflict need not always be negative. An Oxfam study found that:

...so long as the social and political processes provide channels for dialogue, participation, and negotiation (such as community development work seeks to foster), conflict plays a constructive role. Where such channels are blocked, and yet basic needs go unmet, then resentment and desperation build up. The outcome is protest, repression and violence (Agerbak, in Eade 1996b:27).

In its most extreme and destructive expression, a response to crisis may thus take the form of organised violence, armed conflict, or war. This may be associated with a collapse in the state's authority or capacity to function, or with campaigns to take over national power or achieve regional secession. Contemporary warfare also tends to involve efforts by at least one of the warring parties deliberately to destroy the wider social fabric through means such as forced displacement, the gross and systematic abuse of human rights, the devastation of homes and property, and the destruction of markets and livelihoods. Civilians become a military target. Conflict may involve sustained hostility among different sectors within a population, or systematic abuse of or discrimination against certain groups. A major political crisis may be triggered by a natural event. For example, the 1974 earthquake in Guatemala unleashed a campaign of military terror that ended only with the 1996 Peace Accords. Or a single act, such as the assassination of the Burundian President in 1994, may precipitate chaos. Whatever its scale and dimensions, crisis represents a turning point, and change is inevitable.

The vast majority of the emergencies in which agencies such as Oxfam are involved are on a relatively 'manageable' scale in terms of the numbers of people affected, and the dimensions of their interventions. Occasionally, however, a crisis may result in, or exacerbate, suffering on such a scale that all that can be done is to ensure that survivors continue to survive. The role of the international community in Rwanda in 1994 has been criticised on many grounds (Millwood, 1996). The UN agencies and other official bodies are thought to have done too little, too late. By contrast, many NGOs tried to do too much, and too soon to have been able to assess their role in sufficient detail. Although perhaps as many as a million lives were saved as a result of swift and efficient provision of medical services and clean water, some lives were probably lost or endangered because of indecisiveness and inaction on the one hand, and through misguided or uncoordinated aid programmes on the other.

Where information is lacking or confused, it is difficult to decide how to act in the face of overwhelming need. However, if humanitarian aid is seen *only* in terms of material inputs, such as food aid, shelter, and medical supplies, vital as these are in many situations, it may weaken and undermine existing local capacities: economies, organisational forms, and self-confidence. There is also increasing evidence showing that humanitarian assistance may not only prolong the violence by feeding a 'war economy', but also affect the politico-military outcomes and even reinforce the underlying causes of the crisis (eg Duffield, 1995:24–25 and 27–31; Bryer and Cairns, 1997). In terms of social survival, emergency assistance may be just as critical in 'non-relief' areas such as agricultural production, employment, micro-enterprise, education, training, networking, lobbying, organisational development, awareness-raising — even leisure and cultural pursuits. Central Americans called this 'development for survival', Eritreans referred to it as 'bringing strength out of weakness'.

Since resolving a crisis entails negotiation between conflicting interests, the question of who has the power to make and enforce a decision is central. In earlier Chapters, a capacity-building approach to development has been described as one that aims to optimise poor people's chances 'to have a say in shaping critical decisions affecting their lives, through open and accountable political structures ... [and so] to be active participants in the process of social change' (Watkins,1995:15). Reducing the vulnerability of those who face real or potential threats, or who are marginalised within their societies, is another aspect of capacity-building. This calls for a subtle mix of short- and long-term responses, rather than an artificial division between relief and development assistance.

It is beyond the scope of this Chapter to dwell on the role(s) of humanitarian aid in 'complex political emergencies'. The principal lessons that concern us here are first, that aid agencies require a high level of understanding of the political, social, legal — and ethical — complexities in order to intervene in a responsible fashion, as well as to monitor the impact of their interventions. Second, that however effective in its own terms, humanitarian assistance cannot substitute for political action; and is seldom the most significant factor in ensuring people's security and well-being. And third, that humanitarian aid cannot be 'neutral'. Neutrality may be perceived by one side as opposition, by another as support for its political or military agenda (Thompson, 1996:327); and material aid will to some extent be part of the political economy of war. Far from having impartial observer status within civil conflict, civil society is 'part of the field of battle' (Duffield, 1995:36; Ardón, 1997). This does not mean that civil society organisations cannot be effective channels for the delivery of humanitarian assistance, but that aid agencies need to understand how they themselves, as well as their potential counterparts, fit into the wider dynamics of the conflict (Slim, 1997). (An annotated bibliography to the current literature can be found in Eade (ed) 1996b: 98–109.)

The Chapter's opening section describes in greater detail the Capacities and Vulnerabilities Analysis (CVA) referred to in Chapter 2. This is followed by a discussion of some of the issues to consider in channelling humanitarian assistance through, for example, government structures as opposed to grass-roots organisations. The third section sketches out five areas (apart from their material welfare) in which people are vulnerable to crisis, and where well-designed assistance can be provided to reduce this vulnerability. These areas are: security and protection; information and contacts; social and cultural organisation; access to power and decision-making; and building for a future. The intention is to emphasise the potential to strengthen the capacities of poor communities, even in times of crisis.

Examples are drawn from Oxfam's own experience in supporting humanitarian relief work, though the issues raised are not peculiar to emergencies. Although these focus on assistance at the grassroots level, it may also be important to strengthen local government capacity: this is particularly so in operational programmes, where there is a strong risk of by-passing or undermining local authorities, with negative long-term consequences. Similarly, if assistance is channelled through local CBOs or NGOs, these may also require support for their own organisational development. There is a danger that the availability of resources may encourage them to expand rapidly and in ways that are unsustainable (see, for instance, Zetter, 1996; Goodhand and Chamberlain, 1996; Alvarez Solis and Martin, in Eade (ed) 1996b). Other chapters of this book deal in more detail with approaches to building the capacity of organisations.

Reducing people's vulnerability to crisis

Capacities and Vulnerabilities Analysis

In the late 1980s, a major inter-agency project was set up to establish a framework within which to combine development and relief activities (Anderson and Woodrow: 1989). This recommended that aid agencies analyse both the long-term factors affecting people's ability to respond to major political or physical events and their susceptibility to crisis, as well as the resulting needs (the immediate requirements for survival or recovery from a crisis). People's underlying vulnerabilities intensify the severity of disasters, impede response, and continue beyond the crisis. Examples are a lack of resources for subsistence, such as land; or forms of social and economic exclusion. Needs may be immediate and short-term, such as for food or medicine; and also relate to specific vulnerabilities. For example, while an entire refugee population may need supplementary food, the needs of children who were malnourished prior to the crisis may be acute.

... the concept of vulnerability is the starting point — and an important guide — for programming. As we identify certain groups as vulnerable and needing assistance, we must also identify the sources of their vulnerability. Why are these people in this context vulnerable? What decisions and choices have been made — and by whom — that have created the circumstances and put them at risk? (Anderson, 1994:331).

Poverty invariably makes people more vulnerable to the linked phenomena of variable climatic conditions, inadequate or degraded land, conflict, and population displacement. Each of these may be compounded by political questions. In analysing vulnerabilities and needs, it is important to:

• be aware of problems that are likely to arise, and avoid activities that may compound them;
• be alert to how conflict or aid could be used,whether by the state, armed factions, or other governments, to further their own ends;
• know who is providing support (financial, moral, ideological, logistical or military) from within and outside the area.

While this awareness will not enable aid agencies to predict the future, it will enable them to identify potential dangers and interests to be recognised in designing responses to crisis.

A Capacities and Vulnerabilities Analysis (CVA) relates both to material or physical factors, and also to the less tangible aspects of what makes some people stronger or weaker in the face of crisis — for example, their level of social organisation and motivation. In a crisis, a society's vulnerabilities are more noticeable than its capacities. Within a given set of people, these strengths and weaknesses vary according to factors such as gender, age, wealth, class, and cultural identity. They also evolve as people adapt to changes in their situation. A capacity-building approach aims to enable people to retain and build on their existing capacities, and to identify and address factors which undermine their security.

When assistance is provided to people 'to meet their needs' without regard to their existing capacities, very often the capacities that they possess are undermined and weakened by the overpowering presence of the aid giver. When this occurs, vulnerabilities are often increased rather than reduced by aid. An adequate notion of vulnerability, then, must take account of people's capacities (Anderson, 1994: 328).

CVA stresses the links between a society's past, present, and future. To respond effectively to today's crisis means looking at its underlying causes as well as how a given intervention may affect different people's capacities in the future. Project-based aid interventions (not only in emergencies) have often served to make people more vulnerable in the long term, by encouraging dependency, for example. Or they have strengthened some people at the expense of others, as for instance when men take over responsibility for resources previously controlled by women.

Lessons from 41 case studies

Programming decisions

1 To do nothing is better than to do something badly. Agencies should not intervene in a crisis unless it is to support local capacities.

2 There is no such thing as relief projects that are neutral in terms of development. They either support it or undermine it.

3 Indigenous agencies are in a better position to respond developmentally than outside agencies. Outside agencies that are already present are better able to respond than those arriving to deal with the crisis.

4 Agencies that identify themselves as development agencies can provide creative relief in an emergency, especially in areas where they are already involved in long-term work.

5 Development agencies that work in areas prone to crisis should understand the need not only to anticipate the effects of disasters on their long-term work but also to address people's vulnerabilities through that work.

Principles

1 Relief work should be held to development standards. Thus every disaster response should be based on an appreciation of local capacities and should be designed to support and increase these.

2 Development work should be concerned with long-term sustainability. Thus every development programme and project should anticipate and be designed to prevent or mitigate disasters. Thus, they should identify and address the vulnerabilities of the people with whom they work and ensure that these are reduced over time.

3 Both relief and development should be more concerned with increasing local capacities and reducing vulnerabilities than with providing goods, services or technical assistance. In fact goods and services should be provided only insofar as they support sustainable development by increasing local capacities and reducing vulnerabilities.

4 The way that such resources are transferred must be held to the same test.

5 Programming must not be solely pre-occupied with meeting urgent needs but must integrate such needs into efforts that address the social/organisational and motivational/attitudinal elements.

(Adapted from Anderson and Woodrow, 1989.)

Pre-crisis support

... the lives of many millions of poor people are lived out in a state of permanent emergency— families are evicted from their dwellings by force, women are beaten and raped in their own homes, children are abused and exploited by adults. Arguably, if basic rights to representation, to a livelihood and to security are addressed before the eruption of armed conflict, the outcomes may be different (Williams (1995:23).

People may or may not be aware that they are exposed to major hazards, or to situations that place them or their families at risk, or that their rights are being violated. But their lack of power and resources prevent them from either reducing the risks, pressing the relevant institutions to do so, or escaping from an oppressive situation. The most effective responses to the violation of rights will involve a combination of organisational support, education, awareness-raising, and lobbying. In terms of physical hazards, once the risks have been identified ('risk-mapping'), it may be possible at least to reduce them through disaster preparedness and mitigation activities. These could be such measures as early-warning systems to enable economic and logistic steps if food shortfalls are likely; and the construction of dykes or embankments to protect against flooding.

Pre-crisis support can also strengthen people's economic and social capacity to cope with recurring and predictable events such as drought. So-called 'coping mechanisms' or 'survival strategies' are a response to dwindling resources which are both anticipatory (insurance mechanisms) and reactive (disposal of assets). Their effectiveness depends on how well people can guarantee their entitlements to a range of commodities and resources. These strategies and mechanisms may in turn be linked with actual or potential conflict (Keen, 1993; de Waal, 1991), and include:

diversification: of crops, foods, livestock, markets, occupations;

exchange: acquiring cash or goods through sale, barter, borrowing, or charity from richer relatives and neighbours;

dietary adjustments: eating less or poorer quality food;

migration and employment: individual migration in search of work, to increase incomes, decrease the demand on the household's resources, or avoid or avert political repression, such as forced recruitment of boys and men — mass migration is a last resort;

changes in intra-household resource distribution: certain household members (usually women and often girls) eating less, or being given less to eat, in order to protect others' (usually men's, and sometimes boys') consumption.

Such strategies may help to prevent famine in the short-term, but may damage long-term food security, be environmentally destructive, and in themselves involve a degree of suffering. When the next crisis threatens, survivors have fewer assets, and may be in poorer health, and so will be more vulnerable than before (Keen,1993). The aim of intervention measures, whether economic or environmental, is to support existing strategies in ways that also help to reduce their potentially adverse consequences.

Post-crisis rehabilitation and reconstruction

The underlying causes of avoidable vulnerability are generally political and economic — lack of assets, work, land, education, food, markets, or health care; and the inability to press for these needs to be met. Rehabilitation needs may be for help in coping with practical problems, and also support to develop organisational, political, economic, material and technical capacity. This may mean, for instance, simultaneously supporting an organisation of displaced people or returned refugees to lobby the government for housing

173

subsidies to which they are entitled, and funding an NGO specialising in low-cost housing.

The experience of war, as well as its practical consequences, affect people profoundly. Both during and after an armed conflict, reconstruction entails a vast range of adjustments (Ardón, 1997; Chirwa, 1997; Pearce, 1997; Thompson, 1997a and 1997b). New strategies and skills may be needed, because people's previous way of life may no longer be viable or attractive to them. Land titles may have changed hands; savings and belongings may have been lost or destroyed; families and communities may no longer be intact. Most people have experienced loss and emotional trauma; some may be physically disabled as a result of war injuries.

Social relations and expectations may also have changed. Refugees may return with new skills, resources, and attitudes. Children who have never lived in their home country, or outside a refugee camp, must adapt to an unfamiliar reality. Demobilised soldiers (including child-soldiers), ex-combatants, or former detainees must re-adjust to civilian life — and most find this a difficult process (Ardón, 1997; Castelo-Branco, 1997; Tunga, 1997). There may be resentment towards those who were involved in the violence, or towards those who are thought to have escaped it. Further, the 'price' of peace and reconciliation is often to confer amnesty on the perpetrators of human rights violations, as in Argentina, El Salvador or Guatemala. The victim-survivors may see this as a denial of their own right to basic justice, as some have argued in the case of the Truth and Reconciliation Commission in South Africa. Others may argue that the past must be buried in order to move forward. Rehabilitation is not so much a question of returning to normality, as of creating consensus around a new set of norms (Chirwa, 1997). This may pose dilemmas for aid agencies, whose counterparts may be calling for legal action or for reparation, while the government regards this as disrupting a fragile peace. Most post-war societies find that negotiating the transition process itself takes a great deal of time, energy, and diplomatic effort.

Rehabilitation and reconstruction assistance should therefore focus on helping people to function within a new social, economic, and political environment rather than on trying to return to the past. For example, during a war women often develop the skills and experience to fulfil non-traditional civil and economic functions. Among the combatants, women may fight alongside men — in El Salvador as in liberation wars in Ethiopia and elsewhere, there have been women at the highest ranks. As combatants are demobilised, they may not wish to revert to being subordinate to men. However, it is not uncommon for women to be expected in peace-time to return to the home and leave the public domain (with higher status and better paid employment) to men — a line that is often reinforced by pro-natalist state policies in the post-war period. Gender-based conflicts may thus be a feature of post-war reconstruction.

Channels for responding to crisis and conflict

A wide range of inter-related bodies are involved in shaping a response to a major crisis, from UN agencies and peace-keeping forces to national or local government, mandated bodies such as ICRC, specialised NGOs contracted by official agencies, human rights or election monitors, religious structures, independent NGOs, civil society organisations of various kinds, armed groups, and political parties. In addition, there may be numerous NGOs, some highly experienced and others less so.

By 'focusing on the relief activity while eschewing analysis of the external crisis' aid agencies may contribute to a process whereby 'complex situations are depoliticised and presented as technical issues' (Duffield, 1995:23). In highly politicised settings, there are major implications in providing assistance through a government-approved channel as opposed to an NGO that is (or is thought to be) politically affiliated to the opposition, or to a community in a region that is contested militarily. It may make a significant difference to support a provincial or regional government structure, rather than going through central government. A welter of organisations may spring up in response to the availability of funds and material aid. Some of these exist largely in order to 'articulate the infinite local demand for patronage and external resources' (op.cit. p32). Choosing between them on the basis of little or no prior knowledge, and little or no access to the areas in which they claim to work, may present aid agencies with very difficult choices: by opting to channel assistance through a particular institution, a donor or aid agency may be implicitly signalling its own political position with respect to the crisis.

Although civilians are often military targets in contemporary warfare, people usually prefer to stay close to their homes even when this exposes them to danger. Non-combatants may be assumed to have certain political sympathies simply because of where they live, or because of their ethnic or cultural identity. In extreme cases, areas of a country may be closed to outsiders, while 'scorched earth' or 'search and destroy' operations are mounted, with the indiscriminate deployment of anti-personnel mines, to terrorise the local people, or force them to leave the area. If found, they may be tortured, killed, or imprisoned. Atrocities go unwitnessed, unreported, and are denied. Civilians may depend for their survival more on energetic human rights work than on humanitarian relief.

At the same time, these civilians may be in great physical need. Even if crops and livestock have not been destroyed, they may have been neglected as people are forced to move from place to place. It may be necessary for aid agencies to work through trusted intermediaries if they are unable to make first-hand assessments. For instance, during the worst period of the civil wars in El Salvador and Guatemala:

Oxfam channelled humanitarian aid for civilians in the conflict zones mainly through intermediary NGOs and church-based organisations (Catholic, ecumenical, and protestant). The basic criteria were that they had unique access to people in these areas, and that they were highly trusted by the affected population. Their analytical capacity and ability to engage at a political level were especially critical during the early 1980s, when Oxfam and similar agencies had virtually no access to the regions in which this humanitarian work was being carried out, owing to the high levels of armed repression (Ardón, 1997:121, my translation).

Armed conflict interferes with existing 'coping mechanisms', even when the population remains relatively stable. For example, an Oxfam-commissioned study on Africa found that the disruption of strategies on which semi-subsistence economies depended seriously exacerbated the effects of famine (Keen, 1993). Other research has also revealed the ways in which war and survival strategies inter-relate (de Waal, 1991). Disruption may include restrictions on people's freedom of movement or right to bring in goods such as seeds, fertilisers, medicines, or household items, making people more vulnerable in the longer term. For instance, farmers may be forced to adopt high-cost and unsustainable agricultural practices since they cannot use methods which require stability, such as integrated pest management. Under fire, their immediate options are to sacrifice sustainability in order to ensure physical survival, or to seek asylum and become dependent on international assistance.

Conflict may also be associated with a breakdown in social norms and sanctions. Rape and sexual abuse is often part of a strategy of terror, humiliation, and social destruction, during and after war — and was deplored as such at the 1993 UN World Conference on Human Rights (WCHR). Long-term conflicts — lasting for decades in Angola, Guatemala, or Lebanon — have left a legacy of social as well as material dislocation that will take decades to heal (Ardón, 1997). But victims are also survivors: resourceful people who engage actively with those around them. Rather than transplanting Western models of individual counselling, aid agencies should:

... aim to augment efforts to stabilise and repair the war-torn social fabric and to allow it to regain some of its traditional capacity to be a source of resilience and problem solving for all. Self-organisation, empowerment, work and training, support to traditional forms of coping and healing: these terms may be truisms in the social development lexicon, but they remind us that people cannot fully regain control of their lives, and recover from war, as mere recipients of charity and care (Summerfield, 1996:30).

Assessing diverse needs

Formal or extensive consultation may be unfeasible in the midst of war, in the initial stages of a relief programme, or where local social structures are weak or non-existent. However, establishing the *principle* of consultative planning makes it possible to build on imperfect beginnings (see, for instance, Neefjes and David, 1996).

Most adult refugees and displaced persons are women. They have ideas and opinions, even if they do not express these in public. The priorities defined by men may not coincide with what women would identify, were they able to express their views. However, formal or traditional leaders are likely to be men, as are camp officials. Most local government, senior agency personnel, and technical staff are male. Decisions may thus be made by men, even when these concern women's needs, or areas of work for which women are mainly responsible. A 1993 internal report from by Oxfam's office in Sudan said:

Approaches to emergencies as they currently stand blatantly hand the power over women's traditional affairs to men ... running food distribution, water programmes, blanket, jerrycan and other distributions ... re-assigning the women's traditional responsibilities for food and shelter provision to men.

Women may be consulted about proposed washing facilities, or about their children. But even in 'normal' situations, women are not always treated as adults with their own rights, needs and perspectives; much less as active agents of social stability or transformation. Aid agencies may know very little about women's previous lives; and even less about how these have changed, or will have to change, as a result of crisis (Pearce, 1997). To build on women's capacities, it is vital to:

- pay attention to their views in assessing an emergency;
- take into account their actual responsibilities, both domestic (household subsistence, health, child care) as well as economic, in determining consultation processes;
- include them at all levels of planning, decision-making, implementation, and evaluation;
- consider the problems faced by women-maintained households when designing and implementing relief programmes;
- consider the situation faced by unaccompanied women, lone parents, and widows;
- identify and address issues of legal, sexual, physical and emotional protection.

Women may also have little free time for meetings, or be unable to read and write, or to speak the national language. Their involvement may be facilitated by arranging for women-only meetings at a convenient hour, and providing childcare; and by using methods that do not rely on literacy.

Gathering and interpreting information is always a sensitive issue: further, victim-survivors of rape, torture, or other physical abuse may be reticent to confide in others. Indirect ways of allowing their experiences and feelings to be expressed might be in a discussion circle on health, or a mutual support group for widows or lone mothers. Women's concerns may be to do with reproductive health or with fear of abuse or harassment, matters which they would prefer not to discuss with men present. Equally, men may not feel able to talk about their experiences of atrocities in front of women.

Local organisations

Two basic criteria for considering any organisation as a potential channel of relief assistance are, firstly, that it has access to the population that needs help, and is trusted by and accountable to it; and, secondly, that it will offer humanitarian assistance in a fair and efficient way. Existing CBOs or local NGOs are often keen to be involved. While their technical experience may be limited, they know the context, and enjoy the trust of at least some, if not all, of the people in need. They usually have a more sensitive understanding of the situation than have outside aid agencies, and can move around more freely and discreetly than can foreigners.

Such organisations may, however, lack experience in project management, or in handling large budgets, or managing rapid growth. They may need support in the form of office equipment and stipends for aid workers or volunteers. Assistance in training, financial and other planning, project design, and organisational management may also be needed. The aim should be to build on existing skills rather than displacing them with skills and services brought in from outside. It is equally important to avoid building up a resource-driven infrastructure, with no provision for how to 'wind down' or consolidate when the pressure is off (Zetter, 1996). In their study of how donor policies were reflected in the behaviour of NGOs in Afghanistan, Jonathan Goodhand and Peter Chamberlain concluded that 'capacity building should not be limited to "skilling up" organisations, or providing a technical fix. It implies a wider dialogue, based on shared values and ethics' (Goodhand with Chamberlain, 1996:206). This call for dialogue and 'accompaniment' has been echoed by aid workers in other long-term conflicts (Ardón, 1997; Thompson, 1996, 1997a).

Local organisations given a role in distribution may come under considerable pressure to favour certain groups and individuals over others. Any existing biases — for example, in favouring members of a particular political faction, religious faith, or ethnic group — are likely to be intensified with the advent of significant resources. Relationships of patronage may develop where they had not existed before.

Community-based solidarity: beyond the assumptions

Oxfam UK/I responded to floods in Bangladesh in 1995 with a programme that reached about 200,000 people. Oxfam consulted and offered assistance through seven long-standing partners, who in turn worked directly at the community level. An internal evaluation conducted by Tahmina Rahman found, however, that the community structures had actively discriminated against those who most needed help; and that the soft-loan programme had unwittingly benefited men, and not women.

Firstly, community groups were asked to identify the people they thought were most vulnerable. A large number of these people who were not in fact receiving assistance were girls aged nine to 15 years, elderly men and women, and disabled children. The community groups recognised that these individuals were the ones most at risk and unable to take care of themselves. They explained, however, that they did not qualify for assistance as they were not formal group members. Existing members felt that they had first claim on any resources because they had put in time and work; while the more vulnerable people did not participate in any group activities because they could not pay subscriptions or attend meetings.

Secondly, soft loans given to women as part of the rehabilitation programme had been used mainly to create economic activities for their husbands and sons, with the women's role being that of intermediary and repayers of the credit. It is doubtful that these loans helped to empower women. Further, the loans set up dependency patterns (for example, on women's capacity to negotiate loans for the benefit of men) that outlived the short-term relief component of the programme.

(Based on a summary of Tahmina Rahman's report in *Links*, June 1996.)

Supporting relief work through local organisations enables them to gain experience which will be of use in the future, and may reduce the risk of inappropriate action by foreign agencies that are working in an unfamiliar environment. It also defuses the resentment that may arise when local people are disregarded by outsiders confident that they know best how relief should be organised.

However, we should not always assume that local organisations are necessarily the most appropriate intermediaries, just because they are indigenous. Building relief programmes on bad development leads inevitably to bad relief!

Local authorities

In the case of so-called natural disasters or catastrophes, government and civil authorities usually have formal responsibilities to undertake relief work, co-ordinate operations, and protect the affected population. For instance, following major earthquakes in Mexico and in India, the respective governments insisted that the civil authorities handle the immediate search and rescue phase, and coordinate the subsequent relief efforts. International agencies were expressly requested not to intervene at this stage. Sensitivities over the causes of the crisis, and over the official response to it, may be heightened by media attention and international pressure.

Although they may welcome international aid, local authorities may resent NGOs which operate autonomously. Equally, NGOs may be frustrated by regulations, delays and restrictions hampering what they believe to be urgent work. Where feasible, NGOs should at the earliest opportunity consult the competent local authorities and establish working protocols and scope for collaboration in order to avoid undermining their capacity and authority (see Chapter 2). Government departments, for instance, often have trained professionals who could be offered secondments to assist in the relief programme. However, when they offer better salaries and career opportunities to experienced and qualified government staff, agencies should reflect on the overall impact of reducing the number of high-quality personnel in government departments, and consider ways to meet this deficit. Looking to the impact of relief assistance in the longer term, and particularly in a post-crisis period, there are often creative ways to strengthen the capacity of government departments. As Oxfam found in Zambia, even something as simple as facilitating direct contact between government officials and grassroots groups can make a difference to the way in which the former perceive the problems (Pushpanath, 1994).

Clearly, there are many situations in which it is inappropriate to coordinate humanitarian relief programmes through local authorities or government structures. In the case of civil war or a counter-insurgency campaign, where the government is one of the warring parties, it may be impossible to work on both sides of the conflict, or even to work openly at all. The main concern for a humanitarian organisation must be to identify the channels that offer the best hope of reaching people in need. In some settings, that may mean working through organisations that are directly or indirectly in opposition to the government.

Specific vulnerabilities in crisis

Personal security and protection

Crisis may involve actual or threatened infringements of people's basic rights and fundamental freedoms as outlined in the Universal Declaration of Human Rights (UDHR) and subsequent Protocols and Covenants (see Eade and Williams, 1995:pp 27–46). States bear the ultimate responsibility for guaranteeing these rights. However, it is frequently states and governments themselves that either fail to provide adequate and equal protection to every individual, or curtail, abuse or violate the rights and freedoms of some citizens.

Refugees are *by definition* people whose rights are not guaranteed by the government of their country, and who have a 'well-founded fear of persecution'. Every human being has the right to seek asylum when faced with such a fear. In doing so, refugees appeal to the international community (often via UNHCR) to protect their rights and well-being. Persons displaced within their own country have no such automatic right to international protection, since this raises issues of national sovereignty. However, UNHCR may, and often does, seek a mandate to work with people 'in refugee-like situations', including those who are internally displaced or who are returning to their country or place of residence after having been forced to flee.

This protection entails, among other things, attention to physical welfare and provision of legal protection and documentation. Refugees and displaced persons may not be able to produce important personal papers such as birth or marriage certificates, or passports, or other proofs of identity. Often such documents are held by or in the name of the male 'head of household', who may not be present. Registration or ration cards may not be issued to adult women, but to their husbands or partners. Without documents of their own, women and children become more vulnerable to harassment or exploitation. Without proof of identity or qualifications, it may be harder to find paid employment or to travel within a country, or across borders. Children born in exile may become effectively stateless — denied the nationality of their host country, and without papers from their parents' country of origin. While the UDHR stipulates that every person has the right to a nationality, for refugees and displaced persons this right is easily eroded in practice.

The right to seek asylum is also one that is easily disregarded, as governments focus on what they perceive as *their* right to stem immigration. The number of asylum-seekers arriving in industrialised countries rose sharply in the late 1980s and early 1990s: almost ten times as many people applied for asylum in the UK in 1991 as in 1985 (though this number had almost halved by 1996). This period also saw increased restrictions on immigration, particularly in the USA and Western Europe; and ever harsher treatment of asylum-seekers.

The EU enacted legislation placing the burden of responsibility for asylum on the country of 'first safe arrival'. Airline companies have become subject to government-imposed fines if they carry passengers whose documents are not in order. In the UK, asylum-seekers must establish their claim on arrival, and face serious hardship because their rights to housing and social benefits were all but removed by the former Conservative government. In 1996, only six per cent of applicants to the UK were granted asylum; many of the remaining 94 per cent are likely to be caught up in lengthy and expensive appeals for years to come.

Until recently, another disregarded protection issue was that of *sexual violence*. The systematic use of rape and sexual violence in contemporary conflicts has brought a greater awareness of the extent of a problem that has always been a fact of war — not only before and during flight, but also in the very place of refuge. Victims are usually women and girls; the extent to which boys and men are subjected to sexual torture by their captors is little known (Large, 1997). Refugees most at risk are unaccompanied women, lone female heads of household, children who are unaccompanied or in foster-care arrangements, and anybody who is held in detention or detention-like situations.

Sexual violence covers 'all forms of sexual threat, assault, interference and exploitation, including molestation without physical harm or penetration' (UNHCR, 1995: 3). It can involve the use or the threat of force, including that of forcing a person to witness or participate in acts of sexual violence. As a form of torture, it is intended to 'hurt, control and humiliate, violating a person's innermost physical and mental integrity' (ibid, p 3). Fear — whether of reprisals by the assailant(s) or of ostracism by the victim's own community — feelings of shame and guilt, or the knowledge that the perpetrators will not be prosecuted, contribute to under-reporting. Apart from the physical and emotional damage for any victim of sexual abuse, the consequences for women may include unwanted pregnancies, and for both sexes the risk of STDs and HIV/AIDS.

The perpetrators of sexual violence are almost always men. They may be members of the security forces in the country of origin or of refuge; smugglers who assist refugees in exchange for sexual favours; camp or international aid officials; members of the local community in the host country; other refugees, or members of their own family. In addition, 'coercive prostitution' or sex-trafficking may occur (ibid, p 5).

Surviving sexual violence

Amina had had to cross the border [into Bangladesh] with her children as the members of the Burmese paramilitary force 'Lone Htein' started raiding their villages to collect the able-bodied people as forced labour.

'Lone Htein' were not happy with only able-bodied men, they took the women as well in their camps for 'household' work. They targeted women-headed families as the easiest sources when they were looking for young girls to take advantage of. First they asked for money in lieu of male labour, then livestock, then poultry. If nothing was available, they would take a girl. This happened to Amina. First they took her life-savings of 500 kyats, two goats, and gold earrings. The second time, when she had nothing to offer, they asked her to hand over her 12-year-old daughter just for two or three days. 'I refused and cried. Then they took me to their camp and they kept me there the whole night. Next day they released me but took me again the following day for another two nights.'

Many of the women arrived with a history of rape, and came from divided families with lost husbands or children. They may have been unaccompanied, possibly pregnant or with VD, but they had little hope of being treated sympathetically by male doctors. They have found themselves in camps where the space for them to lead anything but the most restricted lives is unavailable, and where the level of curiosity at what they had been through made them the object of unwelcome attention from the media and local population.

It became very hard to find a safe place for women who suffered at the hands of the forces on the other side of the border; the same vulnerability followed them like a shadow, even in a friendly country. We have heard allegations of harassment of women by security forces at the water collection points, and regular sexual abuse of refugee women by the security forces has also been reported. It is not easy to address these problems in a situation when all the camp officials are men and they work through the — mostly male — Mahjhis. (Wahra, 1994:47).

UNHCR stresses the role played by its own protection and legal officers as well as health workers in sensitising the refugee and local population and the security forces to the issues, in order to create a climate which does not tolerate sexual abuse, in which victims can trust that their needs will be met sensitively and confidentially. Once the reality of sexual violence is recognised, it is easier to take steps to reduce its incidence. UNHCR has found that community self-protection is critical in every respect: from involvement in ensuring that the location and layout of a camp enhances their physical security (for example, by not grouping women-headed households together unless they can be adequately guarded, or ensuring that women's washing and toilet facilities are near to their homes, and that paths to them are well-lit), to finding mechanisms for discussion and settling disputes, providing opportunities for work and leisure, taking steps to combat drug and alcohol abuse, or running public information campaigns and training sessions.

These approaches both depend on, and reinforce, a level of organisational capacity among the refugee or displaced population — men as well as women. In this way, addressing the source of people's vulnerability can also become a way to build their capacity to organise to protect their interests.

Information and contacts

The lack of access to reliable information concerning one's current situation or future options is profoundly disempowering. At best, it undermines people's capacity to determine their own interests; at worst, it leaves them prey to rumours or to the deliberate manipulation of information for political or military purposes. Rwandan refugees in former-Zaire were in this situation, with propaganda and disinformation being used to spread fear and division among them (Lumisa Bwiti, 1997).

Further, when people are ignorant of their legal rights, it is easier for these to be denied or blatantly violated by others. Repressive régimes will go to great lengths to maintain certain population groups (such as detainees or marginalised minorities) in ignorance, and to isolate them from the outside world. People who know what their rights are, and which national and international organisations will defend them, are in a better position both to insist on these rights and to denounce violations. The committees of families of the 'disappeared' throughout Latin America, or of war widows in countries like Peru and Guatemala, are extraordinary examples of how 'ordinary' people have mobilised around human rights issues.

Access to information and contacts i thus not only a need, but also a powerful tool for mobilising and effective response to crisis.

Alliances for advocacy

In Colombia, indigenous organisations in conflict areas had excellent community and regional organisation, but weak national alliances and no international relations. They were capable of strong opposition, in their region, to large extractive projects which threatened to dispossess them of their land and livelihoods. However, they were unable to get negotiations with the national government and élites who were determined to gain access to the oil, gold, and hardwoods which the indigenous land held. This heightened tension was leading to increased use of violence by élites. By expanding their contacts to a Canadian indigenous organisation (who had a weak organisational base but strong national and international presence), the Colombian organisations gained significant international profile, including press and seats at the UN to denounce their situation: this forced the national government to negotiate. (Bloomer in Buell, 1996: Appendix B.)

The importance of information for refugees is overlooked by aid agencies, who may initially be more concerned with extracting information from those affected than with providing it to them. Information may also be filtered by outsiders who decide what refugees 'need' to know. They may be given details about a feeding programme, but not be able to find out what is going on in their home country, or internationally. Rationing information in this way can deprive people of the right to make their own political judgements.

Similarly, aid agencies are often sought out by the media and by international bodies, to speak 'on behalf' of the affected population. Their motives may be tactically sound: if an aid agency can help to resolve a crisis by acting as an advocate for those affected by it, it should of course do so. But in strategic terms, it should also ask how far speaking on behalf of others actually empowers *them* to speak out for themselves — and what more could be done to enable this to happen.[2]

Information and empowerment

Oxfam's approach to the 1992–93 drought in Zambia also showed that when local people steer their own campaigning and advocacy work, the results are more far-reaching than if this had been organised on their behalf by international aid agencies:

Communication is a vital component of relief work, and ... our investment repaid positive dividends, in helping people to gain greater control over the relief efforts. The voices of ordinary people were heard, loud and clear, placing those in power under pressure to respond quickly and sensitively to their demands.

Villagers and civil servants for the first time experienced the power of the media and other communication channels to influence events and bring about positive change for the benefit of disadvantaged and voiceless people. It was a significant departure for Zambian NGOs to see, appreciate, and make use of these opportunities. ... The way in which the district volunteers were dealt with by the village participants in a recent workshop, especially by the women who stood their ground in wanting direct dealing with Oxfam, is a case in point. Their new-found self-confidence had come from the actual experience of doing things, having access to information, confronting those in positions of superiority, and removing those who obstructed the smooth running of the programme. All this does not mean that villagers have for ever overcome their powerless and silence, and will never revert to the obedience and meekness of the past. Rather, the experience has shown that there are alternatives, and has given them confidence to believe that these are possible. That is perhaps the most important lesson to learn from this experience (Pushpanath, 1994:88–90).

Social and cultural organisation

Forms of social and cultural organisation are dynamic. They develop over time, and in response to external change. In situations of crisis, existing organisations, such as co-operatives or unions, may collapse or even become the target of attack. Alternatively, they may be reinforced as people seek security within them, as were the Christian Base Communities in El Salvador throughout the 1980s. New forms of organisation may emerge in response to the crisis. Tradition may sustain certain aspects of a society, while rapid adaptation to change may also be a survival mechanism: if most refugees and displaced persons are women and children, they must necessarily take on new or untraditional roles, including those previously undertaken by men.

Organisational capacities may already exist, which may be adapted to enable men and women to deal with change constructively. People may simultaneously be taking on new roles, and needing to cling to old traditions, such as customs related to the status of elders, special forms of clothing, initiation rites, or other ceremonial acts. 'Moving on' may be possible only if some cultural certainties remain. New social structures (for instance, the formation of zonal committees in a refugee camp) may be overlaid on others. This is in part what happened in the case of the Sudanese refugees in Uganda described in Chapter 3 (Neefjes and David, 1996). A delicate balance may need to be struck on whether and how to support those organisational structures that are oppressive for a significant element of the community, but which may also enable that community as a whole to maintain a sense of integrity and continuity. The case of the male-dominated Councils of Elders in Somalia provide a good example of the dilemma (El-Bushra and Piza-López, 1994: 53).

While conflict and its aftermath may open up new opportunities for women, and enable them to challenge limiting sexual stereotypes, these changes have generally been a temporary 're-arrangement' of gender roles rather than a transformation: 'In Eritrea, for example, women are concerned about the assumption by male leaders that they should now return to their traditional gender role' (ibid, pp 30–31). Changes and structures that emerge as a response to crisis will usually be sustainable in the long term if their benefits are to everyone's advantage.

Organising for survival

One of the major achievements for Saharawi [refugee] women has been their empowerment within the context of camp life, and the development of women leaders in many fields. During their time in the camps they have built up an impressive schooling system for girls as well as boys, and run literacy classes for the whole camp population. Many women have themselves undergone skills training and are now teachers, nurses, and clerical assistants within the camps.

Saharawi women found that they had to take on the running of the camps because the men were absent, and they have risen to the challenge and become managers — running schools, clinics, agricultural projects and neighbourhood committees. This ... was an entirely new area for women.

These women have survived by organising: their lives, the distribution of aid, work, and responsibility. They have organised in such a way as to include everyone, to ensure no-one feels marginalised or excluded. This has built up social cohesiveness, in a context where conditions could so easily have fragmented the entire community (Wallace,1994:51–53).

Power and decision-making

Crisis may exacerbate existing inequalities, and reinforce top-down or authoritarian power and decision-making structures. On the other hand, a response to crisis may also be to provide mutual support and solidarity, or to co-operate across previous divides. However, the ways in which human-itarian assistance is offered do not always encourage the participation of the affected population in deciding the priorities or how they should be met. It is not uncommon for refugees to be excluded from policy and decision-making processes that deeply concern them. To be thus marginalised is an affront to people's dignity. In a self-fulfilling fashion, their disempowerment is also likely to intensify the passivity and dependency that then provide another pretext for continuing to exclude them from the decision-making processes.

It is always problematic to identify organisational structures that can adequately and legitimately represent people's interests. As in the case of the Elders' Councils in Somalia, and the community groups in Bangladesh, existing structures may favour certain groups at the expense of others, or be run on authoritarian, patriarchal, or paternalistic lines. New structures may be regarded as less legitimate than the traditional ones; or be simply a mechanism for getting access to relief assistance. Thus, if an aid agency supports projects that provide credit to women, men may push their wives and sisters forward. Survival and aid become intertwined, but in a more complex way than aid agencies necessarily realise.

In a crisis, aid agencies may suspend some of their declared commitments, for instance, to gender equity or participatory approaches. Speed of response, while on occasions important, should not outweigh all other considerations. Promoting equality between women and men should not be seen as something that can be put off until after the crisis, but as a dimension of that crisis and of its resolution. Similarly, instead of seeing broad participation by the affected population as a way to overcome obstacles, it is sometimes perceived almost as a threat — something to be kept under strict control. Yet it is far harder to introduce gender-fair criteria into a context in which patriarchal structures have become consolidated via control of resources. And it is difficult to encourage people to take responsibility if their dependence has been fostered and *rewarded* by unconditional access to resources. As one Nicaraguan NGO worker commented, the international aid agencies helped to promote dependency, especially among the displaced populations, and yet will not share responsibility for the consequences (Ardón, 1997). Far better to seek ways to enable the affected population to develop its potential, acquire new skills, and build for its future.

Refugee self-management

In the early 1980s, as a brutal civil war swept through El Salvador, thousands of poor and illiterate rural people sought refuge in neighbouring Honduras. About 9,000 formed a camp at Colomoncagua, 5 km from the border.

It was clear that these refugees wanted to keep their enforced dependence to the very minimum. Within months, six experienced tailors were busy altering the old clothes that had been donated. Soon, with a couple of sewing machines and material given by a local church agency, they began teaching others how to make shirts, trousers and dresses. Nine years later, every single item of clothing — including underwear, hats and shoes — was manufactured within the camp, in collective workshops which boasted 150 semi-industrial machines and 240 trainees, virtually all of them women and youngsters.

The pattern repeated itself across a comprehensive range of activities — building, carpentry, tin-smithing, hammock-making, car mechanics, literacy, administration, horticulture, and health care, as well as teaching and communication skills. On the eve of their return to El Salvador in 1990, their numbers included 350 health workers, and over 400 teachers and trainers.

From the outset, the refugees insisted that their survival depended on more than mere material welfare. Investing in the future of their community was essential to their human dignity and sense of purpose. For many of the international relief agencies, however, this vision could not be reconciled with their own priorities and ways of working. Accustomed to delivering relief programmes, they were unable or unwilling to hand over any management responsibility to the 'beneficiaries'. In one extreme case, a relief agency withdrew rather than change its way of working. Donors too made sharp distinctions between relief and development: giving out second-hand clothes was acceptable, supplying fabric for refugees to make their own was not.

The implicit message was that to qualify for relief assistance, the refugees had to *remain* both dependent and disempowered — a message that this group resisted and overcame. But why is relief given in a way that weakens people's resolve, and undermines what limited capacities they possess to control their own lives? (Eade, 1995:20).

Forms of organisation and approaches to decision-making vary greatly depending on the cultural and social context. The way these Salvadoran refugees organised themselves depended on a combination of very unusual circumstances; such a degree of self-management is rare even in 'normal' circumstances, but nevertheless shows what can be achieved even in adversity.

Building for a future

Crisis affects the future: the present is unsustainable, and the need is to ensure that change brings about something better. Yet 'crisis management' is concerned primarily with the present, with damage limitation: what must be done now to ensure that the situation does not get any worse? A sudden and major crisis — an earthquake, an epidemic, an industrial accident, an air-raid — demands a swift and decisive response. Other crises may be very long drawn-out, and their resolution remote.

However uncertain their future, people still have their own ideas and aspirations. A capacity-building approach to development in crisis involves helping people to act to bring about positive and sustainable changes in their situation. The experience of acquiring new skills and abilities, and being able to organise more effectively and make common cause with others, may in itself inspire people to see themselves in a new light, relate to others more confidently, and so envisage a different kind of future.

Reading for the future: The case of Bhutanese refugees

Both the Bhutanese Women's Association (BWA) and Oxfam staff were sensitive to the fact that women were suffering stress from both pre-flight atrocities and post-flight insecurities in a new environment, but culturally had difficulty in meeting with others and sharing concerns. In Bhutan mobility was fairly restricted for most women. The Non-Formal Education (NFE) compounds provided a 'semi-public space' that most men found acceptable for their wife and daughter to use, giving some of the women their first taste of interaction with a range of people outside their own homes...

Literacy skills enabled women to communicate and express themselves better; it meant that they were able to write simple letters, read sign-boards, medicine labels, newspapers, bulletin-boards, do simple calculations and distinguish currencies. For the first time in their lives women were in a position to tutor their little ones at home. All this made an enormous difference in the way refugees, particularly women, perceived their future. For instance Shila Rai and her group wrote in an essay: '... if possible women should move forward. We want to have equal rights with men. We have now become literate and we want to participate in the development of our country ...' (Rahman, 1996: 29).

Belief in a better future for themselves and their children can help to sustain people through the most desperate situations. Instead of passively waiting until their situation is more certain, people can come to see crisis as an opportunity to expand their horizons, envisage their own future, and take positive steps to realise their aspirations.

Building the capacities of others: questions for donors

Where donors are the major source of income, and where these donors set the rules by limiting their interventions to short-term, package-oriented, single-intervention project grants, the flexibility to change and improve is severely hampered. Where donors pay scant regard to the capacity building requirements of the grantees themselves, and prefer to disregard the most basic requirements of organisation like sustained funding for administration costs, the game becomes largely self-defeating (CDRA, 1995:19).

Introduction

This Guideline has stressed that, for Oxfam, capacity-building is an approach to development that is based on respect for all dimensions of human rights, and hence on the just distribution of resources. In a more equitable world, diversity would be a source of strength rather of privilege or oppression. Relationships among the many individuals, groups, organisations, and agencies involved in development — in North and South alike — would centre on mutual learning and growth, rather than being dominated as at present by the one-way transfer of resources. This approach would foster participation *and* responsibility, both individual and collective; and promote human creativity and solidarity, instead of reinforcing power and patronage.

It has also been emphasised that efforts to build the capacities of poor people so that they can participate fully and fairly in shaping *their* vision of a healthy society, need to start not by focusing on their perceived weaknesses, but by identifying and reinforcing their existing strengths. Analytical, social, organisational, and motivational capacities are vital. Similarly, more tangible achievements — such as learning to read and write, earning a better income, or winning a place on the municipal council — may be important practical gains, and can motivate people to persist in their efforts even in the face of relentless hostility. Capacity-building is a process of shared growth and learning through people's attempts to create societies in which their needs are met and their interests fairly represented. Specific inputs, such as training for one group, or transport costs for another, make sense only if these are likely ultimately to 'shift the centre of gravity' in favour of those who are poor or excluded. This approach calls for a long-term vision and commitment, not one that is project-bound and anxious simply to claim 'results' within a period of grant funding.

Most development professionals at whom this Guideline is aimed work in aid agencies and NGOs that support development and capacity-building activities; or in organisations that are directly involved in capacity-building for development. Some readers, particularly those whose job it is to allocate grants and report on how these are spent, may see capacity-building as something that others need to do, but that they and their organisations are somehow 'above'. In fact, nothing could be less true. Agencies promoting gender or racial equality, empowerment, and participation must expect to be judged on the extent to which their own organisation and performance demonstrate these values. How many would pass the test? Yet an organisation that does not itself possess certain qualities and capacities cannot realistically promote these in others. An agency's ability to *learn from and respect* the experience of the women and men it aims to serve may be the most important capacity of all.

Yet, as we have repeatedly seen, the donor-recipient relationship is not one that lends itself to reciprocal learning. The structures and bureaucratic mechanisms an agency requires to administer funds are often quite different from (and even inimical to) those needed in order to identify and act on critical insights from the recipients of those funds. Financial and project management systems are for controlling resources; capacity-building is concerned to establish sustainable relationships of trust and solidarity that do not revolve solely around the transfer of money. To become a 'learning organisation' would require a major transformation in the culture of most funding agencies:

> *... staff need to feel secure that in making time and space for reflection and learning they are not going to be punished; learning has to be legitimised by senior managers and the necessary resources protected. Learning has to be built into job descriptions (for senior managers as well as for front-line staff), and rewards for experimentation and inquiry should be built into staff appraisal systems, rather than (as is common today) action being taken to get rid of those who are seen as disruptive or subversive* (Edwards,1996:9).

Agencies may deal with the tension by separating the learning function from the everyday business of raising, spending, and accounting for money.

But in this way, 'institutional learning' becomes compartmentalised, instead of being a central part of responsible development work and an institution-wide responsibility. Learning is seen as an 'optional extra', which can be cut when money is tight. Indeed, many NGOs (Northern and Southern) fear that their donors or constituencies may not regard 'learning' as having anything to do with development.

Similarly, 'administration', which includes information gathering, storage, retrieval, and analysis as well as the monitoring of resource flows, is generally seen as something to be kept to a minimum. This pressure leads to debates within NGOs about whether to classify their fieldwork as administration or as part of their programme. An underlying problem here is that NGOs have made such a virtue of their supposedly lower costs and greater efficiency at delivering aid, that they have helped to create the misleading impression that development can be done cheaply.[1]

A vicious cycle may be set up, whereby aid agencies compete against each other to keep their overhead ratios down, rather than working together to educate their donors and constituencies about the costs *necessarily* involved in trying to reach those who are on the margins of society. This also affects the agencies' counterparts. Southern organisations complain that no-one will fund them to spend time on reflecting on what they are doing; and that they are then penalised for their failure to prioritise or update their thinking (see, for instance, Ardón, 1997).

If there is no mechanism for feedback, and no obligation to distil and disseminate lessons from practice, and if systems for recording information remain poor, and efforts to analyse it under-valued and under-resourced, the institutional memory becomes fragmentary and short-lived. Any link between past experience and future practice is weak or non-existent. As a result, its broader policies and practice remain only partially informed by experience.

Disincentives to learning in NGOs

The regular reporting system in most large NGOs is shaped by demands for information which pass down the structure from upper to lower levels, starting from the board or senior management, and terminating with the staff in the programme offices. A good deal of financial data is required in the form of budgets, monthly accounts, and annual audits. There is also quite heavy demand for more narrative accounts of past or proposed activities, which may be satisfied through programme or annual reports, and strategic plans. Information may be needed for a variety of purposes, including reporting to donors and trustees, keeping managers abreast of developments, presenting the organisation's work to the public in order to raise funds, or by policy makers who seek to distil wider lessons ...

The primary purpose of these exercises is generally seen by programme staff as satisfying the demands emanating from higher up in the system. There is thus a bias towards what those lower down perceive that those higher up want to hear. Achievements tend to be highlighted rather than problems, in the process filtering out some of the more valuable lessons ... Even where a format makes specific provision for problems to be discussed, the emphasis tends to fall on difficulties arising in the environment, of which admittedly there may be many, rather than on those inherent to practice or strategy. In all this, it is unusual for any additional analysis and syntheses to take place which could provide new insights to inform programme management. *Formal reporting, in other words, does little to facilitate a learning cycle at this level* (Howes and Roche, 1996:4–6).

As we have seen, downwards accountability (to recipients and ultimate beneficiaries) is far less developed than upwards accountability (to donors and trustees). In reality, changes are more likely to occur through pressures exerted by the agency's domestic constituency (both internal and external) and donors, than through feedback from the distant and often unknown recipients of its assistance. This is particularly evident in the case of large-scale emergency programmes, which are likely to be funded by official donors, and must conform with their extra reporting requirements. But it is also broadly true of an agency's relationships with Southern counterparts. 'Short-term, package-oriented, single-intervention project grants' described in the opening quotation by a South African NGO, often create avoidable dependency rather than build capacity.[2]

This Chapter draws out some of the things that development agencies should consider if they are serious about taking a capacity-building approach. It starts by looking at a characterisation of the various kinds of learning that NGOs might adopt for different purposes, and then explores some of the organisational and cultural constraints that NGOs (particularly NGOs that are also acting as funders) experience in trying to promote capacity-building among their counterparts in the South. Returning to some of the ideas outlined in Chapter 3, it concludes with some reflections on how NGOs might develop more collaborative and long-term relationships.

Learning to learn: a pre-condition for capacity-building

In his work on NGOs as learning organisations, Michael Edwards identifies five types of learning that are especially relevant to them. Each meets a different need, and has distinct requirements in terms of human and financial resources, and timescales. He argues that while participatory learning 'is the bedrock of any NGO learning system', and is by definition owned by the people who generate and will use it, other forms of learning may be needed for other purposes. Some of the basic questions to ask are:

- Who learns in the organisation and how?
- What kind of learning is rewarded?
- To what degree are errors admitted and analysed?
- What forms of knowledge are legitimated and how?
- How does information flow in the organisation?
- How is institutional memory constructed, and how accessible is it — to whom?
- What changes occur through self-learning as opposed to other influences?
- How does the organisation react to learning which challenges its assumptions ('dissonant information')?
- What changes are being made to the organisation's learning systems?
- Will these equip the organisation to anticipate and adapt to external changes?

The five types of learning he identifies are: participatory, project-based, policy-related, advocacy-related, and scientific research or visionary thinking (Edwards, 1996). The main points about each are summarised below:

Participatory learning in the field

- Lessons from grassroots experience are fundamental for development NGOs. Practitioners (in field offices, in projects, in counterpart organisations) should be encouraged to reflect on their experience in an analytical way.

- Such reflection need not necessarily be presented in written form. For example, a workshop or exchange visit may be of more direct practical use than an elaborate report.

- The purpose of such learning should be to bring about change *at the same level*. Providing information to the NGO's headquarters (eg for advocacy work, or case-study material) is a secondary aim.

Project-based learning

- Projects are still the main currency of NGO practice, and learning in the form of monitoring and evaluation of projects is necessary, in order to develop a body of institutional knowledge about good practice. This in turn should shape the development of operational policy.

• At an organisation-wide level, project-based learning must be backed up with adequate systems for recording, storing and retrieving analysis of local experiences. These systems need not be sophisticated, but they must be accessible if they are actually to be used.

• NGOs must invest in creating opportunities for field staff to systematise and share their knowledge: for example, through secondments, sabbaticals, transfers, or contract extensions.

• Further training and support may be required in order for field staff to develop 'the depth of analysis required to pull together the lessons of project experience and synthesise them into a form which is usable'.

Policy-related learning

• Policies will be influenced by project-based findings only if these are sufficiently generalised to have wider application. Yet it is difficult to make valid generalisations about situations that are intrinsically diverse, dynamic, and uncertain.

• Ways of developing general lessons from localised experience include: establishing common elements in patterns of experience, rather than aggre-gating the experiences themselves; focusing on experiences that challenge the 'norm'; exploring differences in interpretation of the same experience among stakeholders, to find out more about what is happening and why; making a strategic selection of project-level experiences, to try to reduce bias; and bringing together long-term project experience and local research, to build up a richer interpretation.

• NGOs may select policy issues in a top-down way, and then gather project-related material in a systematic and rigorous fashion. There is a risk of bias ('selecting information that proves the case while discounting other evidence'), but there have also been examples of influential work, eg by Save the Children Fund (SCF) in collaboration with the Institute of Development Studies (IDS) at Sussex. There is a danger that, while the research is academically respectable, the findings and outcomes are not 'owned', and therefore may not be used, throughout the organisation.

Advocacy-related learning

• NGOs wishing to use lessons from their experience in advocacy and campaigning work must be able to make useful generalisations, but be able to support these with specific examples.

• Since advocacy is by definition concerned to argue a particular standpoint, it is vital that NGOs check these 'lessons' against external sources. No NGO can rely solely on its own sources if it wishes to be a credible advocate.

Scientific research and visionary thinking

• Scientific learning and research is not the natural preserve of NGOs, who lack the resources to carry it out. Nevertheless, 'methodological standards and notions of rigour' do influence the world in which NGO learning and policy development take place.

• Since international development assistance is declining, and is not the only (or even the major) way in which development is promoted, NGOs must consider how their own roles might change. To do this may involve establishing new relationships in new territories; and envisioning alternative value systems and forms of international solidarity. NGOs may not 'dream up alternative futures on other people's behalf', but should engage in 'dreaming of new worlds, thinking the unthinkable, and learning outside of the normal parameters of NGO roles, interests and agendas'.

Within Oxfam, for instance, a greater concern with capacity-building is itself generating a more systematic approach to learning, backed up with a Cross-Programme Learning Fund (CPLF). A range of methods include *focused desk research*, to develop a more grounded understanding of the theory behind concepts such as 'democratisation' and 'civil society', and to learn more about what Southern counterparts and other NGOs are thinking and doing. *Field research* is planned 'to develop methods and tools to appraise and assess organisations and their potential impact on poverty in ways that strengthen their own ability to assess their impact' (Roche, n.d.). This would draw on contemporary approaches such as PRA and Participatory Organisational Analysis, revive older techniques such as Theatre for Development, use secondary data more systematically, and test different combinations of these.

There are many different ways of learning, though there needs to be a high level of commitment to it if learning is to take place throughout the organisation. Within Oxfam's CPLF, three ways of promoting learning are:

• *The 'Wandering Minstrel' approach*, whereby an individual has a brief to focus on a particular issue in several countries, and to convene meetings and workshops to discuss the findings. The advantages are a sense of ownership among the participants, the opportunity for 'cross-pollination', and some agreed outputs. Oxfam's Regional Offices in Latin America and the Caribbean developed this way of working in the 1980s, as a means of ensuring region-

197

wide coherence in areas such as popular education, human rights, and work with refugees and displaced persons. More recently, the approach has been adopted in East Africa, involving three separate Country Offices (Birch, 1996)

• *Informal learning packs* which bring together writings from practitioners as well as discussion papers from inside and outside the organisation, and bibliographies on a theme of current concern. Oxfam's *Gender and Development Packs* started doing this in the mid-1980s, when it was important to involve as many programme staff as possible in what was then a new debate. In 1996, *Exchanging Livelihoods* was a learning pack on urban issues bringing together contributions from Oxfam's field staff. In 1997 a pack on food security is being developed. Learning packs are flexible (both in production and in terms of how they are used), and serve to validate the ideas and experiences of staff whose opinions might not otherwise be heard outside their immediate working environment. For contributors, they may seem less daunting than a formal publication.[3]

• *Bringing people together* through inter-project or inter-programme exchanges and workshops has always been part of Oxfam's approach to development: the current guidelines on exchange visits have changed little since they were drafted in 1975, though the visits themselves are now often on a larger scale. The wider institutional interest in promoting inter-regional learning has also encouraged a more systematic approach to linking activities. The most ambitious of these were the South-South Linking Projects associated with Oxfam's 50th Anniversary in 1992 (see Chapter 5, and also Reardon, 1995; Sweetman (ed) 1995; de Wit, 1995; Nelson, 1995). While the links did not generate networks that outlived Oxfam's funding, some lasting relationships have nevertheless evolved at national and regional levels.

Oxfam is hoping that such learning processes will generate 'data on organisational change over time, which would then be correlated with changes in material poverty, social relations, and vulnerability as assessed by local people' (Roche, ibid.). Related work would involve collaborative research with other NGOs, training, and a range of activities to disseminate the findings, such as workshops, publications, and conferences.

Information, learning, and impact

Traditionally, learning within Northern funding agencies has not really been about themselves, but about the organisations and work they fund. When things go well, the agency congratulates itself. When they go wrong, it is as likely as not to be the local staff who are seen as having 'failed' to assess and monitor the situation; while Southern counterparts may be penalised by not having their grants renewed.

Learning depends on information, but information in itself does not guarantee learning. Nor do organisational changes necessarily take place on the basis of what has been learned (see Chapter 5 and Chapter 7 for more discussion on the conditions that will encourage change in response to feedback or learning). In international aid agencies, demands for information about projects or other funded activities — more commonly in the name of accountability than of learning — emanate from the top. As higher levels of official aid are being channelled through Northern NGOs, relationships between them and their Southern counterparts are changing (Powell and Seddon, 1997; Ardón, 1997).

The question here is not so much whether 'partnership' is possible between unequals, but whether the relationship that exists is based on values and trust, or on contractual obligations. The language of partnership may remain (though some agencies use terms such as 'client', 'user', and 'provider' instead) but the reality is shifting. The spectrum of attitudes, and layers of information demands on NGOs (Northern and Southern) is summarised by Rick Davies as follows:[4]

Laissez-faire: Funded NGOs should be trusted to do what they say they will do and not be harassed by donors.

Minimalist (defensive): Donors' demands for information can distract and undermine an NGO's effectiveness and should be minimised.

Minimalist (self-interested): Donors are too busy to read and use information about project activities and impact, and so do not wish to ask for much more than they already receive.

Apologetic or realist: Donors have obligations to their own donors and must, unfortunately, ask for information.

Facilitating: Information is needed from funded NGOs so that others might learn from their experiences and support other activities, such as development education.

Interventionist: The process of supplying information can have a positive impact on a funded NGO's institutional development, defined in terms of the ability to relate and respond.

Hard-line: Funded NGOs have signed a contract with their donors and so have an obligation to produce the goods.

Difficulties that NGOs face in becoming 'learning organisations' include, then, a mismatch between the organisation's own structures, obligations, and priorities, and the experiences and insights of those whom they support, and from whom they must learn. These are compounded by the problems in translating experience from one setting to another, across major social, political, cultural, and often linguistic divides. Yet without some effort to monitor and learn from experience, there can be no genuine evaluation. And without evaluation, all an agency can do is carry on and hope for the best (Riddell, 1996).

What transferable lessons can be drawn about capacity-building and how can it be measured? Impact assessment is notoriously difficult, particularly where there are multiple and dynamic objectives. Even in more straight-forward cases, the input of a single NGO seldom leads to one clear outcome. Further, capacity-building for development is both an end in itself and a means to achieving a world in which all human beings can fully exercise their rights and responsibilities.

Proving and measuring impact is hazardous even when information is easily gathered, and where there are unambiguous links between inputs and outputs or outcomes. Processes — such as capacity-building, empowerment, organisational development, or networking — are not usefully defined just in quantitative terms. Clearly, development agencies cannot justify supporting any vague activity on the grounds that this will somehow 'build capacity'. There needs to be agreement between those involved about what each hopes to achieve through collaborating, and how they will review progress — a process of negotiation and trust-building that takes time and effort. As was stressed in Chapter 7, it may be counter-productive to seek fixed definitions of, for instance, 'poverty' or 'exclusion', since people's perceptions of these may well alter in part as a result of the activities in which they are involved. In addition, the likelihood of *proving* causal links between, say, assertiveness-training for community leaders and a successful public campaign for consti-tutional reform, is remote. It is more realistic to employ the tests of 'probability, observation, and the balance of evidence' based on the perception of those directly involved.

Together with Oxfam, the Ghanaian NGO, IDOSEC has developed the following principles for impact-related research or information-gathering. This should:

- not be an extractive process, but should generate insights for the communities and individuals involved, as well as for the NGOs;
- not demand a disproportionate amount of time from NGO staff, community groups, or individuals;
- seek the views of those not involved in community groups, and those least able to promote their opinions in the normal course of events;

- actively seek the views of men and women in every aspect;
- cross-check findings through different methods, respondents, and researchers where possible, as well as verify them with respondents, key informants, and community groups;
- attempt to avoid raising expectations regarding future funding or projects;
- allow multiple perspectives to be compared, and similarities and differences — among men, women, and children as well as group and non-group members — to be explored; and also allow for negotiation and agreement to be reached between different groups, and differences of opinion and perception to be expressed and recorded (Kamara and Roche, 1996:10–11).

This approach means that funding agencies need to accept the existence of diverse, and contradictory, perceptions of the impact of their support; and be willing to draw conclusions on the basis of 'optimum ignorance' rather than incontrovertible evidence. Intuition and interpretation may be as important as factual evidence.

Building mutual capacities

Do Northern aid agencies have the skills and qualities to recognise and build the capacities of others, particularly those from different cultures? A survey of European NGOs into their views on how to strengthen Southern NGOs, revealed how far most were from defining appropriate roles for themselves, and admitting to their own limitations (James, 1996). While the survey focused on Northern NGOs, the insights apply equally to Southern NGOs, and to official aid agencies. This section draws out the findings, pointing to areas in which agencies might go about self-critical examination of their own practice.

Roles and functions

• Given the tendency for Southern organisations to follow the demands and agendas set by their Northern donors, the latter should separate funding and operational roles in capacity-building. In general, Northern NGOs and donor agencies should fund the process, not direct it.

• Few NGO staff have formal training in organisational management, and rely largely on empirical knowledge. Such knowledge is highly valuable. However, an organisational process and its outcomes can only be properly managed and interpreted by people who understand it.

Information and skills

• If an agency's central role is to 'strengthen the capacity of their partners (as many European NGOs have now redefined their core purpose)', then it must recruit and train staff in matters concerning organisational behaviour and management. This should backed up with clear policies: for as those working on gender know only too well, occasional workshops will not alone shift the dead-weight of an agency's thinking and practice.

• The 'depth of engagement in terms of quality of information and level of trust' needed if an agency and its counterpart are serious about capacity-building, cannot be provided just through completing project application forms and observing rigid management controls. Formal systems of organisational assessment are seldom used in the NGO sector. However, 'as the organisational strengthening needs change dramatically over time, this does not fit easily into one-off Logical Frameworks' or other 'off-the-shelf' tools now prevalent among NGOs. This points to a need for training in appropriate assessment and monitoring techniques.

• As is clear from experience in gender training or policy-related advocacy work, it is vital to develop a strong local or regional capacity for training and supporting local organisations. This both provides the possibility of a sustainable relationship, and helps to ensure that the advice and methods used are culturally sensitive.

Programme strategies

• Capacity-building is demanding. No NGO can maintain uniformly intense and long-term relationships with hundreds of counterparts worldwide. Relationships also evolve, and are affected by staff changes. One strategic option is to concentrate on fewer counterparts, and make a far longer commitment to them than the standard annual grant. For example, in Senegal Oxfam supported the gradual evolution of local peasants' organisations over many years, until they became a strong, national federation (see Chapter 3).

• Organisations cannot understand each other by means of 'rushed field-visits and bland project proposals'; nor can outsiders easily assess the potential sources of support that are available in the country or region, or how these might link up together. The cost of maintaining locally-based staff is great, particularly for agencies that work in many countries. Nevertheless, some kind of sustained 'presence' is needed, in order to facilitate two-way communication.

Funding procedures

• DfID (formerly ODA) in the UK, and USAID, calculate that organisational strengthening may take over a decade, though this depends on the scale of the organisation, and what it is expected to achieve. The strategies for strengthening a national institution, such as a civil-service bureaucracy, or a union for small farmers, are clearly very different. However, there is a huge mismatch between the aim to build the capacities of some of the poorest people in the world, and the method of giving one-to-two year grants that is common in the NGO and official aid sector. NGOs urgently need to review creative ways to make multi-annual commitments, and alternatives to the project grant. Financing mechanisms that offer the possibility of longer-term stability are endowments and guarantee funds.

• While the project-bound approach is inappropriate for capacity-building in all but the most limited sense (eg a one-off programme or activity), NGOs have traditionally raised their funds through 'selling' projects to their supporters and donors. It would be more consistent with a capacity-building approach to raise financial support for *programmes*, within which a range of activities could be supported. This was part of the thinking behind Oxfam's PROF experiment, referred to in footnote 2 in this chapter.

• It is a common lament among Southern NGOs that their Northern counterparts are reluctant to fund their core costs, such as administration, recurrents, and certain capital costs (such as purchase of premises). Yet if these costs are not met, the NGO is forced onto a 'project treadmill', which in turn impedes its capacity to act strategically. Overcoming this reluctance may enable Northern NGOs to project their *own* administration costs in a more positive light.

Collaborating for change

Competition among agencies may be good for their institutional profile; but does not necessarily translate into 'better' work on the ground, and may discourage learning and capacity-building, because it appears to rule out the possibility of collaboration. For instance, if NGOs are assumed to be 'better' than governments at channelling assistance to very poor communities, this may have the effect of undermining a government's capacity to provide essential services — and also foster antagonisms that make collaboration and mutual learning more difficult.

Second, a competitive environment means that agencies necessarily risk seeing themselves as being at the centre of the development stage, rather than as just one actor among many. This may reinforce the tendency to see their dealings with counterparts in one-dimensional 'project-bound' terms, rather than as part of a web of relationships. Yet it can be extremely damaging if agencies fail to consider the cumulative effect of their actions as a sector. Most development workers have witnessed the 'honey pot' syndrome, whereby several agencies are buzzing around the same small set of 'fundable' local groups. Many Southern organisations have been damaged by over-rapid, donor-led growth. Yet agencies seldom take individual or collective responsibility for this (Ardón, 1997). Conversely, agencies may also leave their 'partners' in the lurch when they decide to re-order their funding priorities. Since Northern agencies are likely to be responding to similar pressures (shortages of funds, or competing demands), it is not surprising that they make similar decisions; but if half a dozen agencies decide unilaterally to close down their programmes in a given region, the total impact may be devastating (Parasuraman and Vimalanathan, 1997).

Finally, a competitive environment tends to breed opportunism rather than long-term solidarity. Agencies may thus be more susceptible to funding a given project because it promises to yield what their donors and constituencies will recognise as results, rather than for moral considerations such as 'keeping faith' with a local organisation during difficult times, or 'accompanying' its slow process of growth. As has already been stated, major official agencies consider that capacity-building may take a decade, not just a couple of years; ironically, some of the pressure on NGOs to demonstrate tangible impact is perceived as coming from these same quarters.

In Chapter 3, we stressed the importance of seeing the whole picture. Here, we would reiterate similar points. For development agencies do not and cannot stand alone. They are part of a complex and dynamic web of relations both within 'civil society' and with the state. Thus, to have an effect on inequality and injustice, they must be prepared to collaborate with each other and with other sectors, on several levels. And they need to develop a common sense of what constitutes good practice.

The only way that we can retain a holistic, multi-faceted, and diverse approach to capacity-building — and develop the specialisation and skills required for particular purposes, such as micro-finance, community-based coastal resource management, research, or para-legal work— is to work more in partnerships and alliances with like-minded agencies, where the whole is more than the sum of the parts.[5]

In other words, rather than trying to be all-embracing in their scope, agencies would do better to concentrate on their own areas of strength, and complement these by teaming up with others. While this happens occasionally, agencies seldom collaborate both among themselves and with their counterparts to develop a coherent set of long-term activities. For example, one NGO might concentrate on micro-level support, or on the 'pump-priming' role of building and supporting local movements; another might work with organisations that were already at some level of maturity, helping them to develop their skills. Maintaining such partnerships and alliances would entail a larger investment in negotiating, planning, and managing a range of groups and inputs. Agencies would need to overcome fears of losing flexibility, in order to take on long-term obligations. However, the potential benefits would be in two areas. Local organisations would learn to handle a wider set of relationships, and call on support from different quarters as needs arose, while also being released from the 'project treadmill'. Meanwhile, the agencies providing financial and technical assistance would together develop a more global picture of the complex working environment, within which the contribution of each would be recognised and respected, and also be subject to peer scrutiny. While concentrating resources in this way might mean working in fewer areas, it is likely that the quality both of the agencies' work and of their working relationships, would be enhanced.

This more collaborative way of working might also inspire greater levels of trust among co-operating organisations. National and international NGOs could make fuller use of their experience and expertise. Northern NGOs have the responsibility to help their donating publics to see the links between their own societies and the forces of poverty and disempowerment, North and South. Southern NGOs have a similar role to play in raising awareness, particularly in societies whose internal divisions foster profound ignorance about the lives of those who are marginalised, whether because they are rural, or slum-dwellers, or unemployed, or from oppressed castes or ethnic groups, or simply because they are poor.

It has often been observed that those countries which actively foster social cohesion, equality, and solidarity at home, tend also to show greater solidarity on an international scale — not only in terms of aid flows, but also in terms of political action and awareness. The challenge facing development NGOs is both to contribute to helping those who are excluded to become full and active citizens in their own societies, and so to promote informed and responsible world citizenship.

Notes

Chapter 1 Introduction

1 The United National Development Programme (UNDP), one of the major proponents of both 'sustainable human development' (SHD) and 'people-centred development' (PCD) uses the two terms interchangeably. It defines the former as 'the development of the people, by the people, for the people', and the latter as 'empowering poor people rather than marginalising them by enlarging their choices and providing for their participation in those decisions that affect them' (quoted in Nicholls, 1996). For a lively critical debate on these terms between David C Korten, President of the People-Centered Development Forum, and Raff Carmen, see 'Dialogue on David C Korten's 'Which Globalization?' in *Development*, Vol 40, No 2, 1997, pp 55–66.

2 *The Copenhagen Declaration and Programme of Action of the World Summit for Social Development*, Chapter 5, Section B, paras 85 c and e. It is worth noting that both the French and the Spanish versions in this and other UN documents — *renforcer les capacités* and *fortalecer las capacidades* — emphasise the idea that these capacities already exist; and that outsiders can only help to strengthen these. For this reason, some agencies have adopted the term 'capacity-enhancing' (Hudock, 1996). We agree with this position, but adopt 'capacity-building' here simply because of its wider usage by donors and development NGOs.

3 Carmen Malena, *Working with NGOs — A Practical Guide to Operational Collaboration between The World Bank and Non-governmental Organizations*, World Bank, 1995, p64

4 'Capacity building: Myth or reality?', *Community Development Resource Association Annual Report 1994/95*, CDRA, South Africa.

5 Deborah Eade and Suzanne Williams (1995), *The Oxfam Handbook of Development and Relief*, Oxford: Oxfam. While the present *Development Guideline* reflects Oxfam's own experience in capacity-building, for an account of its overall approach to development and relief *The Oxfam Handbook* remains the most comprehensive and detailed source.

6 Oxfam's Memorandum of Association defines its charitable purpose as '[the] relief of poverty, distress and suffering in every part of the world without regard to political and religious beliefs'.

7 See Rick James (1996), *Organisational Strengthening of European NGOs*, INTRAC (paper delivered at Development Studies Association Conference, September 1996). Interestingly, 'capacity-building' has gained favour among official donors during a trend of decline in official development assistance (ODA), though ever more of this assistance that is channelled through NGOs. For instance, ODA from OECD members dropped in 1995 by over nine per cent in real terms over the previous year, and was overall the lowest as a percentage of GNP since the UN established a target of 0.7 per cent. (German and Randel, 1996). Three possibilities come to mind: that NGOs are intrinsically associated with capacity-building (and hence are the vehicle of choice for donors interested in this approach), that donors regard capacity-building as a more efficient form of aid (allowing dwindling budgets to stretch further), or that their support for it may be more rhetorical than substantive.

8 These principles are discussed in Chapter 1 of *The Oxfam Handbook of Development and Relief* (1995).

9 There is a vast literature on both institutional and organisational development, and much ink has been spilt on the meaning of the terms, and how they relate to each other. The debate is not one in which many NGOs or other development actors have become centrally involved.

Chapter 2
Capacity building: where has it come from?

1 See the Annotated Bibliography in Eade (1996a) for further reading.

2 The Ford Foundation, for example, began to foster such analysis through its Women's Direct Action Program, thanks to which research institutes began to establish Women's Studies or Inter-disciplinary Studies Departments. (See Eade (1991) in Wallace and March (eds), 1991, pp 306–310).) However, few major NGOs were taking gender analysis seriously into account until the mid-1980s: Oxfam was a pioneer among British NGOs, establishing its Gender and Development Unit (GADU) in 1985.

3 I am grateful to Lilly Nicholls for drawing my attention to Sen's important contribution to the thinking of UNDP and others on capacity-building; and also for pointing to feminist critiques of Sen's work that stress the difference between capability building and capability use, and the immense changes that would be required truly to put people at the centre of development.

4 See Mary B Anderson, 'Understanding difference and building solidarity: a challenge to development initiatives' in Eade (ed), 1996a. Mark Duffield (1995) takes this further, arguing that 'libertine developmentalists' have contributed to undermining a belief in universal values and, by extension, a belief in the universality, indivisibility, and inalienability of human rights.

5 The 1992 Rio Conference on Environment and Development (UNCED), the 1993 Vienna International Conference on Human Rights, the 1994 Cairo International Conference on Population and Development (ICPD), the 1995 Copenhagen World Summit on Social Development (WSSD), the 1996 Habitat II International Conference in Istanbul, and the Rome World Food Summit also in 1996.

6 For a short, sharp overview of what these trends mean, see Powell and Seddon (1997). The authors argue that 'the shift to a pro-NGO policy, often justified — at least by the NGOs themselves — on the grounds of getting closer to the poor, has not been accompanied by any lessening in the centralised Northern control of the industry but rather by the reverse. Northern NGOs are imposing tighter parameters on their local in-country staff and in turn are increasingly obliged, in seeking funding for their work, to operate through highly structured bureaucratic procedures. Once such procedures become the norm, then not only are the much vaunted flexibility and cultural appropriateness of the NGOs denied expression but they are vulnerable to strong pressure that NGOs should now recognise the desirability of competing for development contracts with other organisations, including private sector consultancy companies.'

7 Between 1990 and 1995, official spending on relief assistance rose four-fold, to nearly US$2 billion. Yet the proportion of emergency assistance allocated by the EC to governments fell from 95 per cent in 1976 to only six per cent in 1990. See Macrae (1996), pp18–19.

8 Moser (1993) quoted in Razavi, S and C Miller (1995).

9 In a review of David C Korten (1995) in *Development in Practice*, Volume 6, Number 4, pp371–2.

Chapter 3 What is capacity-building?

1 Similarly, agencies often manage their bilateral dealings with their counterparts in isolation from the cluster of relationships in which these may be involved. For instance, as Oxfam was preparing to wind down its programme in Southern India, local organisations complained that since other funding agencies were pulling out at the same time, their work would be seriously damaged (Parasuraman and Vimalanathan, 1997). The cumulative impact of the rapid withdrawal of external support may be far greater than any one of the funding agencies might have imagined or intended. That similar problems have been reported in Central America (Ardón, 1997) and South Africa (Pieterse, 1997) suggests that this is not an isolated phenomenon.

2 This section follows an internal 'Discussion Paper on Modelling Oxfam's Ways of Working', 23 October 1995 by Chris Roche, who leads Oxfam's Gender and Learning Team.

3 For a brief account of Kebkabiya, and the difficulties in implementing a transfer of management responsibilities, see Strachan, 1996: 208–216; and for a fuller description, see Strachan,1997. For a background to ALIN, see Graham, 1993:83–91.

4 Parasuraman and Vimalanathan (1997:ii) also found, for example, that the planned withdrawal of funds 'meant loss of employment of several hundred middle level and grassroots level workers, most of them receiving subsistence income of between Rs 200 to Rs 600 per month. These workers had neither a redundancy package nor job-search assistance'. The authors proposed in such cases that Northern funders should consider continued assistance to enable the organisations and individuals concerned to make alternative arrangements.

Chapter 4 Whose capacities?

1 An obvious example is gender, where development agencies (official and non-governmental) that employ gender equity criteria in assessing requests for funding seldom reflect this commitment in terms of their own management or staff structures. Such divergence between rhetoric and practice exposes them to accusations of hypocrisy — both from those who view such policies as a form of imposition from outside, and from those (inside and outside the agency) who are genuinely committed to gender equity. See, for example, Longwe (1997).

2 For reasons of space, this is a highly abbreviated discussion. For a fuller account, see Eade and Williams (1995), Chapter 2.

3 Some people within the disability movement take issue with these definitions, arguing that impairment implies the loss or abnormality together with its effect on a particular function, such as the loss of an eye as well as the blindness this entails. They see disability or handicap as the social construct placed on the impairment; thus, the denial of particular educational options to blind people constitutes the disability or handicap. Since no languages make identical semantic distinctions, it is more important to be sensitive to the issues than dogmatic about the terminology.

4 In Sen and Grown, 1988.

5 This is true not only in the context of development. Social policy is often based on assumptions about, for example, why women work or have children, normative myths that may never have been correct for most families, and/or which have ceased to be representative of the social fabric. This may be to do with the lack of available data, or with the delay in translating this into policy terms. Often, it has to do with denying or refusing to legitimise certain changes.

6 In fact, women's income generation projects (IGPs) have a high rate of failure. A group whose activities increase its members' workload without material benefits is unsustainable and damaging. This will be discussed further in Chapter 6. Since IGPs are often supported instrumentally as a means to enable women to organise, increase their self-confidence, and bring them respect, this poor record raises questions about what kind of development they are thought to represent.

Chapter 5 Investing in people

1 Several reasons explain this decline. Some of these relate to whether the original statistics were reliable — for instance, nationwide illiteracy may not have been as high as was thought, and CNA achievements may therefore not have been quite so impressive. For example, some of the adults who enrolled in the Crusade had already had some previous schooling — and so were technically literate. However, the Crusade was only meant to be a stop-gap measure as the Sandinista Government was committed to universal primary education. The real reason for the lapse back into illiteracy is because many social investment policies were undermined or abandoned because of the *contra* war throughout the 1980s. Thus, there was little opportunity for many poor people to consolidate new literacy skills. In addition, under the centre-right Chamorro government, primary and secondary schools began to charge parents registration and exam fees.

Chapter 6 Investing in organisations

1 See, for example, Nichols (1991), Cammack (1992), Pratt and Loizos (1992), Rubin (1995), Elliot (1996), and Millard (1996); *Motor Vehicle Management Handbook* (1991).

2 The growth in the NGO sector is almost matched by that of the literature on NGOs, a sample of which is listed in Further Reading).

3 All of these arguments were variously expressed by certain NGOs whose health promoter training programmes Oxfam funded in Honduras and El Salvador during the 1980s, in order to block the formation of national associations of community health workers, who would then become independent affiliates of the Regional Health Committee. What these NGOs did not say was that they feared that their own primacy in the Committee would then be challenged from below. Fortunately, the 'beneficiaries' showed greater political acumen than they, and simply organised themselves without waiting for permission to do so — and Oxfam phased out support for the NGOs in question.

4 Chris Roche comments that since hierarchy, 'old boy' networks, and compartmentalisation are increasingly seen as inefficient within the more dynamic private sector organisations, NGOs should learn from this rather than repeating the mistakes of an earlier and less flexible form of management (personal communication, May 1997).

5 A related tool is the 'organisation ranking grid', which seeks to identify and analyse how different stakeholders construct their assessment of an organisation, in order to develop the basis for mediating between them. (Zadek and Evans, 1993).

6 In the early 1990s, strategic planning (SP) became fashionable among Northern NGOs. As they faced challenges to their *raison d'être* and traditional ways of working, as well demands for ever greater 'transparency' and accountability, they saw SP as a means to review their basic assumptions and directions, and often their organisational structures. Restructuring, decentralisation, delevelling, and downsizing entered the NGO lexicon, even as 'scaling-up' was still in vogue. The incursion of such boardroom language should not be surprising, since SP emerged from the Northern private sector, within which it was a tool for setting and monitoring the central direction and 'competitive edge' of an enterprise. Indeed, one of the main criticisms against it is that in practice, SP has been associated with top-down and rigid systems of upwards accountability at the expense of the more flexible, diverse and 'bottom-up' approaches that Northern NGOs claim to favour.

7 The 'user evaluation' that formed part of Oxfam's participatory review of its Ikafe programme revealed differences among the various users, specifically the Ugandan host population and the Sudanese refugees (Neefjes and David, 1996). Even though it may not be within Oxfam's scope to overcome these conflicts, the review helped to lay bare some of the underlying tensions.

8 In 1996, the Geneva-based secretariat of one international NGO had to resort to cutting salaries, and then laying off staff, when its expected grant-funding did not materialise — a situation that objectively reduced the organisation's capacity, and significantly undermined staff morale (personal experience). Voluntary sector organisations often have no provision for pensions, life assurance, or redundancy — a major problem when social security systems are also weak or absent.

9 All development agencies in a sense live off the poor (Hancock, 1989). Nevertheless, many would distinguish between living off money that is raised (largely in the North) for the eradication of poverty, and adopting a 'user fee' approach which expects the poor to pay for services they need but cannot afford. Whether, given the resources, people would 'buy' the services of the development agencies is a moot point.

Chapter 7 Investing in networks

1 Address at the 1995 7th World Telecommunications Forum and Exhibition, quoted in *South Letter*, No 24, Autumn/Winter 1995, The South Centre, Geneva.

2 According to *The Economist*, October 19–25 1996, congestion on the Internet is caused by the huge growth in non-text transmission, such as making telephone calls or viewing film clips: 'to send 15 seconds of high quality video munches as much bandwidth as the text of a 700-page book'. Many users are now opting to bypass 'the Net' and set up private 'intranets' within single locations and 'extranets' with branches and partners. A group of US research universities plans to build Internet II, 'dedicated to academic traffic and free of commercial users, very much as the Internet itself was just a few years ago'.

3 The Director of the Centre for Communication and Human Rights, Professor Cees Hamelink, observes that the 'democratic' nature of the Internet may be more significant than most realise: 'The pluralism of a market-driven [Global Information Infrastructure] may indeed reflect Athenian democracy: a highly exclusive system that left most people (such as slaves and women) out' (Hamelink, 1996)

4 The People's Communication Charter 'articulates a shared position on communication from the perspective of people's interests and needs;...and [sets out] people's fundamental right to communicate.' Some of the rights listed in the Charter are the right to freedom of expression; the right to receive opinions, information, and ideas; to be informed about matters of public interest; the right to gather information, including the right of access to government information; the right to distribute information; the right to reply; the right to express themselves in their own language, and to protect their cultural identity. The Charter affirms that people have the right to acquire the skills necessary to participate fully in public communication, which requires programmes for basic literacy and critical education about the role of communication in society. Journalists should be accorded the full protection of the law in carrying out their professional duties. The media should be accountable to the general public and submit to firm ethical principles.

5 Two examples are:

The Essential Internet: Basics for NGOs: a how-to directory that explains key terms and concepts, and offers simple instructions on how to access the Internet. From: InterAction, 1717 Massachussets Ave NW #801, Washington DC 20036, USA.

@t ease with e-mail: A Handbook on using electronic mail for NGOs in developing countries UN-NGLS and Friedrich Ebert Stiftung, 1995. A question-and-answer publication designed to introduce newcomers to e-mail by explaining basic terms and concepts, offering advice and contacts, listing existing computer networks and service providers, and suggesting ways to benefit from these. From: NGLS, Palais des Nations, CH-1211 Geneva 10, Switzerland.

Chapter 8 Building capacities in crisis

1 Hugo Slim (1996), 'Planning Between Danger and Opportunity: NGO Situation Analysis in Conflict-Related Emergencies', paper based on 1995 training presentations for ActionAid and VETAID.

2 Some observers attribute less noble motives to international aid agencies, accusing them of seeking the television lime-light in order to raise their own profile and fund-raising capacity. The criticism has also been made that aid agency representatives, newly arrived on the scene themselves, are not always knowledgeable about the situation in which they find themselves. The relationship between humanitarian aid and the media is examined in Rotberg and Weiss (eds), 1996.

Chapter 9
Building the capacities of others: questions for donors

1 NGOs may have created a rod for their own backs, in that if they spend more than they claim on necessary overheads — and informed sources suggest that spending is more in the region of 25 per cent than the 15 per cent or less they commonly claim — then they may be accused not only of inefficiency, but also of dishonesty (Sogge et al, 1996:88).

2 Of course, not all grant-funding is of this 'stop-go' type; and even within the annual grant framework, there are many examples of longer-term 'accompaniment' of local counterparts (see for instance, Ardón, 1997; Thompson, 1996). Oxfam has also experimented with moving *in practice* from a project to a programme approach, for example in its attempt at joint-planning with local organisations in Nicaragua, known as PROF. However, such experiments can only thrive if the resources are assured over a period of years — something that very few funding agencies are able or willing to guarantee.

3 The Gender and Development Pack evolved into the journal, *Gender and Development* (formerly *Focus on Gender*). While some of the advantages of flexibility have been lost, benefits include: reaching a wider audience, being subject to peer-review, and recovering some of the editorial and production costs through subscriptions. It is a myth, however, that informal means cheap. 'Exchanging Livelihoods' cost as much to compile, produce, and translate as a formal publication would have done; but with no means of recovering these costs. It may well be that truly 'informal' publications are better handled as electronic conferences.

4 Davies, Rick (1996), *Donor information demands and NGO institutional management*, paper delivered at workshop entitled 'Institutional strengthening of Southern NGOs: What is the role for Northern NGOs?' at Centre for Development Studies, University of Wales, Swansea, 3–5 July 1996, summarised by Chris Roche.

5 Chris Roche, personal communication, 30 May 1997

References

Agerbak, Linda (1991), 'Breaking the cycle of violence: doing development in situations of conflict', *Development in Practice*, Vol 1, No 3, reprinted in Eade (ed) 1996b

Alvarez Solís, Francisco and Pauline Martin, (1992) 'The role of Salvadorean NGOs in post-war reconstruction', *Development in Practice* Vol 2, No 2, reprinted in Eade (ed) 1996b

Anacleti, Odhiambo (1995), 'The mills that were wanted but not required — and another story', *Development in Practice*, Vol 5, No 3

Anderson, Mary B and Peter J Woodrow (1989), *Rising from the Ashes: Development Strategies in Times of Disaster*, Paris/Boulder CO: UNESCO/Westview Press

Anderson, Mary B (1994), 'The concept of vulnerability: beyond the focus on vulnerable groups', *International Review of the Red Cross*, Number 301, July–August 1994

Antrobus, Peggy 'Postscript: Women in Development' in Wallace and March (eds) (1991), *Changing Perceptions*, Oxfam: Oxford

Archer, David and Sara Cottingham (1997) 'REFLECT: A new approach to literacy and social change', *Development in Practice*, Vol 7, No 2.

Ardón, Patricia (1997) *Los Conflictos en Centroamérica*, unpublished mimeo, Oxford: Oxfam

Barrig, Maruja and Andy Wehkamp (eds) (1995), *Engendering Development — Experiences in Gender and Development Planning*, Amsterdam and Lima : Novib and Red Entre Mujeres

Bebbington, Anthony and Roger Riddell (1995) *Donors, civil society and southern NGOs: new agendas, old problems*, London:ODI.

Bebbington, Anthony and Diana Mitlin, (1996), *NGO capacity and effectiveness: a review of themes in NGO-related research recently funded by ESCOR*, London:IIED

Birch, Isobel (1996), *Learning about Learning: Lessons from East Africa*, unpublished report, Oxford: Oxford.

Boal, Augusto (1979), *Theatre of the Oppressed*, London: Pluto Press

Brown, Deryck R (1997), 'Sustainability is not about money!: the case of the Belize Chamber of Commerce and Industry', *Development in Practice*, Vol 7, No 2

Bryer, David and Edmund Cairns (1997), 'For better? For worse? Humanitarian aid in conflict', *Development in Practice*, Vol 7, No 4

Buell, Rebecca (1996), *Oxfam's Work in Conflict Situations*, unpublished report, Oxfam: Oxford

Butegwa, Florence (1995), 'Promoting women's political participation in Africa', in Reardon (ed).

Caine, Glenda (1997), 'Training for peace', *Development in Practice*, Vol 7, No 4

Cammack, John (1992), *Basic Accounting for Small Groups*, Oxford: Oxfam

Carmen, Raff (1996), *Autonomous Development: Humanising the Landscape*

Carney, James F (Padre Guadeloupe) (1985), *Honduras: Un sacerdote en la lucha*, Mexico: Claves Latinoamericanas

Carson, Wendy Jo (n.d.), 'Rhetoric versus reality: a case study of the international division' in unpublished *Case Studies Pack: Strengthening a gender perspective in Oxfam UK/Ireland's work*, Oxford: Oxfam

Castelo-Branco, Viriato (1997), 'Child soldiers: the experience of the Mozambican Association of Public Health (AMOSAPU)', *Development in Practice*, Vol 7, No 4

CDRA (1995), 'Capacity building: Myth or reality?', *Community Development Resource Association Annual Report 1994/95*, Woodstock, South Africa

Chambers, Robert and G. Conway (1992) *Sustainable Rural Livelihoods: Practical Concepts for the Twenty-first Century*, Brighton: IDS Discussion Paper 296.

Chicuecue, Noel Muchenga (1997), 'Reconciliation: the role of Truth Commissions and alternative ways of healing', *Development in Practice*, Vol 7, No 4

Chirwa, Wiseman Chijere (1997), 'Collective memory and the process of reconciliation and reconstruction', *Development in Practice*, Vol 7, No 4

Clark, John (1991), *Democratizing Development: the Role of Voluntary Organizations*, London and West Hartford, CT: Earthscan and Kumarian Press

Coote, Belinda (1996, rev), *The Trade Trap: Poverty and the Global Commodity Markets*, Oxford: Oxfam

Cornia, Giovanni Andrea, Richard Jolly, Frances Stewart (1989), *Adjustment with a Human Face*, Oxford:OUP.

Crush, Jonathan (ed) (1995), *Power of Development*, London: Routledge

de Waal, Alex (1991), 'Famine and Human Rights', *Development in Practice*, Vol 1, No 3, reprinted in Eade (ed) 1996b

de Wit, Dorien (1995), *An Evaluation of the Oxfam Women's Linking Project (WLP): An important step in the process*, Oxford: De Buek and Oxfam

Drisdelle, Rhéal (1997), *Mali: A Prospect of Peace?*, Oxford: Oxfam

Duffield, Mark (1991), *War and Famine in Africa*, Oxford: Oxfam

Duffield, Mark (1995), *The Symphony of the Damned: Racial Discourse, Complex Political Emergencies and Humanitarian Aid*, Birmingham: Centre for Urban and Regional Studies

Eade, Deborah (1992) 'How far should we push?' in Wallace and March (eds).

Eade, Deborah (1995) 'Development for Survival', *Red Cross, Red Crescent*, Issue 2, 1995

Eade, Deborah and Suzanne Williams (1994) 'Emergencies and development: ageing with wisdom and dignity', *Focus on Gender* Vol 2, No 1.

Eade, Deborah and Suzanne Williams (1995), *The Oxfam Handbook of Development and Relief*, Oxford: Oxfam.

Eade, Deborah (ed) (1996a), *Development and Social Diversity*, Development in Practice Readers, Oxford: Oxfam

Eade, Deborah (ed) (1996b), *Development in States of War*, Development in Practice Readers, Oxford: Oxfam

Eade, Deborah (ed) (1997), *Development and Patronage*, Development in Practice Readers, Oxford: Oxfam

Edwards, Michael (1996), *Becoming a Learning Organisation, or, the Search for the Holy Grail*, paper commissioned by the Aga Khan Foundation, Canada.

Edwards, Michael (1997), 'Development Studies and Development Practice: Divorce, Unhappy Marriage or the Perfect Union', keynote address at the Seminar on the Study and Practice of Development: Current and Prospective Linkages, Development Studies Centre, Dublin, Ireland, 7 February 1997 (unpublished).

Edwards, Michael and David Hulme, (1992), *Making a Difference: NGOs and Development in a Changing World*, London: Earthscan

Edwards, Michael and David Hulme (eds) (1995), *Non-governmental Organisations: Performance and Accountability— Beyond the Magic Bullet*, London: Earthscan and Save the Children Fund.

Edwards, Michael and David Hulme (eds), (1995b), *NGOs, States, and Donors: Too Close for Comfort*, Save the Children, London: MacMillan Press

El-Bushra, Judy and Eugenia Piza-López (1994), *Development in Conflict: The Gender Dimension*, Working Paper, Oxfam UK/I and ACORD

Elliot, Nicola (1996), *Basic Accounting for Credit and Savings Schemes*, Oxford: Oxfam

Escobar, Arturo (1995), *Encountering Development: The Making and Unmaking of the Third World*, Princeton: Princeton University Press

Escobar, Arturo and Sonia Alvarez (eds) (1992) *The Making of Social Movements in Latin America: Identity, Strategy and Democracy*, Boulder, Colorado: Westview Press.

Farrington, John and Anthony Bebbington et al (1995), *Reluctant Partners? Non-governmental Organisations, the State and Sustainable Agricultural Development*, London: Routledge.

Faure, Denise (1994), 'Women's health and feminist politics', *Focus on Gender* Vol 2, No 2.

Fordham et al, 1995, *Adult Literacy: A Handbook for Development Workers*, Oxfam, Oxford

Fowler, Alan with Liz Goold and Rick James (1995), *Participatory Self Assessment of NGO Capacity*, Occasional Papers Series, Number 10, Oxford: INTRAC

Fowler, Alan (1991), 'Building partnerships between Northern and Southern development NGOs', *Development in Practice* Vol 1, No 1, reprinted in Eade (ed), 1997

Fowler, Alan (1997), *Striking a Balance: A Guide to Enhancing the Effectiveness of Non-governmental Organisations in International Development*, London: INTRAC/Earthscan.

Francisco, Gigi (1996) *Integrating Realities/Uniting Diversities: Program of Oxfam UK/Ireland in the Community-based Coastal Zone Management in the Philippines*, unpublished mimeo, Oxford: Oxfam.

Freire, Paulo (1972), *Pedagogy of the Oppressed*, Harmondsworth: Penguin Books

Freire, Paulo (1973), *Education for Critical Consciousness*, London: Sheed and Ward

222

Freire, Paulo and D Macedo (1985), *Literacy: Reading the Word and the World*, London: Routledge

German, Tony and Judith Randel (1996), *The Reality of Aid: An Independent Review of International Aid*, London: Earthscan Publications, ICVA and Eurostep

Goetz, Anne-Marie (1995), 'Institutionalising Women's Interests and Accountability to Women in Development', *IDS Bulletin*, Vol 26, No 3.

Goetz, Anne-Marie (1996), *Understanding Gendered Institutional Structures and Practices*, presentation for Oxfam meeting on Organisational Change, April 30, 1996 (unpublished)

Goetz, Anne-Marie and R Sen Gupta (1996), 'Who takes the credit? Gender, power and control over loan use in rural credit schemes in Bangladesh, *World Development*, Vol 24, No 1

Goodhand, Jonathan with Peter Chamberlain (1996), '"Dancing with the Prince": NGOs' survival strategies in the Afghan conflict', *Development in Practice*, Vol 6, No 3, reprinted in Eade (ed) 1996b

Graham, Olivia (1993), 'Networking in practice: the Arid Lands Information Network', *Development in Practice*, Vol 3, No 2

Gutiérrez, Gustavo (1975), *A Theology of Liberation*, London: SCM Press

Gutiérrez, Gustavo (1983), *The Power of the Poor in History: Selected Writings*, New York: Maryknoll, Orbis Books

Gwynn, John and Bela Sehgal (1996), 'Questionnaire: Gender policy implementation in the India team' in *Case Studies Pack: Strengthening a gender perspective in Oxfam UK/Ireland's work* (unpublished) Oxford: Oxfam

Hamelink, Cees (1995), *World Communication: Disempowerment and Empowerment*, Zed Books/Southbound/Third World Network: London and Penang.

Hamelink, Cees (1996), 'Alice in Wonderland and the People's Charter', *Culturelink* 19.

Hancock, Graham (1989), *Lords of Poverty*, London: Macmillan

Hope, Anne and Sally Timmel (1995, rev), *Training for Transformation: A Handbook for Community Workers*, Harare: Mambo Press.

Howes, Mick and Chris Roche (1996), *How NGOs Learn: The Case of Oxfam UK and Ireland*, paper presented at the NGO Study Group of the Development Studies Association, July 1996.

Hudock, Ann C (1996), *Institutional Interdependence: Capacity Building Assistance for Intermediary NGOs in Sierra Leone and The Gambia*, paper presented at Development Studies Association Conference, September 1996

Human Rights Watch (1996), 'Silencing the Net — The Threat to Freedom of Expression On-line', *Human Rights Watch Report*, Vol 8, No 2.

James, Rick, (1994), *Strengthening the Capacity of Southern NGO Partners*, Occasional Papers Series Number 5, Oxford: INTRAC

James, Rick (1996), *Organisational Strengthening of European NGOs*, paper presented at Development Studies Association, September 1996

Johnson, Chris (1997) *Afghanistan: A Land in Shadow*, Oxford: Oxfam.

Johnson, Susan and Rogaly, Ben (1997), *Microfinance and Poverty Reduction*, Oxford: Oxfam/ACTIONAID.

Joyner, Alison (1996), 'Supporting education in emergencies: a case study from southern Sudan', *Development in Practice*, Vol 6, No 1, reprinted in Eade (ed), 1996b

Kamal Smith, Mohga, (1996), *Kosovo Trip Report 16–23 July 1996*, unpublished report, Oxford: Oxfam

Kamara, Siapha and Chris Roche (1996), *A Participatory Impact Assessment and Advocacy Project for Poverty Alleviation in Northern Ghana*, paper prepared for the 3rd international workshop on the evaluation of social development, IDOSEC (Accra) and Oxfam

Kaplan, Allan (1996), *The Development Practitioners' Handbook*, London:Pluto Press

Kassey Garba, K (1997), *Towards an Effective Empowerment of Women in Nigerian Trade Unions*, unpublished paper, University of Ibadan, Nigeria

Keen, David (1993), *Famine, Needs Assessment, and Survival Strategies in Africa*, Oxford: Oxfam

Khan, Mahmuda Rahman (1995), 'Women entrepreneurs in the Bangladesh restaurant business', *Development in Practice*, Vol 5, No 3.

Kidder, Thalia (1996), *The Effectiveness and Limitations of Women's Income-Generating Projects: The Impact of Formal Rules and Informal Norms in a Nicaraguan Program*, unpublished Master of Public Affairs dissertation at the University of Minnesota

Korten, David (1990), *Getting to the 21st Century: Voluntary Action and the Global Agenda*, West Hartford, CT: Kumarian Press

Lang, Gillian (1996), *The Oxfam/ODA Programme of Support for PHC in Namibia: What is there to Learn from this Project?*, unpublished mimeo, Oxford: Oxfam

Large, Judith (1997), 'Disintegration conflicts and the restructuring of masculinity', *Gender and Development*, Vol 5, No 2

Leach, Fiona (1996), 'Women in the informal sector: the contribution of education and training', *Development in Practice*, Vol 6, No 1

Longwe, Sara Hlupekile (1997), 'The evaporation of gender policies in the patriarchal cooking pot', *Development in Practice*, Vol 7 No 2, reprinted in Eade (ed), 1997.

Lumisa Bwiti, Godefroid (1997), 'Le Zaire: de la chasse a l'info a la chasse au magot' in Tchaptchet (ed), 1997 *Parole a l'Afrique: presse et democratie*,

Mackintosh, (1997), 'Rwanda: beyond "ethnic conflict"', *Development in Practice*, Vol 7, No 4

Macrae, Joanna (1996), 'NGOs: has the "N" gone missing?', *Red Cross, Red Crescent*, Issue 3.

Malena, Carmen, (1995), *Working with NGOs — A Practical Guide to Operational Collaboration between The World Bank and Non-governmental Organizations*, Washington DC: World Bank

Manji, Firoze (1997), 'Collaboration with the South: Agents of Aid or Solidarity?', *Development in Practice*, Vol 7, No 2, reprinted in Eade (ed), 1997

Maselli, Daniel and Beat Sottas (eds) (1996), *Research Partnerships for Common Concerns*, Hamburg: LIT Verlag

Mda, Zakes (1993), *When People Play People: Development Communication Through Theatre*, London: Zed Press

Mejía, Oscar, Doris Hernández et al, 'A peasant farmers' literacy programme', *Development in Practice*, Vol 2, No 3

Meyer, Marion and Naresh Singh (1997), 'Two approaches to evaluating the outcomes of development projects', *Development in Practice*, Vol 7, No 1

Millard, Edward (1996, rev), *Export Marketing for a Small Handicraft Business*, Oxford: Oxfam

Millwood, David (ed) (1996), *The International Response to Conflict and Genocide: Lessons from the Rwanda Experience*, Steering Committee of the Joint Evaluation to Rwanda, available from Overseas Development Institute, London

Mondragón, Rafael (1983), *De indios y cristianos en Guatemala*, Mexico: Claves Latinoamericanas

Moore, Mick (1995) 'Promoting Good Government by Supporting Institutional Development', *IDS Bulletin*, Vol 26, No 2

Moser, Caroline O N (1993), *Gender Planning and Development: Theory, Practice and Training*, London: Routledge

Movimento de Organização Comunitária, 'On being evaluated: tensions and hopes', *Development in Practice*, Vol 3, No 3, reprinted in Eade (ed), 1997

Neefjes, Koos and Ros David (1996), *A participatory review of the Ikafe refugee programme*, unpublished mimeo, Oxford: Oxfam

Nelson, Valerie (1995), *South South Environmental Linking Programme: Learning from Experience*, unpublished mimeo, Oxford: Oxfam

Nichols, Paul, (1991) *Social Survey Methods: A Fieldguide for Development Workers*, Oxford: Oxfam.

Nicholls, Lilly, (1996), *From Paradigm to Practice: The Politics and Implementation of Sustainable Human Development — The Example of Uganda*, Research Paper 2, Centre for the Study of Global Governance, London School of Economics.

Panos (1995), *The Internet and the South — Superhighway or Dirt-Track?*, Panos Media Briefing Paper 16, London: Panos

Parasuraman, S and J Vimalanathan (1997), *Oxfam South India Programme: A Report on the Status of Projects Administered by Bangalore Office in Preparation of Phase-Out*, unpublished mimeo, New Delhi: Oxfam India Trust

Pearce, Jenny (1993), 'NGOs and social change: agents or facilitators?', *Development in Practice*, Vol 3, No 3, reprinted in Eade (ed), 1997

Pearce, Jenny (1997) 'Sustainable Peace-building in the South: Experiences from Latin America', *Development in Practice*, Vol 7, Number 4

Pixley, Jorge (ed) (1986), *La mujer en la construcción de la iglesia*, San Jose: Editorial DEI

Piza-López, Eugenia and March, Candida (1991), *Gender Considerations in Economic Enterprises*, Oxford: Oxfam.

Postma, William (1997), *Appreciative Inquiry for Organisational Capacity — Interim Report of Listening Workshops (CRWRC & partners)*, unpublished mimeo: Dakha: CRWRC

Powell, Mike and David Seddon (1997), 'NGOs and the Development Industry', *Review of African Political Economy*, No 71

Pratt, Brian and Loizos, Peter, *Choosing Research Methods: Data Collection for Development Workers*, Oxford: Oxfam.

Pushpanath, K (1994), 'Disaster without memory: Oxfam's drought programme in Zambia', *Development in Practice*, Vol 4, No 2

Rahman, Tahmina (1996), 'Literacy for Refugee Women: A case study from Nepal', *Refugee Participation Network*, Issue 21, April 1996

Rao, Aruna and Syed M Hashemi (1995), *Institutional Take-off or Snakes and Ladders? Dynamics and Sustainability of Local Level Organisations in Rural Bangladesh*, Dhaka: BRAC

Razavi, Shahrazoub and C Miller (1995), *From WID to GAD: Conceptual Shifts in the Women and Development Discourse*, Occasional Paper 1, Geneva: UNRISD

Reardon, Geraldine (1995), *Power and Process: A Report from the Women Linking for Change Conference, Thailand, 1994*, Oxfam, Oxford

Riddell, Roger C (1996), *Trends in International Cooperation*, paper commissioned for the Aga Khan Foundation Canada Round Table 'Systematic Learning: Promoting Public Support for Canadian Development Cooperation, available from Overseas Development Institute, London

Riddell, Roger C (1997), *Linking Costs and Benefits in NGO Development Projects*, London: Overseas Development Institute

Rivera, Luisa María (1995) 'Women's legal knowledge: a case study of Mexican urban dwellers', *Gender and Development*, Vol 3, No 2.

Roche, Chris (n.d.), *Revised proposal to SMT to take forward our learning on capacity building*, internal paper, Oxford: Oxford.

Roche, Chris (1998), 'Institutional footprints', in Thomas et al (eds) (1998).

Rotberg, Robert I and Thomas G Weiss (1996), *From Massacres to Genocide: the Media, Public Policy and Humanitarian Crises*, Cambridge, MA: Brookings Institute/The World Peace Foundation

Rowlands, Jo (1995), 'Empowerment examined', *Development in Practice*, Vol 5, No 2

Rowlands, Jo (1997), *Questioning Empowerment: Working with Women in Honduras*, Oxford: Oxfam

Rubin, Frances (1995), *A Basic Guide to Evaluation for Development Workers*, Oxford: Oxfam.

Sandiford, Peter et al (1994), 'The Nicaraguan Literacy Crusade: how lasting were its benefits?', *Development in Practice*, Vol 4, No 1.

Saxby, John (1996), 'Who Owns the Private Aid Agencies?' in Sogge et al, 1996

Schmelkes, Sylvia (1997), 'Basic learning needs of young people and adults in Latin America', *Development in Practice*, Vol 7, No 3

Schuurman, Frans J (ed)., (1993), *Beyond the Impasse: New Directions in Development Theory*, London: Zed Books.

Searle, Denise, 'Whose Net gains?', *The Guardian*, 30 October 1996

Sen, Gita and Grown, Caren (1988), *Development, Crisis and Alternative Visions: Third World Women's Perspectives*, London: Earthscan.

Skinner, Steve (1997), *Building Community Strengths: A Resource Book on Capacity Building*, London: Community Development Foundation .

Slim, Hugo (1997) 'Relief agencies and moral standing in war: principles of humanity, neutrality, impartiality, and solidarity', *Development in Practice*, Vol 7, No 4.

Smith-Ayala, Emilie (1991), *The Granddaughters of Ixmucané: Guatemalan Women Speak*, Toronto: Women's Press.

Smyth, Ines (1997), 'Towards an Oxfam Strategy for Building Capacities on Gender', internal paper (in draft), Oxford: Oxfam

Sogge, David with Kees Biekart and John Saxby (eds), (1996), *Compassion and Calculation: The Business of Private Foreign Aid*, London and Chicago: Pluto Press with Transnational Institute

Smillie, Ian (1995), *The Alms Bazaar: Altruism under Fire— Non-profit Organisations and International Development*, London: IT Publications

Stewart, Sheelagh and Jill Taylor (1995), 'Women Organising Women — Doing it Backwards and in High Heels', *IDS Bulletin*, Vol 26, No 3.

Storey, Andy (1997), 'Non-neutral humanitarianism: NGOs and the Rwanda crisis', *Development in Practice*, Vol 7, No 4

Strachan, Peter (1996), 'Handing over an operational project to community management in North Darfur, Sudan', *Development in Practice*, Vol 6, No 3

Strachan, Peter with Chris Peters (1997), *Empowering Communities: A Casebook from West Sudan*, Oxford: Oxfam

Summerfield, Derek (1996), *The Impact of War and Atrocity on Civilian Populations: Basic Principles for NGO Interventions and a Critique of Psychosocial Trauma Projects*, Relief and Rehabilitation Network Paper 14, Overseas Development Institute, London:ODI

Sweetman, Caroline (ed) (1995), *North South Cooperation*, Oxford: Oxfam

Tábora, Roció (1992), *Democratizando la vida: La propuesta metodólogica de las mujeres del PAEM*, Tegucigalpa: COMUNICA

Tchaptchet, Jean-Martin (ed), 1997 *Parole a l'Afrique: presse et democratie*, Geneva: UN-NGLS

Tendler, J and Freedhiem S (1994), 'Trust in a rent-seeking world: Health and government transformed in North-east Brazil', *World Development*, Vol 22, No 12

Thomas, Alan, Joanna Chataway and Marc Wuyts (1998) *Finding out Fast: Investigative Skills for Development Policy and Public Action*, Milton Keynes: The Open University (forthcoming).

Thompson, Martha (1996) 'Empowerment and survival: humanitarian work in civil conflict' (Part I), *Development in Practice*, Vol 6, No 4

Thompson, Martha (1997a) 'Empowerment and survival: humanitarian work in civil conflict' (Part II), *Development in Practice*, Vol 7, No 1

Thompson, Martha (1997b), 'Transition in El Salvador: a multi-layered process', *Development in Practice*, Vol 7, No 4

Tunga Alberto, Francisco (1997), 'Physical, psychological, and political displacement in Mozambique and Angola', *Development in Practice*, Vol 7, No 4 Turton, David (1993), *Refugees Returning Home*, Geneva: UNRISD

UNDP, *Human Development Report*, Oxford and New York: OUP

UNHCR, (1995) *Sexual Violence Against Refugees: Guidelines on Prevention and Response*, Geneva, UNHCR

UNIFEM/UN-NGLS (1995), *Putting Gender on the Agenda: A Guide to Participating in UN World Conferences*, New York/Geneva

UNRISD (1995), *States of Disarray: The Social Effects of Globalisation*, Geneva: UNRISD.

Uphoff, Norman (1989), *Local Institutional Development: An Analytical Sourcebook*, West Hartford, CT: Kumarian Press

Vincent, Fernand and Campbell, Piers (eds) (1989), *Towards Greater Financial Autonomy: A Manual on Financing Strategies and Tecniques for Development NGOs and Community Organisations*, Geneva: IRED

Wahra, Gawher Nayeem (1994) 'Women refugees in Bangladesh', *Focus on Gender*, Vol 2 No 1

Wallace, Tina (1994), 'Saharawi women: 'between ambition and suffering'', *Focus on Gender*, Vol 2 No 1

Wallace, Tina with Candida March (eds) (1991), *Changing Perceptions: Writings on Gender and Development*, Oxford: Oxfam

Watkins, Kevin (1995), *The Oxfam Poverty Report*, Oxford: Oxfam.

Whaites, Alan (1996), 'Let's get civil society straight: NGOs and political theory', *Development in Practice*, Vol 6, No 3

White, Sarah C (1996), 'Depoliticising development: the uses and abuses of participation', *Development in Practice*, Vol 6, No 1

Whitehead, Christine (1995), 'Emergency Social Funds in Bolivia and Peru', *Development in Practice*, Vol 5, No 1

Williams, Suzanne (1995), *Basic Rights— Understanding the concept and practice of basic rights in Oxfam's programme: a resource for staff*, unpublished mimeo, Oxford, Oxfam

Williams, Suzanne with Janet Seed and Adelina Mwau (1994), *The Oxfam Gender Training Manual*, Oxford: Oxfam

Wolfe, Marshall (1996), *Elusive Development*, London & New Jersey: Zed Books, and Geneva: UNRISD.

Zadek, Simon and R Evans (1993), *Auditing the Market: A Practical Approach to Social Auditing*, London: Traidcraft/New Economics Foundation

Zeleza, Paul Tiyambe (1996) 'Manufacturing and consuming knowledge: African libraries and publishing', *Development in Practice*, Vol 6, No 4, reprinted in Eade (ed), 1997

Zetter, Roger (1996), 'Indigenous NGOs and refugee assistance: some lessons from Malawi and Zimbabwe', *Development in Practice*, Vol 6, No 1